Syd Carpenter

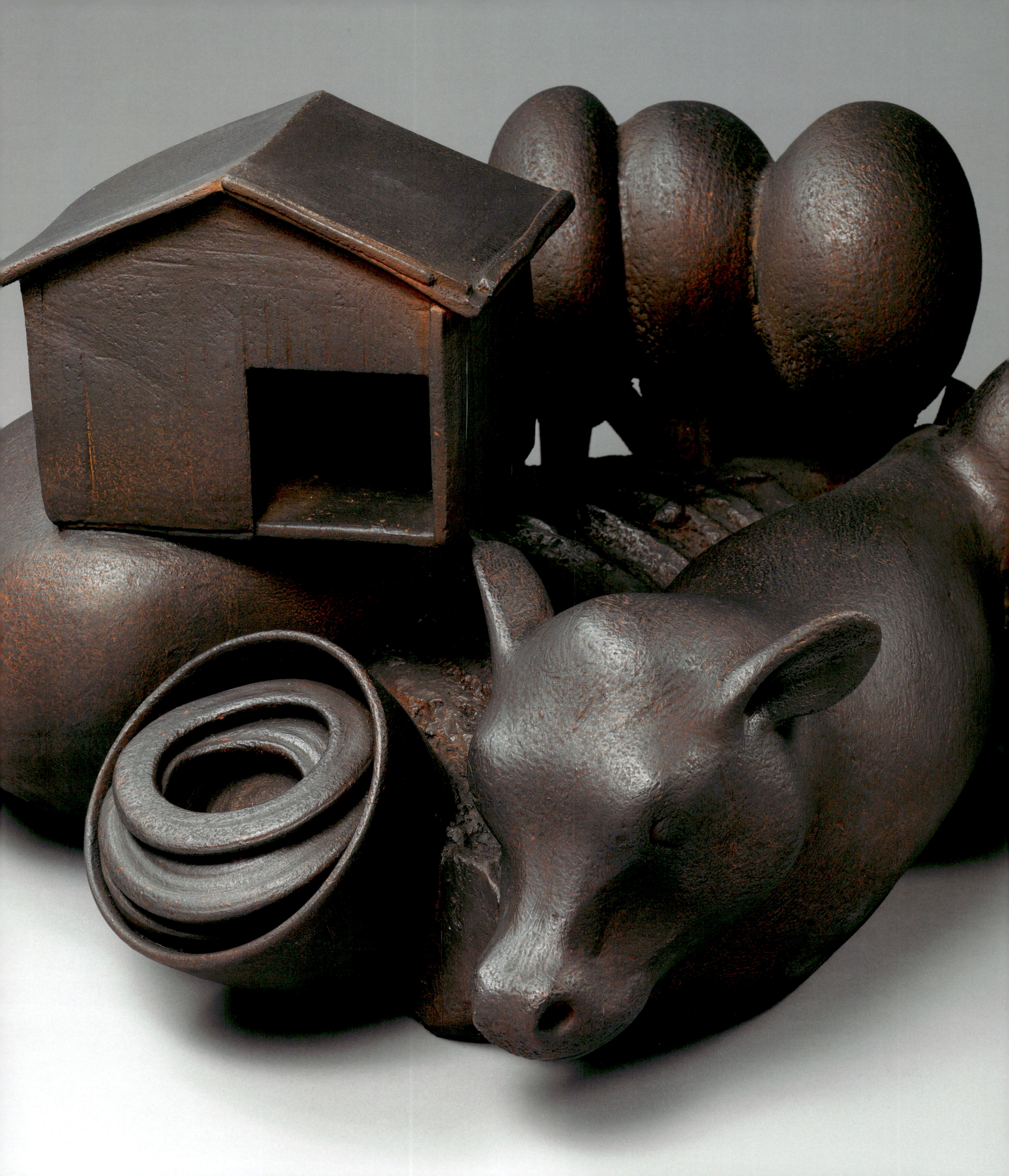

Syd Carpenter

Planting in Place, Time, and Memory

WOODMERE

Distributed by
the University of Pennsylvania Press

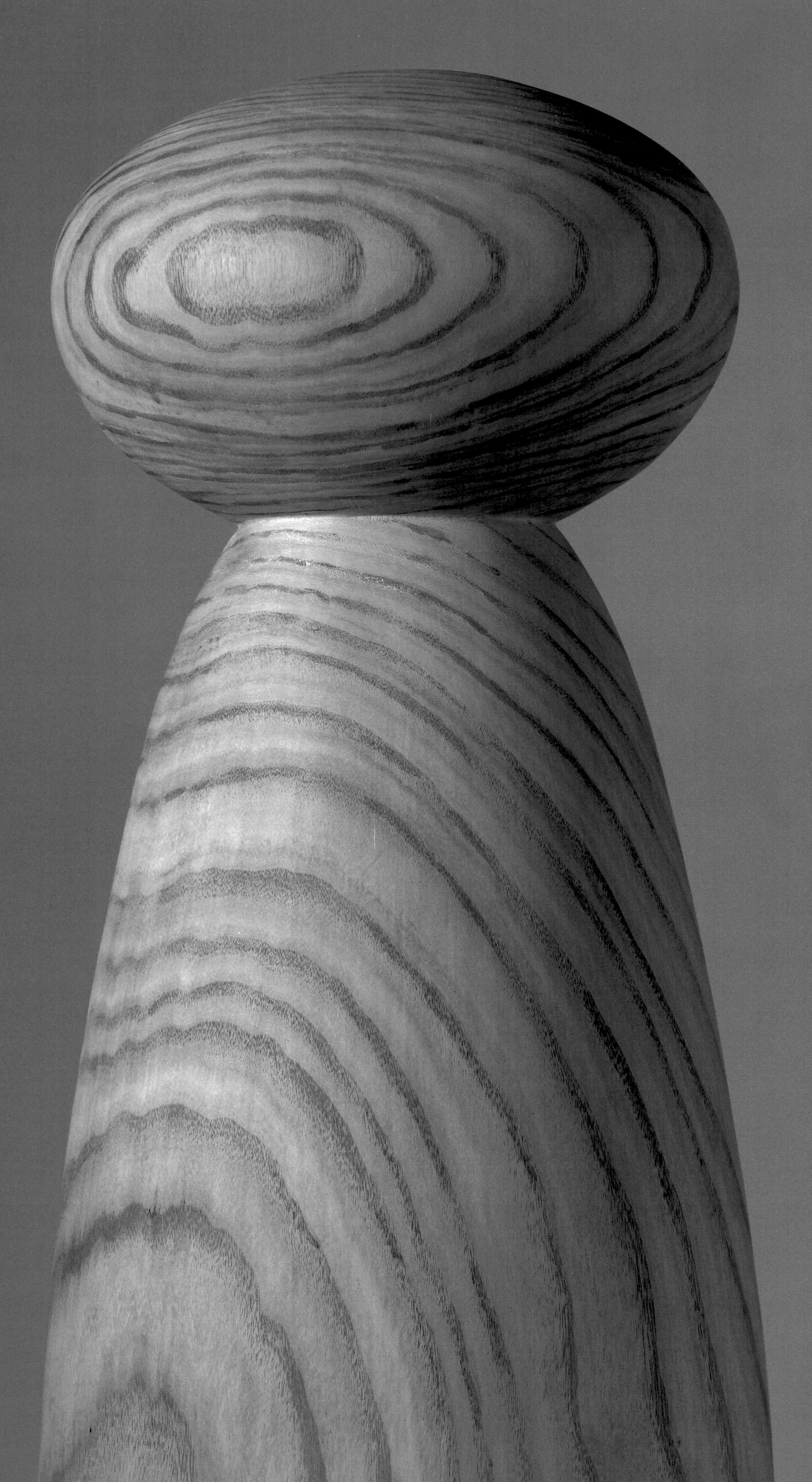

Contents

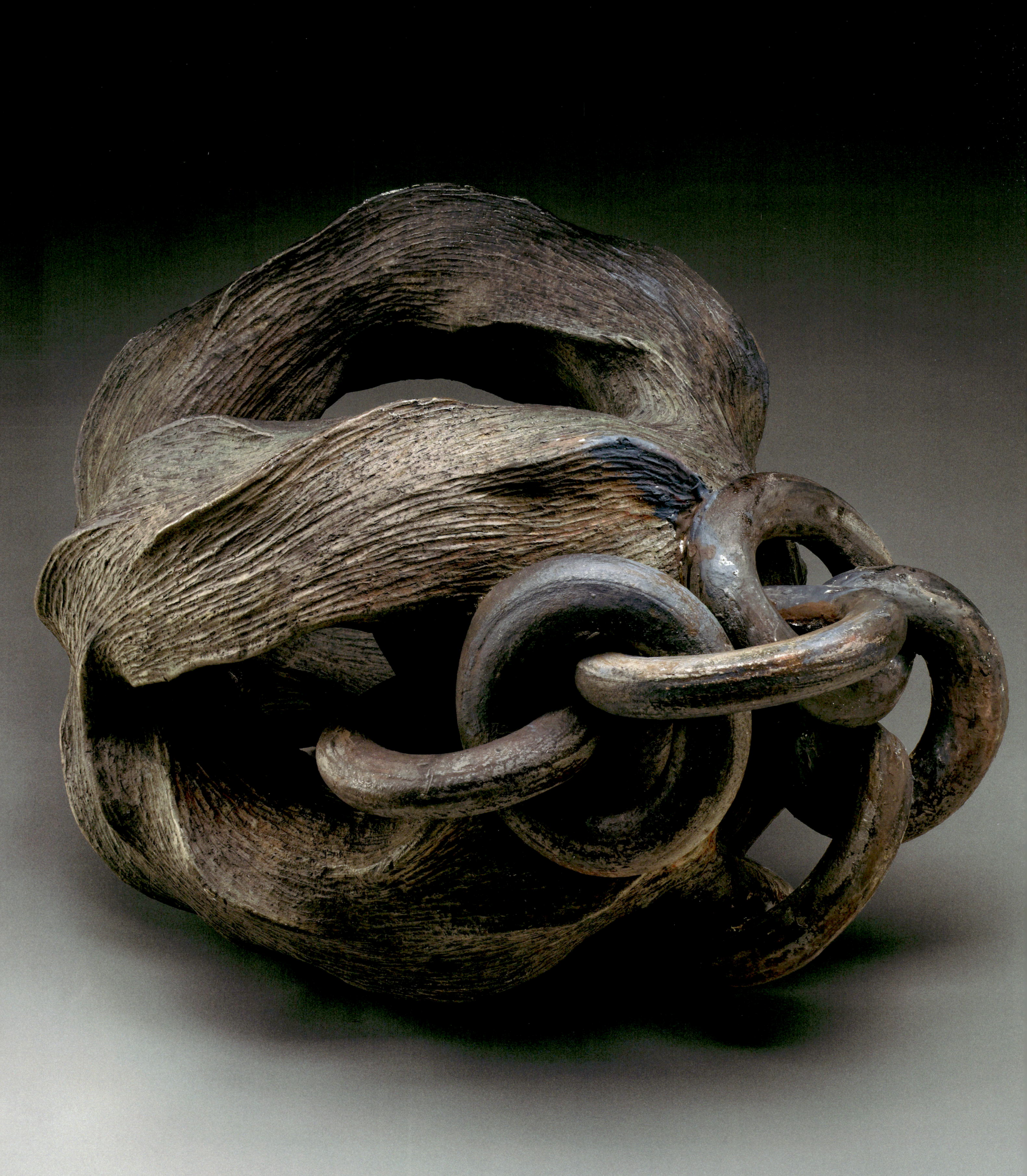

Directors' Foreword

SYD CARPENTER is an esteemed artist and educator whose gravity and creative spirit extend deep into the arts of Philadelphia and across the broader landscape of American art. As a growing list of museums and significant collections acquire her work, the time is right to tell her story and collaborate with the artist herself to establish an understanding of the drivers of her practice over time. With this catalogue and the multivenue exhibition across our three Philadelphia museums—Woodmere, the Philip and Muriel Berman Museum of Art at Ursinus College, and the Frances M. Maguire Art Museum at St. Joseph's University—we have worked with the artist to "plant" her voice in the telling of her accomplishments for future generations, who will doubtless continue to find meaning and give shape to her legacy.

The exhibition is structured as three parts, each offering a different experience and exploring different aspects of the artist's oeuvre. Woodmere presents *Syd Carpenter: Planting in Place, Time, and Memory,* a retrospective that demonstrates numerous through lines in her work over five decades, including a steady but ever-changing virtuosity in the manipulation of clay that is tied to empathy for the physicality of the human condition. At the same time, there are many evolving narratives that seem to strengthen over time: Blackness and the land, womanhood and family, history and community.

The Berman Museum show, *Syd Carpenter: Home Bound in Wood, Steel, and Clay,* presents two large-scale contemporary installations, *Mother Pin Ascending* and *Home Places,* accompanied by related works from earlier periods in the artist's career. Finally, the Maguire Art Museum offers *Re-Union: Syd Carpenter, Martha Jackson Jarvis, Judy Moonelis, Sana Musasama, and Winnie Owens-Hart,* a group exhibition that places Carpenter's work in the context of other female ceramicists who have maintained connections over the past fifty years. Carpenter's work was featured in the first rotating exhibition when the Maguire Art Museum opened in spring 2023, and the museum is deeply grateful for her continued support.

One of the unique aspects of Carpenter's contributions is her parallel and sometimes intertwined activity as an artist and gardener, which makes for a special connection to our three museums, all of which are integrated into the greenspaces and arboretums that are our ongoing partners. Inspired by landscape architect Darren Damone's interest in *hügelkultur*, the centuries-old practice of mounding tree trunks to create hill-like planting beds for farming, Carpenter teamed up with her husband, artist Steve Donegan, to create Woodmere's ongoing hügel installation. Titled *La Cresta,* this earth sculpture makes reference to nearby Ridge Avenue, which follows the crest of the

FIG. 1.1 Syd Carpenter and Steve Donegan with their hügel garden titled *The Instrument*, 2024 (The Philip and Muriel Berman Museum of Art, Ursinus College)

Philadelphia landscape and preserves the routes of the Lenape people across the land. Building on the success of *La Cresta,* Carpenter and Donegan made another set of hügels, titled *The Instrument*, on the grounds of the Berman Museum (fig. 1.1), working with students. A living addition to that museum's outdoor sculpture collection of nearly eighty works by regional, national, and international artists, the gardens resonate with and embody the wide-ranging scope of the liberal arts ethos, celebrating the role of the arts in the experiential learning environment of Ursinus's academic community.

Carpenter also works as an artist-curator. When she juried Woodmere's Annual in 2018, her approach was not merely evaluative; it was a curatorial undertaking with a distinct vision about emerging dialogues in the arts of Philadelphia, both inclusive of voices and earthy in the materiality of the art selected. It was thrilling to see her work at the center of the great range of strong artists, each of whom seemed to engage with some aspect of her streams of thinking. The holistic view of the community in which her art functions is also evident at the Colored Girls Museum in Germantown, where Carpenter designed the entrance path and sculpture garden. The installation of art and plants will evolve, as gardens do, while also serving as a space where community members can gather, reflect, and celebrate shared histories.

At the Berman Museum, Carpenter and Donegan worked collaboratively with faculty, staff, and students in environmental science, biology, and the Office of Sustainability, who helped guide the hügel project from conception to completion. The gardens foster cross-disciplinary opportunities for student and faculty engagement as a deeply rooted traditional practice combining permaculture with aesthetic principles. The project team intentionally incorporated felled trees from the campus grounds and plants that suit the Southeastern Pennsylvania climate.

Carpenter's interest in sustainable land practices has an even further-reaching impact here, though. The communal nature of the garden's design, installation, and stewardship speaks to the specific interdisciplinary academic context for which the work was created, and thereby to Carpenter's approach to gardening as a type of reflective, responsive place-making.

Given Carpenter's commitment to education, it is appropriate that two of the participating museums are at universities. Already she has participated in the student community at Saint Joseph's University, and will continue to do so with this exhibition.

We extend special thanks to our thought partners on this project—Linda Goode Bryant, Leslie King-Hammond, and Lowery Stokes Sims—three powerhouse figures in the arts who inspire us all and have each engaged in a deep way with Carpenter's work, as described in these pages. On Woodmere's staff, Deputy Director of Exhibitions Rick Ortwein and Associate Curator Amy Gillette coordinated this catalogue and the exhibition with Registrar Laura Heemer and Assistant Registrar Julianna Liska. Director of Development Lily Williams was the driving force behind our fundraising. Hildy Tow, the Robert L. McNeil, Jr.

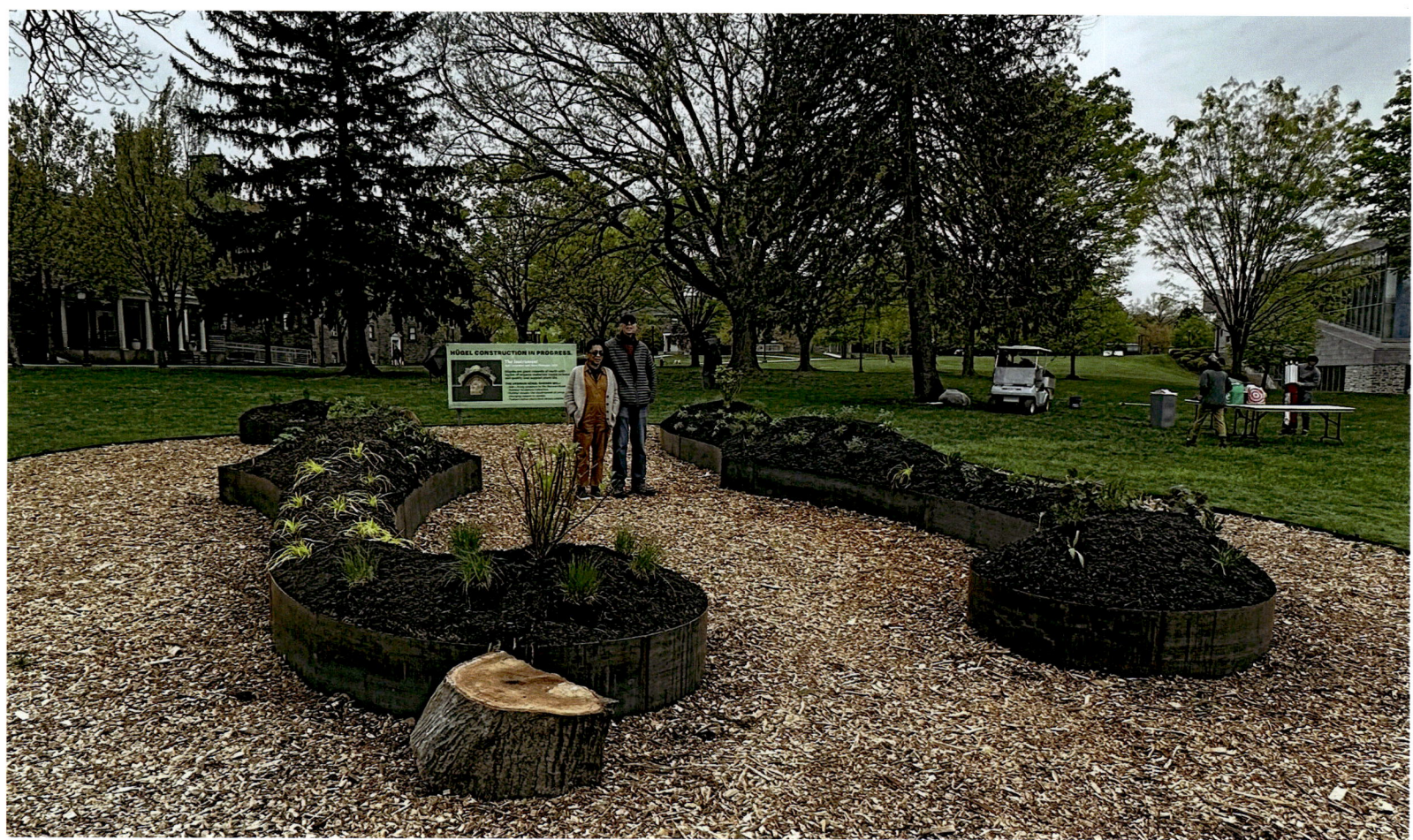

Curator of Education; Amanda Monroe, assistant curator of education; and Lya Rodgers, assistant curator of school and family programs, organized numerous programs for adults, families, and schoolchildren and worked alongside their counterparts at the Berman and Maguire museums. Bryce Long partnered with Carpenter and Donegan in rebuilding the hügels at Woodmere. At the Berman Museum, Creative Director Deborah Barkun, Collections Manager Catherine Sirizzotti, and Operations Manager Betsy Witt were instrumental in bringing the exhibition and related programming to academic and public audiences. On the Maguire Art Museum's staff, Associate Director Jeanne Bracy was involved with all aspects of the show, including coordinating with the artists, developing programming, and installing the exhibition. Assistant Curator Erin Downey played an important role in this capacity as well, and created the museum's interpretive materials. Education and Community Engagement Coordinator Jane Allen developed interactive educational materials and assisted with programming.

We are deeply grateful to our funders, including The Pew Center for Arts & Heritage, with additional support from National Endowment for the Arts (NEA), The Edna W. Andrade Fund, a Donor Advised Fund of the Philadelphia Foundation and the Philadelphia Committee of the Garden Club of America

Thanks to the lenders to the show: James Brantley, Everson Museum of Art, James A. Michener Art Museum, Judy Heggestad and the Lewis Tanner Moore Collection, Andrea Packard, Pennsylvania Academy of the Fine Arts, Petrucci Family Foundation Collection of African American Art, Philadelphia Museum of Art, a private collection, Rhode Island School of Design Museum, Danny Simmons, Frances Young Tang Teaching Museum and Art Gallery at Skidmore College, Martin Weinstein and Teresa Liszka, and Sarah Willie-LeBreton and Jonathan LeBreton.

Carpenter's work inspires and uplifts, fostering a vibrant dialogue about the power of art to transform and unify. Her ongoing work as educator continues to shape the next generations of artists, instilling a sense of purpose and respect for both the roots of culture and contemporary expressions. Our museums are honored to share Syd Carpenter's artistic journeys and contributions to the rich spectrum of American art.

William R. Valerio
The Patricia Van Burgh Allison Director and CEO, Woodmere

Lauren M. McCardel
Executive Director, Philip and Muriel Berman Museum of Art, Ursinus College

Emily Hage
Director, Frances M. Maguire Art Museum, St. Joseph's University

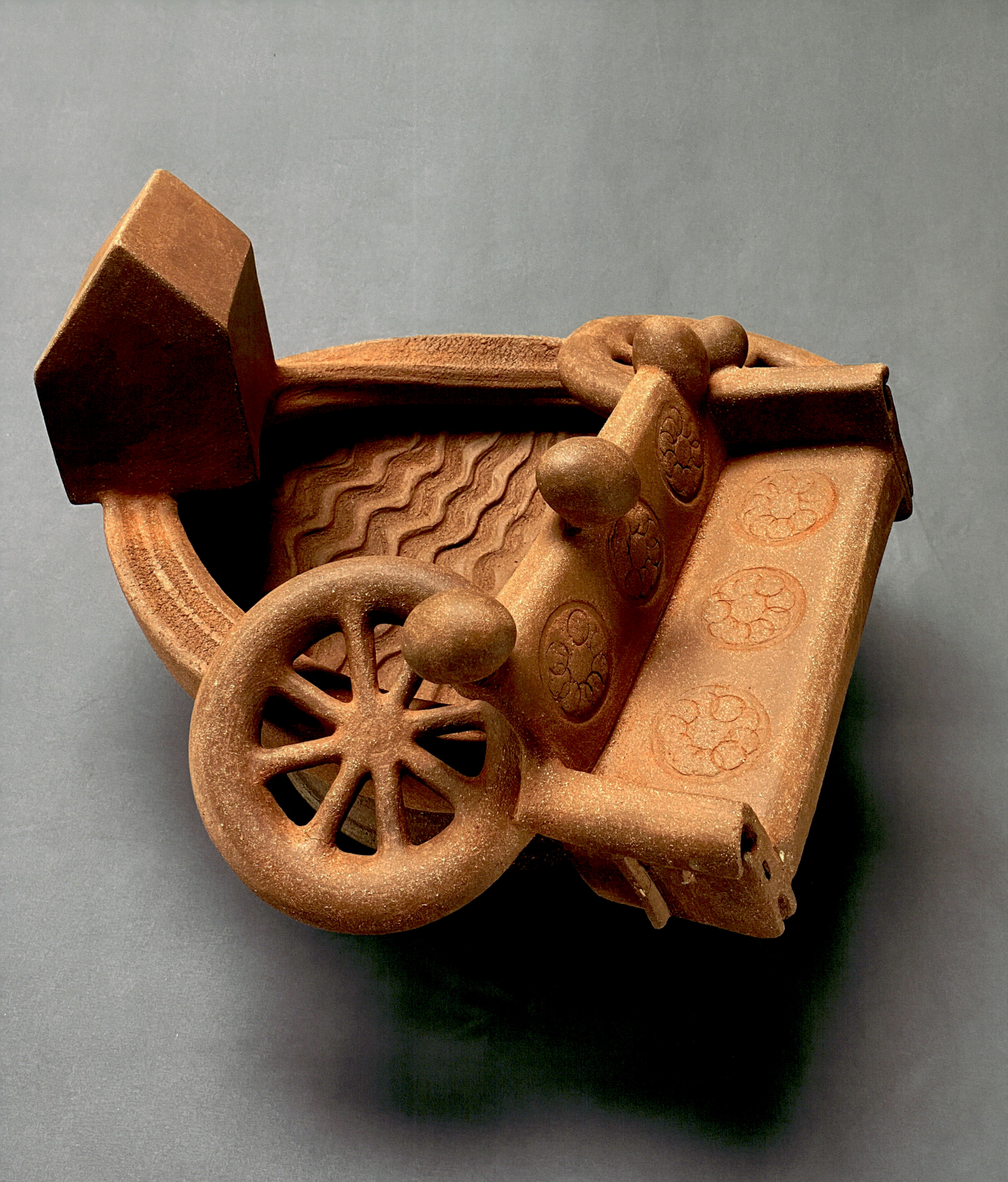

A Conversation with Syd Carpenter

INTERVIEW BY WILLIAM R. VALERIO

ON MARCH 9, 2025, Woodmere Director William R. Valerio joined Syd Carpenter in her studio to discuss the trajectory of her career in the context of this exhibition.

WILLIAM R. VALERIO Syd, it's great to be here in your beautiful studio, filled with art and tools and clay. I also see art by your husband, Steve Donegan, and by artist friends, as well as objects from around the globe and your many wonderful plants. The place is alive with energy!

Our plan is to discuss the evolution of your work: your beginnings, how you found your voice as an artist, how your work grew over time, and your direction as we look to the future. Not that this is going to be a straight-line journey. I'm sure we'll go backward and forward and explore tangents.

There's a great deal written about your work, and several excellent videos, but I've found that these narratives tend to start with the farm portraits you made around 2010. The purpose of our retrospective exhibition is to start at the beginning, in the 1980s, with the first works you were showing as a professional artist (fig. 2.1).

But before we dive in, I'd like to suggest a framework for our discussion that relates to your unique voice as an artist, at least in my eyes. In the *Craft in America* series on PBS, you described your journey to Pittsburgh to find the site that had been your grandmother's garden. You talked about looking out over the Monongahela River, imagining your grandmother's presence, seeing what she saw—the steel mills and factory buildings—and sensing what she may have sensed. From there you built works of art, like the *Indiana Hutson* farm portrait, that channel your lived experience there with humanity, deep-grounded empathy, and connection to your grandmother. Your work grows from your interactions with people. And so, for example, when I look at the rendering of a metal porch glider on the *Mary Howard Farm Bowl* (fig. 2.2), I'm sure it's a translation of an object that was not only actually there, but also that you somehow experienced it in a meaningful way. It represents a connection you made with Mary and her farm. Maybe you sat on that glider with Mary, or if not, it was an important element in the life of the farm. Its presence on the bowl brings the place alive in my imagination.

SYD CARPENTER Yes, that glider was a real piece of furniture at Mary Howard's farm—I remember its pink color. The experience on the land that had been my grandmother's garden was profound, and yes, you can say that much of my work grows from lived experiences I've shared with others, but that's not always necessary for me. I think of the *Ramshackle Fence* (fig. 2.3), my

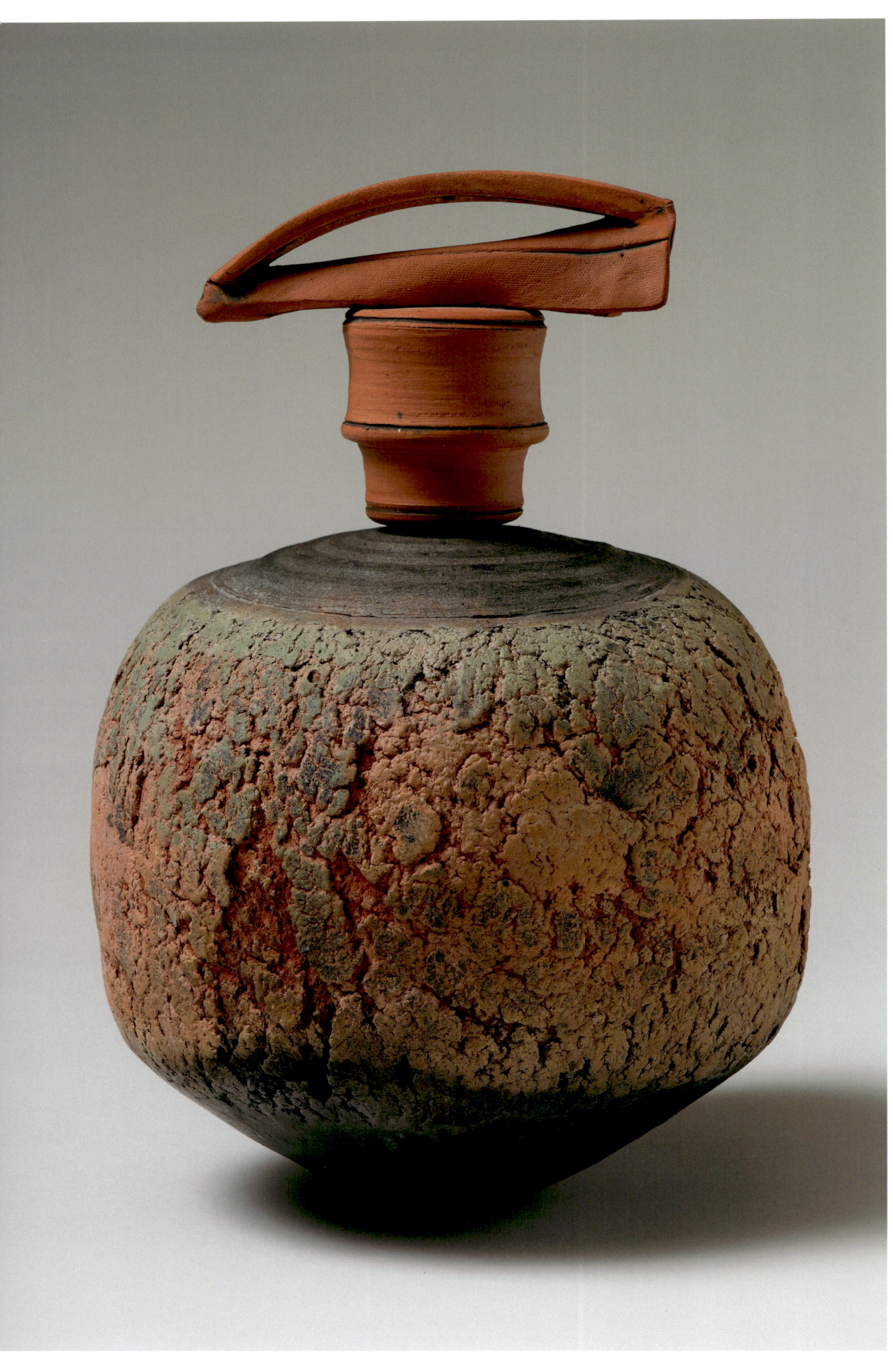

FIG. 2.1 *Untitled (Lorraine's Pot)*, 1985, terracotta and black copper oxide, 15 × 10 × 10 in. (Woodmere: Gift of Lorraine and Benjamin Alexander, 2023)

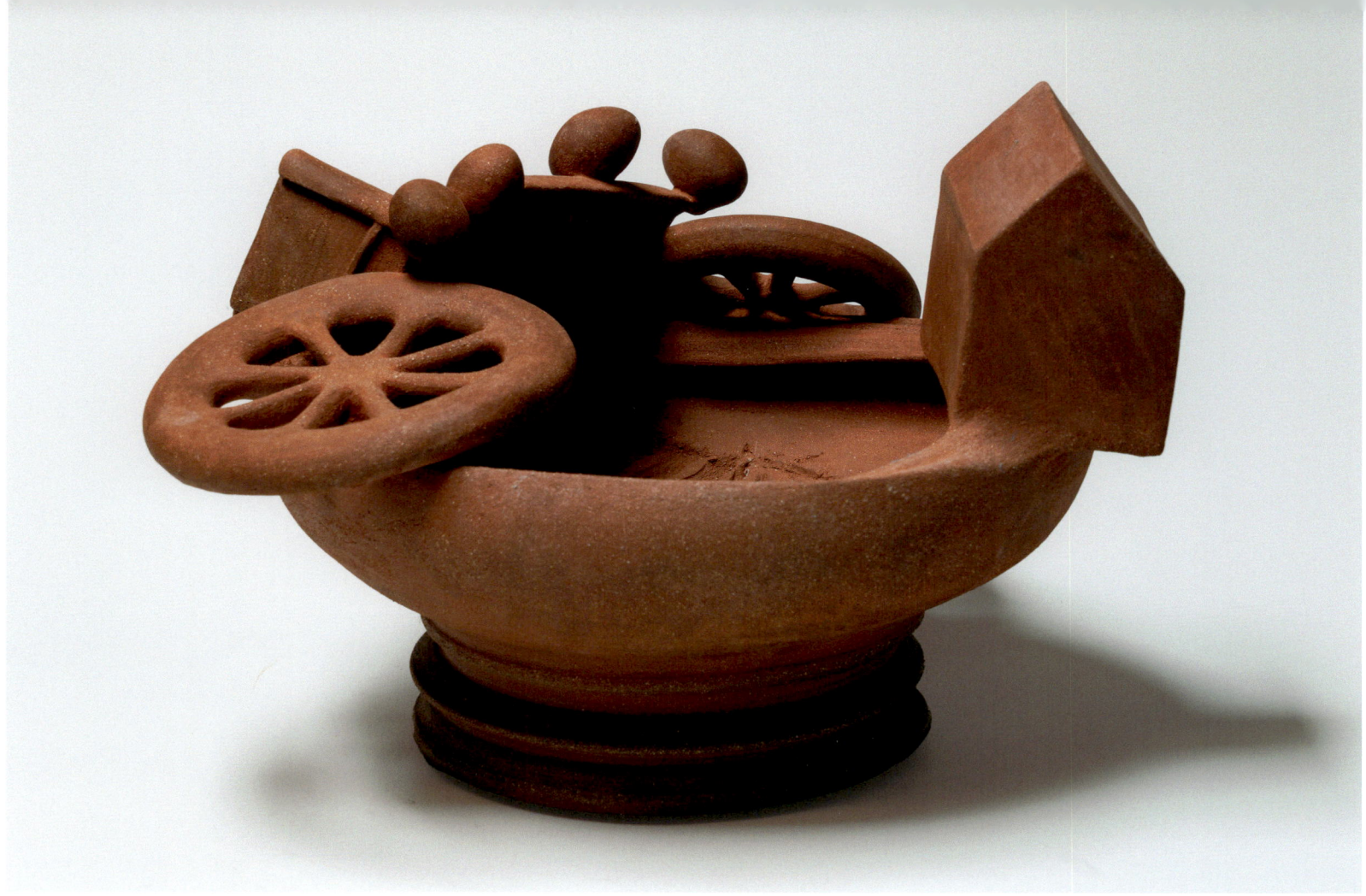

FIG. 2.2 *Mary Howard Farm Bowl*, 2020, stoneware, 15 × 20 × 22 in. (Collection of the artist)

FIG. 2.3 (FOLLOWING SPREAD) *Ramshackle Fence*, 2008–12, earthenware, graphite, and acrylic, 30 × 75 × 9 in. (Everson Museum of Art: Museum Purchase, Deaccession Fund)

most ambitious farm portrait: It's a broad statement about farms as places, about the hundreds of ramshackle fences I've seen, and an amalgamation of memories and ideas about farms. It also includes my first sculpted clothespin, which I modeled after those in my mother's own bag of clothespins—those forms have come to represent my mother in my work. So in a way the connection to people you're describing is there, it's just not always direct.

VALERIO Let's turn back the clock. Can you talk about your experiences as a student at Tyler?

CARPENTER I started at Tyler in 1970 and finished in '76. I was there because my family needed me to be close, but they didn't want me *not* to get away for college, and they knew it was my calling to be an artist and go to an art college. Getting into Tyler was a big deal. Back then, there was Tyler or RISD [Rhode Island School of Design]. There was no good undergrad art program in New York City at the time. The New Yorkers were coming down to Philadelphia. We met our friend Martin Weinstein at Tyler—he's an amazing artist and we have traveled together. Frank Bramblett and Roger Anliker were there too, and, very significantly for me, so was Rudy Staffel.

VALERIO There's no artist I can think of with a more expansive dedication to experimentation with materials than Frank. Roger

Anliker's work combines virtuosity and deep personal resonances. And, if creativity means pushing the boundaries of one's chosen medium, then Rudy Staffel gets the gold star.

CARPENTER They all remain inspiring to me. But I have to mention the women who were teaching there, too. The great Winifred Lutz worked in sculpted paper, and there was an extraordinary fiber artist there at the time, Adela Akers. She came to Philadelphia from Cuba, by way of Spain and Chicago. John Dowell was teaching there as well, so there was a Black faculty member, which was very unusual in those days, but so important, and there was Paul Keene at the Philadelphia College of Art (PCA). It was a good time for me to be at Tyler!

VALERIO My understanding is that your earliest works are the large, textured pots you made in the 1980s, after Tyler. As an art historian, I would place those within a broader conversation about functional "craft" vessels, crossing into the more exalted territory of sculpture.

CARPENTER Well, they're pots with lids and sometimes handles that are sculptural, but in terms of function, they're jars with flat bottoms. They had to be stable. There was a certain kind of symmetry around them. They connect to the vast ceramic history of rounded vessels that relate to nature—gourds, pumpkins—and

A CONVERSATION WITH SYD CARPENTER

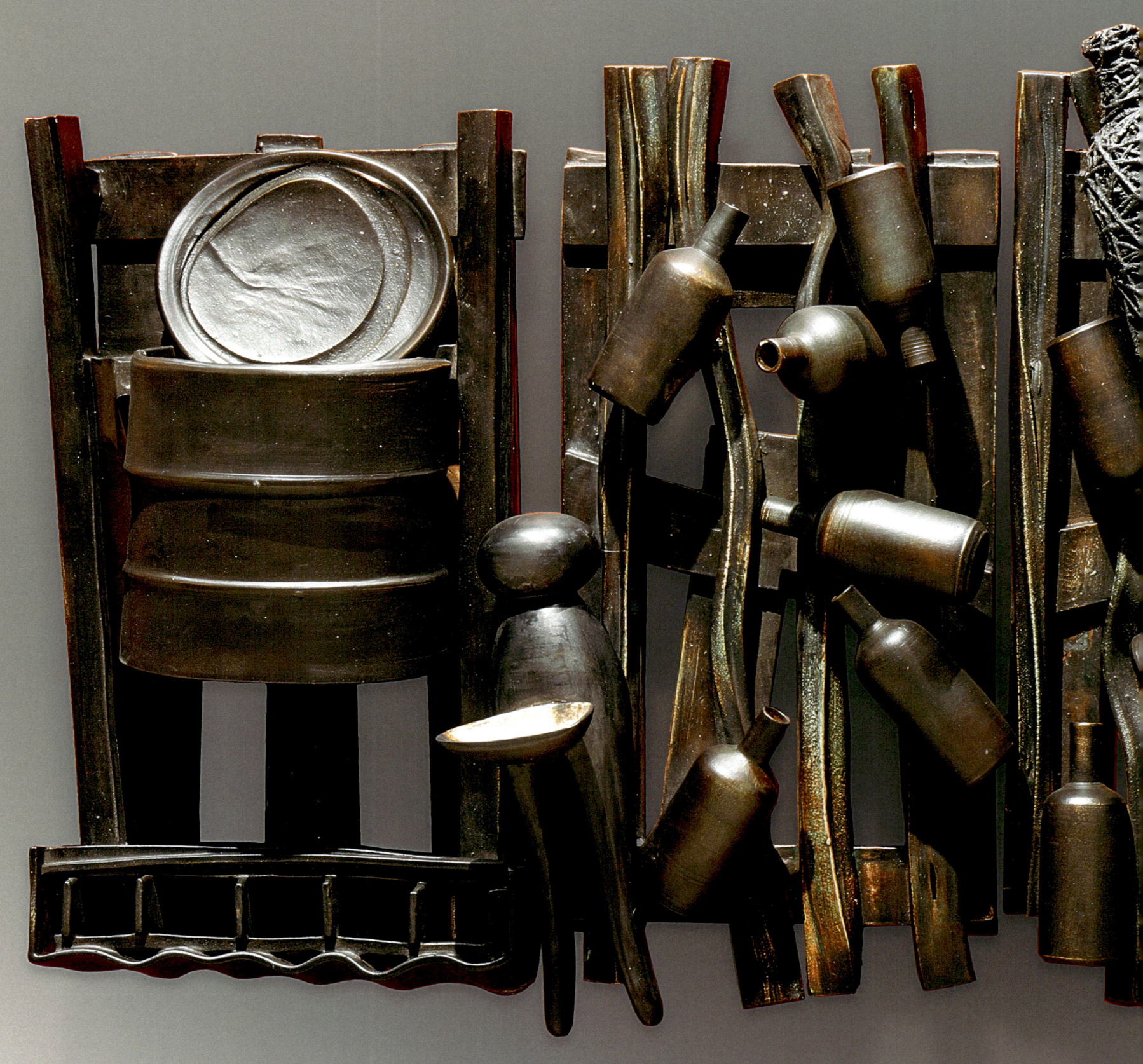

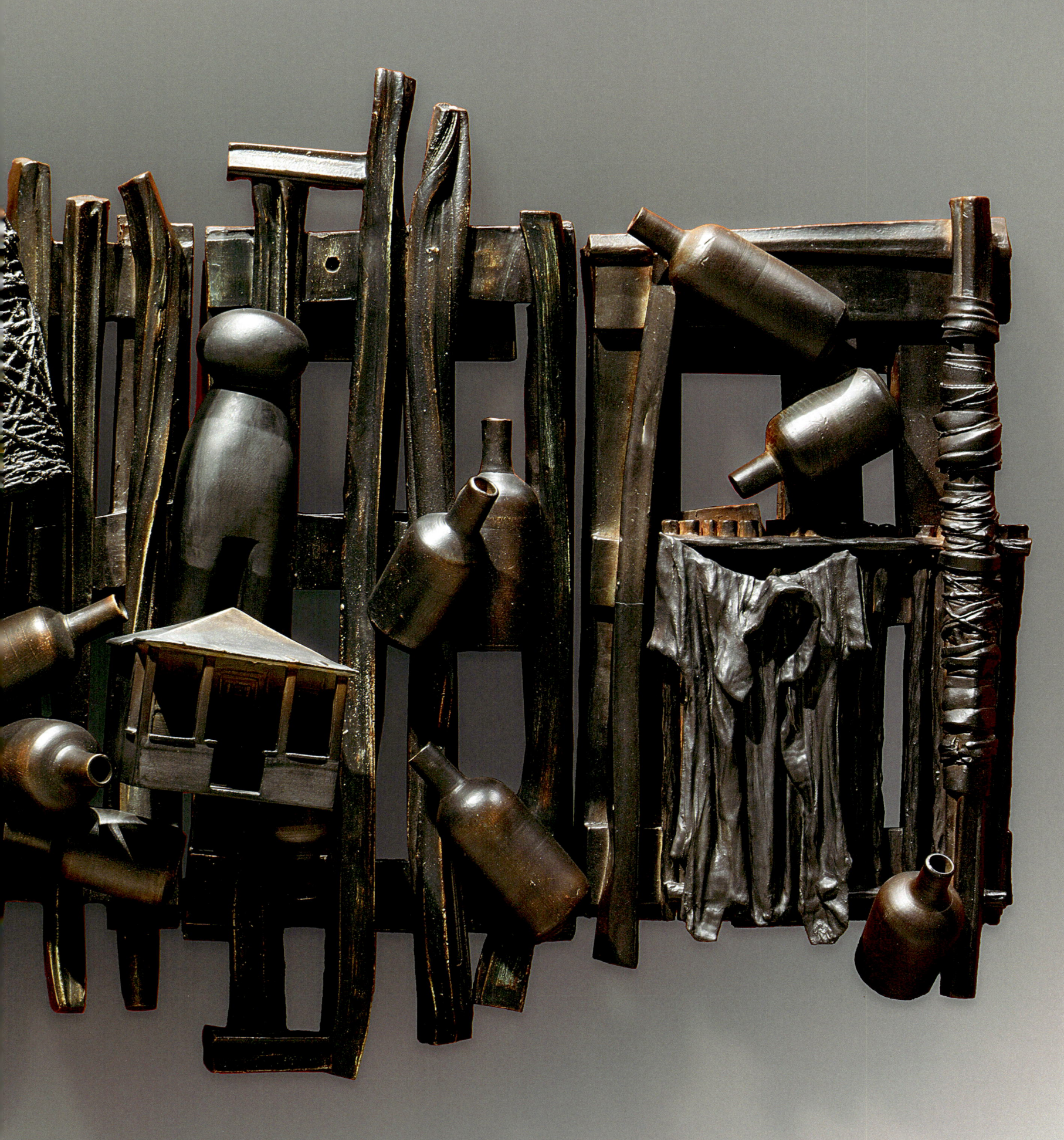

to human anatomy—stomach, uterus, all those. I made the pots partially on the wheel, mostly the tops so I could make the lids, and the bottoms so they would sit properly. But they all began as a slab of clay, and they're hand-built: They're slabs that are turned into cylinders then closed off at top and bottom on the wheel. Then they're shaped, stretched, painted on. You can see the concentric rings that result from finishing on the wheel in the *Untitled* pot of 1985 in Woodmere's collection (see fig. 2.1).

VALERIO That pot sits in my office, actually. I've often pondered its rough, rich, craggy surface—the earth itself. The top piece has a bow shape—an arc under tension—and a directional nose, like the head of a plow, gesturing.

CARPENTER Yes, it's gesturing, that's always it. I'm not playing a model maker there, as I did when I made Mary Howard's glider, but yes, the form on that pot could be a plow or a tool of some kind. The top pieces are little drawings in clay, sketches in three dimensions. I'm not necessarily trying to make a replica of a plow or a hammerhead. It's not going to do that. But I like to look at objects and ask the question, what is it doing? Even as an object that takes up space, there's always some way of describing it actively. So if a mug is just sitting there on the table, well, how is it sitting? Is it sitting low? Is it sitting high? Is it reaching? Is it spiraling? Is it tilting? I always think objects have gestures. And when I'm making something, I'm always asking, well, what's it doing? Is it leaning? Is it about to collapse?

VALERIO That pot was a gift from Lorraine Alexander. She herself was an artist—she showed at Gross McCleaf Gallery—but she also collected. She had an artist's eye for truly interesting objects. Woodmere was given a number of works from her collection. That she was an early collector of your work is significant. That's a pot with a great provenance.

Another pot, owned by James Brantley (fig 2.4), is a wider, round form that suggests a great monumentality, like a mountain-planet with a house for its sole inhabitant.

CARPENTER It relates to a certain kind of topography and landscape and a way of thinking about earth and movement. The architectural form on top is rigid and impenetrable, but the body of the pot itself is in motion because it seems to expand or exert a sense of inner pressure. I always thought about the inner pressure when I was making these pieces because it takes me pressing against the cylinder to make that belly swell and come up. And I have to do that with concentration because if I push it too much the clay will split.

VALERIO What about that house on top, the place itself?

CARPENTER I've been making these little structures forever—they appear on most of the farm bowls—without copying any specific house. It's to evoke architecture without copying architecture. In my new installation at the Berman Museum, I built one of these houses on a larger scale than before, and it's connected to that much earlier house on James's pot. Building the houses is just a continuation of the ideas I was exploring on the tops of these pots.

VALERIO Retrospectives can reveal these kinds of connections over time in the work.

CARPENTER I have stacks of sketchbooks all over the place, along with sketches and drawings—things I was saying to myself and exploring as ideas when I was twenty—and now fifty years later, I'm still murmuring in line about the same things. You evolve as an artist, but there's a core and layers on top of it, like an onion. But the core is still in there. The reality is that I made these pots in my thirties, and now I'm making something like it in my seventies. And so I just think, oh, there's some connectivity, there's a stream that's running—even though it sometimes goes underground, it comes back up.

VALERIO I need to know about the pot titled *House for Mr. Biswas* (see p. 35). Who was he?

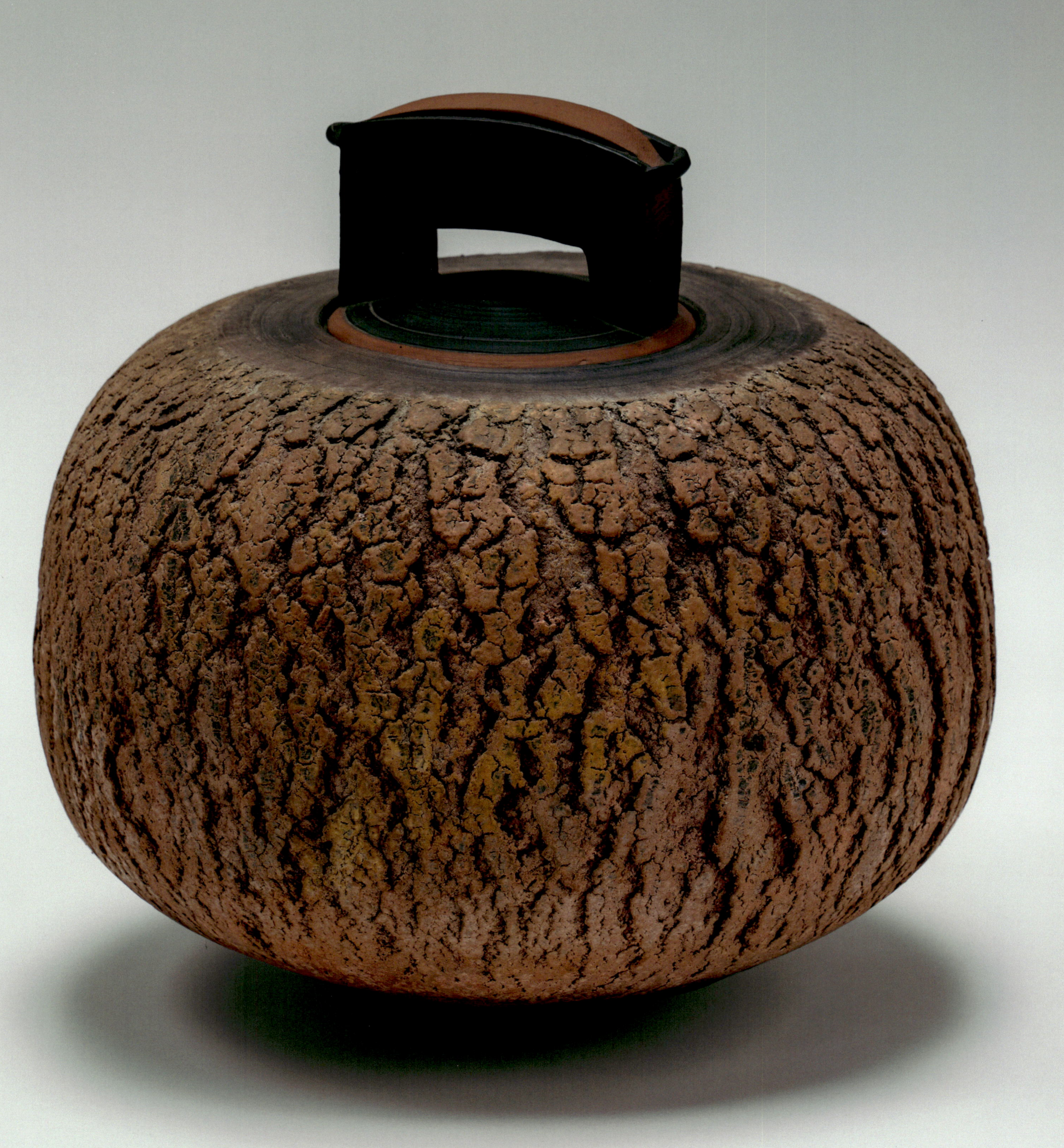

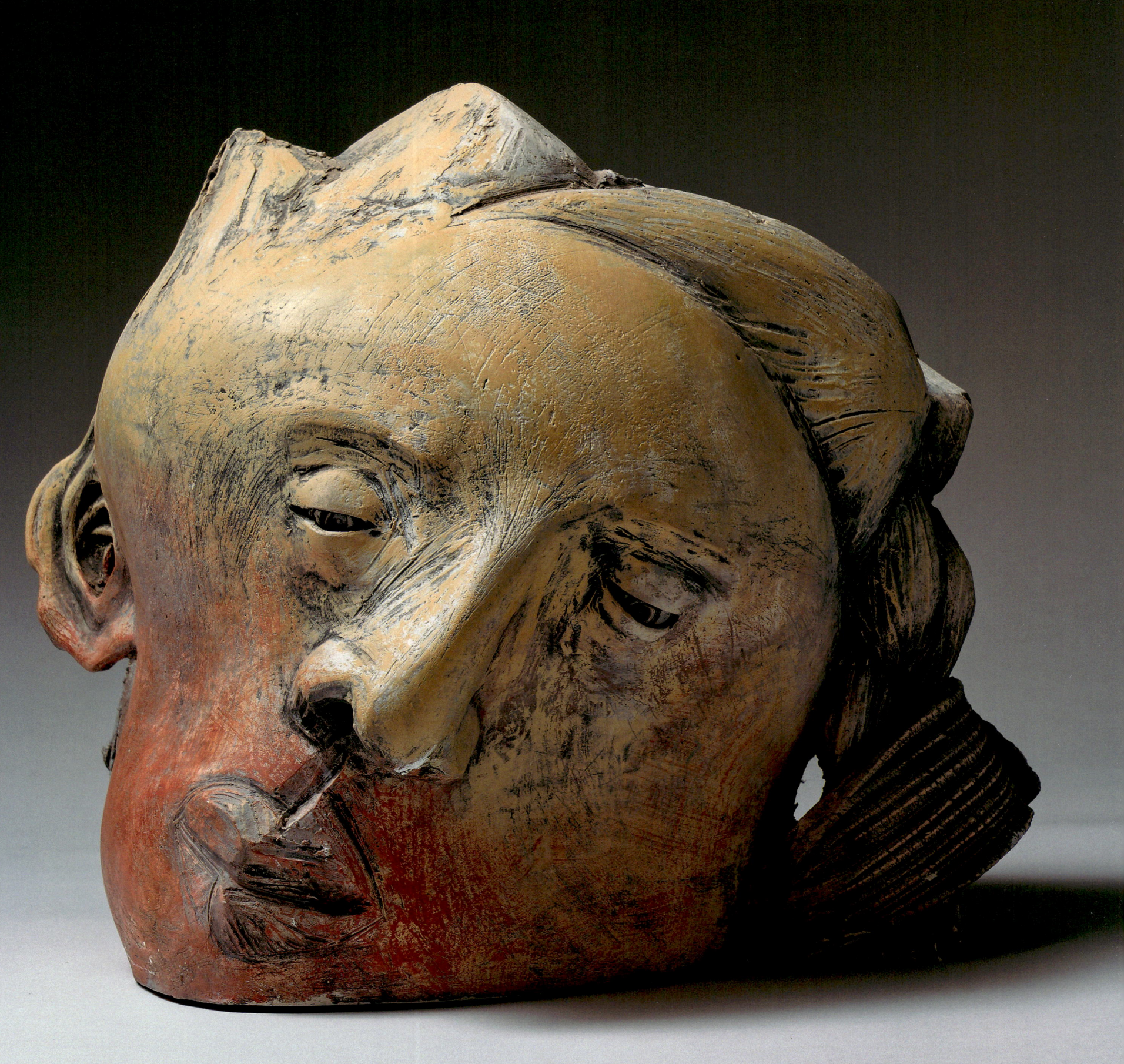

FIG. 2.5 *Child 3*, 1990, clay and terra sigillata, 17 × 21 × 16 in. (Collection of the artist)

CARPENTER That pot was inspired by a novel by V. S. Naipaul about an Asian Indian man in the Caribbean—Mr. Biswas. I read it many years ago, and this was a house for him, this very tall house.

VALERIO And is this a guardian figure?

CARPENTER Yes. It's a furry animal and it's protecting him. These were shown at the Sande Webster Gallery on Walnut Street in Philadelphia. Sande bought many works straight out of my shows in her gallery back in the 1980s. [Webster, wife of James Brantley, had a particular interest in Black artists.] Woodmere's pot is from one of those shows. The pots basically were the beginning of my professional career, getting out there, being public, and actively trying to get the work shown.

VALERIO That statement helps me understand the significance of the 1990s for you. There's only a short time from your professional beginnings as an artist, to a pivotal decade of significant recognition. The next major phase of your career started with the large heads (fig. 2.5, and pp. 36–37). Can you tell me about those?

CARPENTER They're right after the pots, and made in the same way, from a hand-built cylinder with some limited wheel turning to shape the tops and make the bottoms sit right. Then I sculpted and distorted the forms. It started when I noticed that one of the pots in process looked like a face. So really, the pots evolved into heads.

VALERIO Whose heads are they?

CARPENTER I called them children. And when I showed them at Sande's gallery, it was an installation of about a dozen of them: *Child 1* through *Child 12*. They were just talking to each other, gesturing and whispering. They're not specific children, but each time I was making one, I was stretching and improvising, making large sculptural forms that push out from the pressure within. That sense of inner pressure and organic growth was important to the pots we just talked about, and the balloon-like

pressure is important to the children. Life bursting out! They're babies and toddlers that I imagined in communication with each other but caught when their ability to use language is in its formative stages. There aren't social skills, but instead the necessity to communicate for the sake of the needs associated with being alive. It's about being unformed and figuring it out by using whatever tools you may have, making sounds and movements. Kids have a body language and a repertoire of sounds before they have language.

VALERIO Do all of them sit on flat surfaces?

CARPENTER Yes. They were designed to be displayed on pedestals or tables. However, there was a deep relief wall sculpture with a child's face called *Of a Like Mind* (see p. 40).

VALERIO Let's interpret that and its juxtaposition of two distinct elements: the large face of an older child, maybe even a teenager, and—on a different scale altogether—a rectangular box of three female nude torsos. The large face has downturned eyes and raised brow-like forms; it seems turned in on itself, pensive. What about those torsos below, the body as vessel of life?

CARPENTER I didn't know it at the time, but this would become a transition to the next phase of my work, large wall reliefs like *A Part of the Whole* (pp. 38–39).

VALERIO That's a powerful work and a recent gift to Woodmere from the Wind family. From the time Jerry and Dina purchased it in the early 1990s, it was a very strong presence in their home in Gladwyne. It hung over their living room fireplace alongside pieces by Jim Dine, Lynda Benglis, and Tony Cragg, among others. Jerry and Dina fell in love with your work early on—they acquired this from your Wind Challenge exhibition at the Fleisher Art Memorial. Dina was a sculptor, and she saw in you a confidence in working with clay, a mastery of your chosen medium; one time looking at *A Part of the Whole* together, she described that it wears its monumentality with conviction. Jerry is a professor at Wharton School of Business, whose mantra

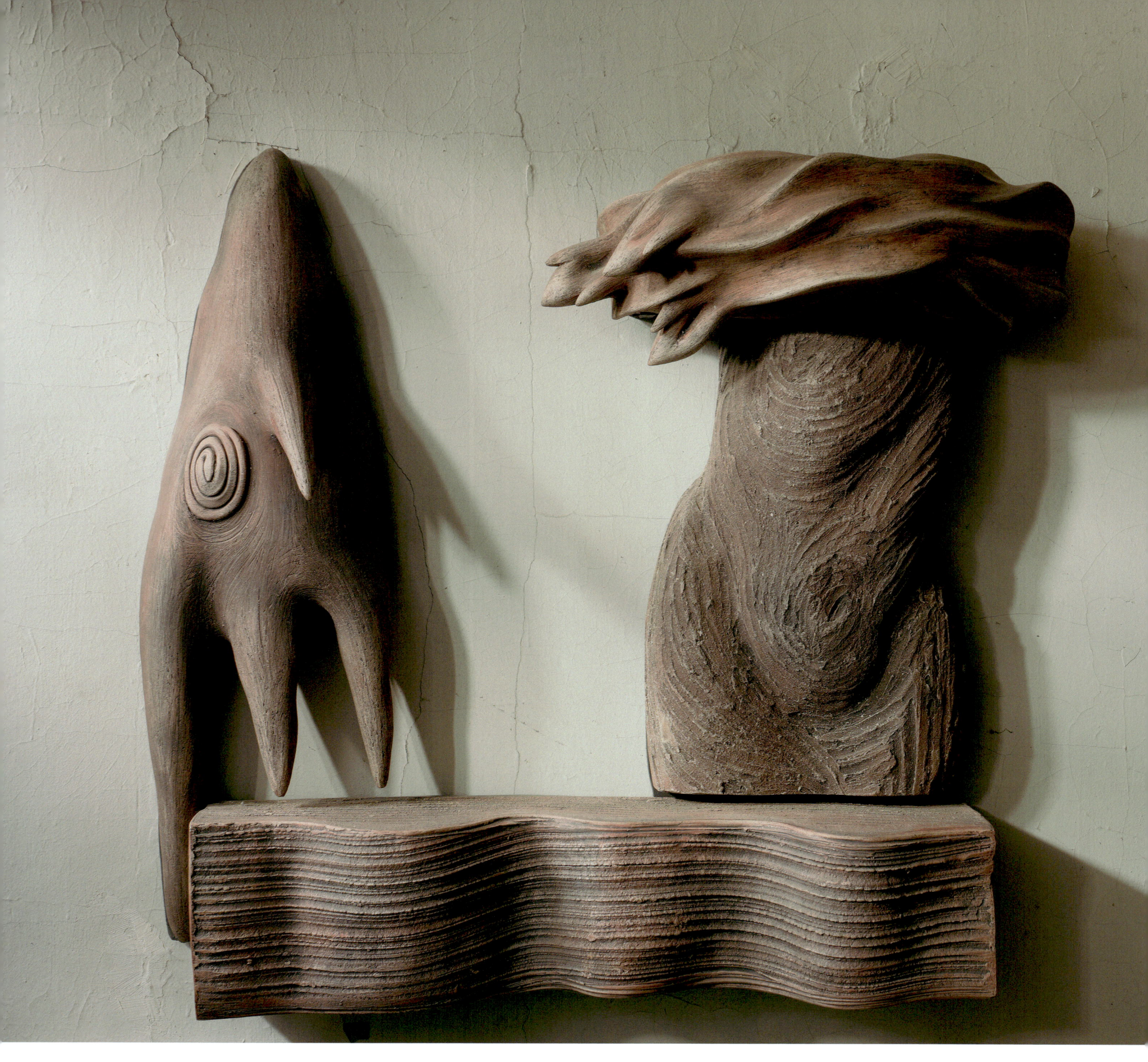

FIG. 2.6   *Then, Now, When*, 1991, clay and slip, 41 × 42 × 12 in. (Collection of the artist)

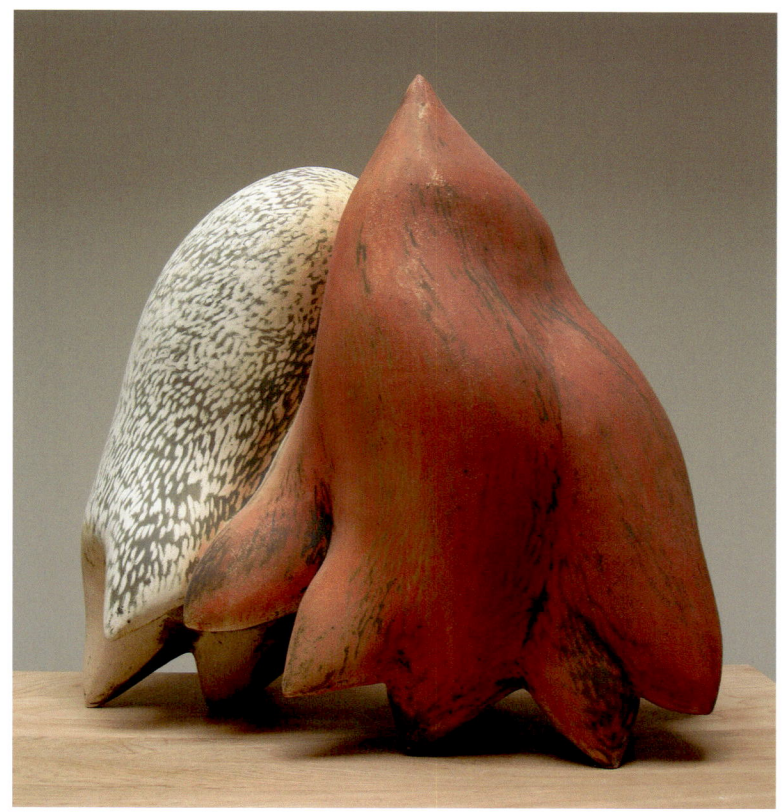

to his marketing students is: Experiment! He and I have often discussed your work, and he greatly admires the experimental nature of your practice, that you're not content to work today in the same ways you did yesterday. What's the subject of this piece?

CARPENTER This is man and the built environment. Houses, architecture, and the constructed world we all live in, juxtaposed with the human form and the mind that creates it. The children of my previous works have now grown up, and the giant figure is embedded in, gives shape to, organizes, and gives structure to the life it creates.

VALERIO A Vitruvian man, of sorts—the work is not just powerful in its forms, but it addresses the larger-than-life themes that have occupied the imaginations of artists for many centuries. Another large wall sculpture from this period is *Then, Now, When* (fig. 2.6). The title suggests the passage of time.

CARPENTER Yes, that was intentional. For about ten years, it hung in the faculty lounge at Swarthmore College. Then, when the space was needed for something else, it came home to me. The circular composition suggests movement. Between the verticals of the amoeba-like shape on the left and the woman's torso on the right are forms that evoke the movement of water below and wind above. I wanted to suggest the movement of nature.

VALERIO Can we talk about that amoeba? Does it relate to your later three-dimensional leaf sculptures?

CARPENTER Yes, there's a continuity in the shape and idea, but they're also different. The "leaf" works I made in the 2000s came from extending the flat shapes of leaves, building a sculpture by exploring the volumes created by pulling the edge lines and flat shapes of leaves into three dimensions. They become new entities, like *Two Birds Dancing* (fig. 2.7).

The amoebic shape in *Then, Now, When* grew out of my interest in microorganisms, you know those squishy, formless beings you can see only with a microscope. I'm entranced by all

that, as are many artists; all life depends on, and started with, those creatures.

VALERIO I've seen many images of the coronavirus in art in recent years! *Check Your Sources* (1990), which Hal Sorgenti purchased from Sande Webster for the game-changing collection of works by Black artists he gave to the Pennsylvania Academy of the Fine Arts (PAFA), also implies the up-and-down trajectory of a living entity: A coiled shell-like form becomes a sleeve on a flexed arm. The arm transfers its energy into a sword-like plant that cascades down.

CARPENTER Yes, that piece is about energy and strength. It's interesting for me to consider these relationships because when I was making *Then, Now, When* and *Check Your Sources*, I was thinking about the nature of relief sculpture. Although I was making very deep relief, it somehow wasn't deep enough for me. As a sculptor, I needed to imagine the parts of the forms that were— by extension—inside the wall. It's the depth of it I wanted, like: Where's the rest of it? The only answer was that it was in the wall. At some point I decided to start making pieces that were more dimensional again, so you could feel the full spectrum of the form, nothing hidden behind the plane of the wall. And so I began making wall sculptures that are full, three-dimensional forms that come off the wall. In the checklist for this show, it would be works like *A Snake without a Head Is Just a Rope* (fig. 2.9), which is in the collection of the Philadelphia Museum of Art.

VALERIO Having your works acquired by PMA and PAFA, and by serious collectors like Lorraine Alexander and Dina and Jerry Wind, is major recognition.

CARPENTER Also, a great number of Sande's clients were designers; she could follow her stars and her vision to provide a platform for Black artists because she was selling a lot of work to interior designers. Her gallery was also a frame shop, and she had a great eye for making unique, expensive frames. I credit her with getting my work into PMA and PAFA, which, don't get me wrong, is really amazing, but *she* did that.

My own sense of community as an artist came from showing at Sande's gallery and from being part of the craft community and organizations like the National Council on Education for the Ceramic Arts. That was my home base in terms of support.

It's so interesting to look at these again and think of them together. I can see how the narratives evolved. Those first pots, there are little narratives—the plow, the house, the characters like Mr. Biswas. And that's perfect for what they are. But then if you're continuing to work with identifying things that are important to you, that respond to what you're observing, what you're thinking, and you want more: well, then what? How do you represent deep thoughts as an object that takes up space, as it imposes itself physically. When you're making a sculpture, you're creating something that has physical agency. It's taking space. It must live a life. It has to be sturdy. It must have a voice and be autonomous. It must live in the space that it eventually ends up in. That amoeba-like entity is a depiction of something alive, and it opened many doors in my sculpture.

VALERIO The Metropolitan Museum of Art's piece—*Familiar Figure* (fig. 2.8)—is part of this same period, roughly chronologically.

CARPENTER That was acquired by Robert Ellison; the Met acquired his entire collection. Back in those days, he got on the train and came to Philadelphia and went to Sande's gallery to see the work (there was no internet for him to scope things out in advance). He bought two works and installed them in his loft in

New York. He later invited me to come up and see his collection and to see my work installed side by side with gorgeous works by George Ohr.

VALERIO I've always read *Familiar Figure* as relating to a woman's body: hips, fallopian tubes, perhaps a belly.

CARPENTER Bill, it's a vagina! But it's also a pair of scissors, and it speaks to the violence of female circumcision. I'm imagining the horror of the vagina sewn shut.

VALERIO I obviously didn't get that—that's intense.

CARPENTER Yeah, there are lots of layers going on there. So that's a painful figure. The title is understood by half of the population. There's the pain, with the scissors, but then it's also a plant form.

VALERIO What's the social context that brought you to *Familiar Figure* and *Check Your Sources*? It's 1991, the first Bush era, the first Gulf War.

CARPENTER I had just gotten a job at Swarthmore, so I was working hard. Yes, the Iraq War and the Bushes coming at us, and people dying of AIDS and the terrible injustices. It was not good. It was a very rough time. I never stopped working, and the stuff was coming out in the work. Sometimes anger, sometimes pain, sometimes other emotions. I couldn't make pieces that were bucolic or conventionally pretty. I could still reference the garden, and that was important. I had also just bought a house in Mount Airy [in Northwest Philadelphia] and I started the garden there, too. My mother had just passed—that was big. So there was a lot going on.

VALERIO You mention your mother—I hadn't thought about this before, but *Familiar Figure* evokes your later *Mother Pins*. There's a formal resonance, a rhyming of forms. Is there a layer of the Met's piece that references your mother, the woman, now gone, who gave you life, who brought you into the world?

FIG. 2.8 *Familiar Figure*, 1991, clay and slip, 49¾ × 21¾ × 9⅞ in. (Metropolitan Museum of Art: Gift of Robert A. Ellison Jr., in celebration of the Museum's 150th Anniversary, 2020)

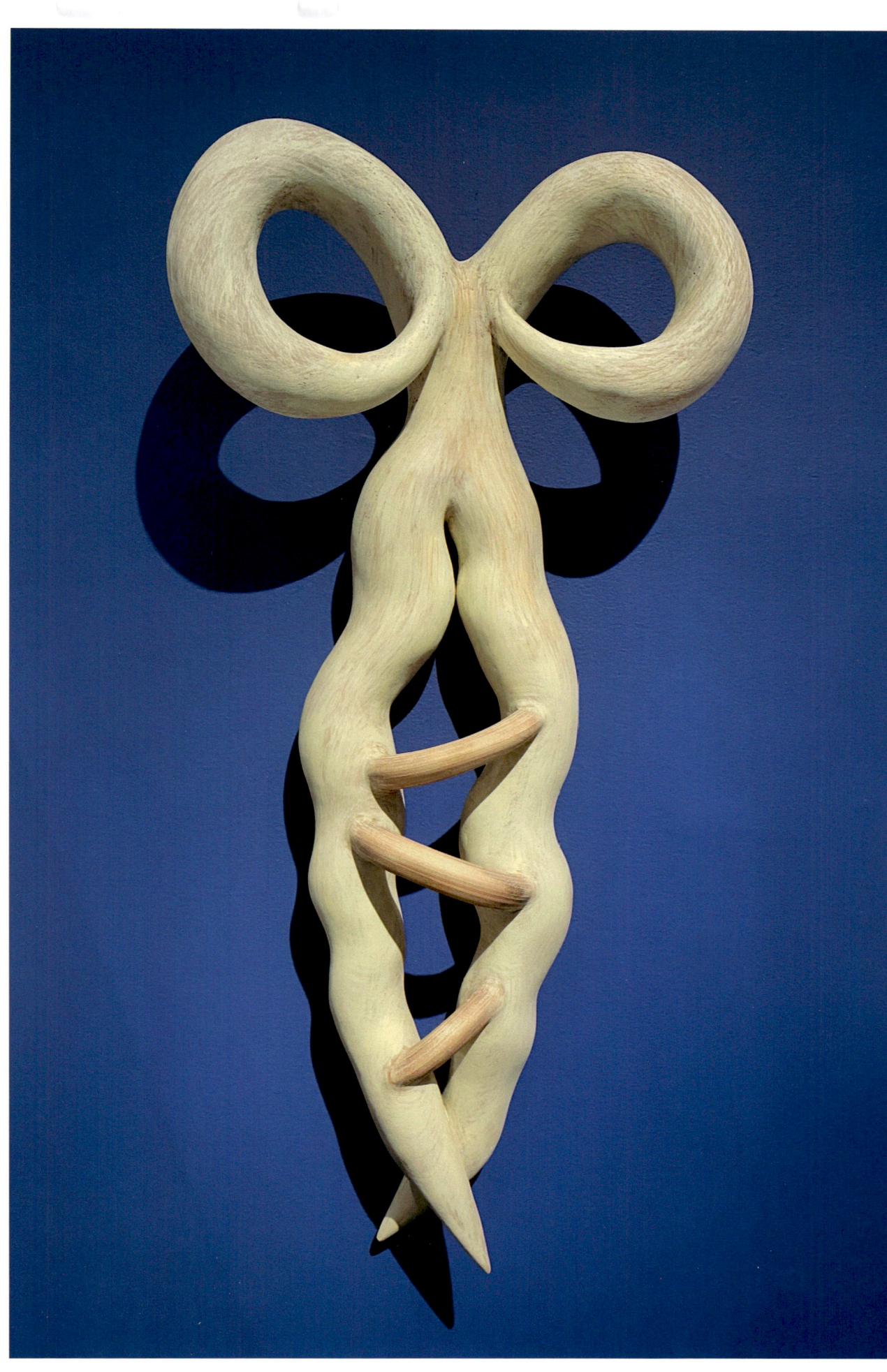

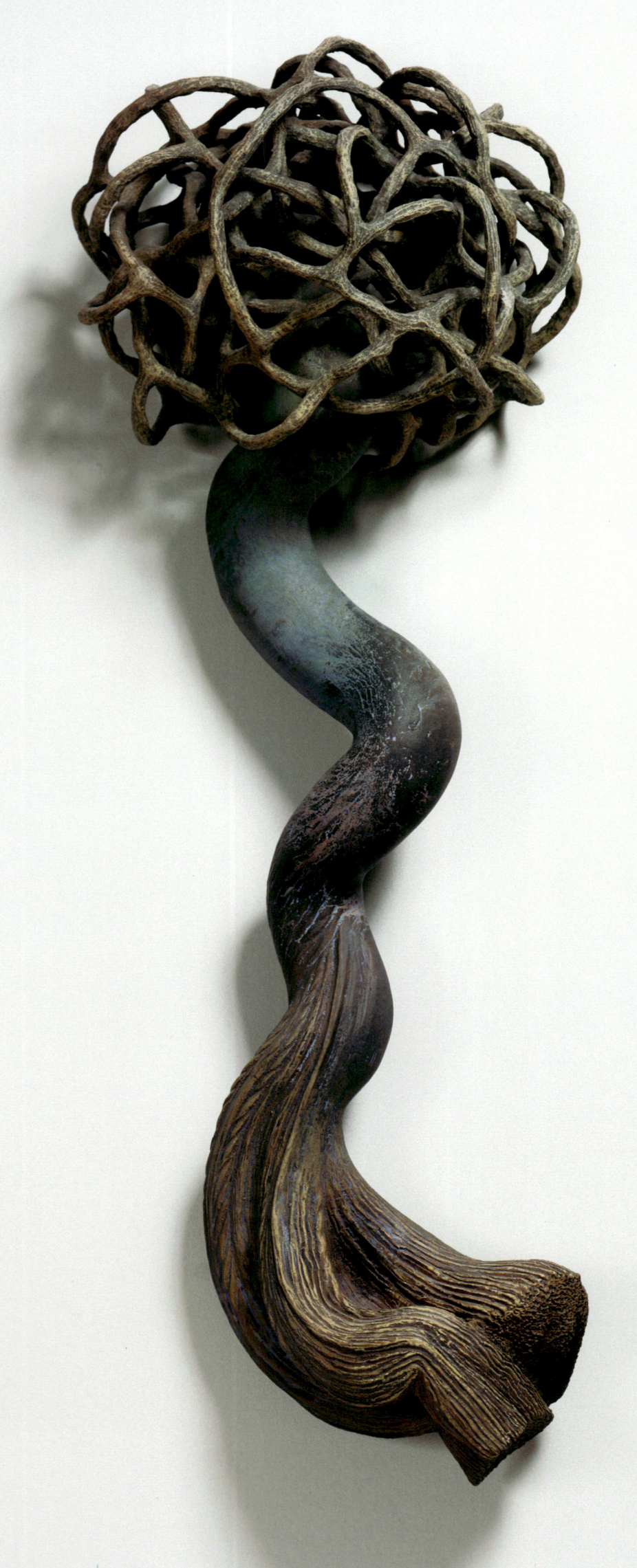

FIG. 2.9 *A Snake without a Head Is Just a Rope*, 1994, glazed earthenware, 59 × 20 × 16 in. (Philadelphia Museum of Art: Purchased with funds contributed by The Women's Committee and the Craft Show Committee of the Philadelphia Museum of Art, 1995-19-1)

CARPENTER I wasn't thinking of my mother when I created *Familiar Figure*, but the sculpture is evocative of the female body, as are the *Mother Pins*. *Familiar Figure* is infused with the suggestion of violence against the female body. The *Mother Pins* represent resistance.

VALERIO Violence is expressed in some of your other works as well. The very title of *A Snake without a Head Is Just a Rope* suggests decapitation. That came slightly later, in 1994, and I imagine it's one of the wall sculptures with no imagined parts existing in the imaginary space behind the wall, as you described earlier.

CARPENTER There is a practice in West Africa known as *asafo* where competing military teams assault each other verbally and visually with appliquéd banners. Many of the insults are metaphors. One team insults the other by saying they are not a snake, just a rope without a head. In a way, you may be right that it's decapitation, emasculation. But that's the rope, and if you look at it, it's unraveling. I was also making nests at the time, and that's one of my nests on top. The rope meets the nest. I should also mention that the piece is made with coiling. The large, coiled tube is hollow, like a coiled pot. I remember coiling and coiling and coiling to make that piece.

VALERIO Let's move on to the twenty-first century. Can you talk a bit about *Frank Portrait* (fig. 2.10)?

CARPENTER That's my baby brother, Frankie. He was in the military, and in about 2000 he was stationed in Turkey. He was in a van, something happened, and the van flipped over. He was rushed from the scene to the doctors and medical units, but the result was that he became quadriplegic. And this was a man who had been incredibly handsome, loved to dress sharp, loved to dance—a ladies' man.

VALERIO The Petrucci Foundation's work is called *Frank in Tow* (fig. 2.11). I'm guessing it's a long, coiled tube like the works we were just talking about. Frank's sculpted likeness is on one side of the central fulcrum, and a large bird stares at him from the opposite end. There's a balancing act, a seesaw quality to the work.

CARPENTER This work is very important to me. My mother loved birds. The bird is my mother, watching over my brother, whom she loved with all her heart. The wheels represent the wheelchair that he was pretty much confined to after the accident. *Frank in Tow* can go on the wall or the floor. On the wall, it's angled so the viewer looks up at Frank. If it's shown horizontally, it's more about him in his wheelchair in relation to my mother.

Frank's Peace (see pp. 42–43) is another portrait of Frank, with a curving, tubular form. He's the stallion nestling with his hat. He's at peace. There's a leaf there, and underneath it is his porkpie hat.

VALERIO Can I ask about *Breathe* (see p. 46), also at Woodmere and a gift from the Winds? Are those wheels related to Frank's wheelchair?

CARPENTER No, no. That form is more of a shell, and it pulls air in, a kind of inhale. Then the breath travels through the tube and comes out as bubbles. It's about giving form to breath as an idea, an elemental process, the foundation of living. Breath as the essence of life. It's related to Frank as a meditation on life.

VALERIO It's wonderful to me that you had the audacity as a sculptor to make a three-dimensional work in earthy clay that expresses something as ephemeral as breath itself! I've been holding back asking you about *Frank as Sun King* (see pp. 44–45). Can you tell me about that?

CARPENTER I was making works that were meditations on Frank and thinking about his dignity and pride in the face of his greatly diminished state. The stature of the Sun King, Louis XIV, who built Versailles, came to me—the most majestic, grandest idea of what a person can be. The wheel is a found object, actually a wooden gear, and it represents everything round and radiant, his life-giving aura, the sun, of course. But it's also a found object

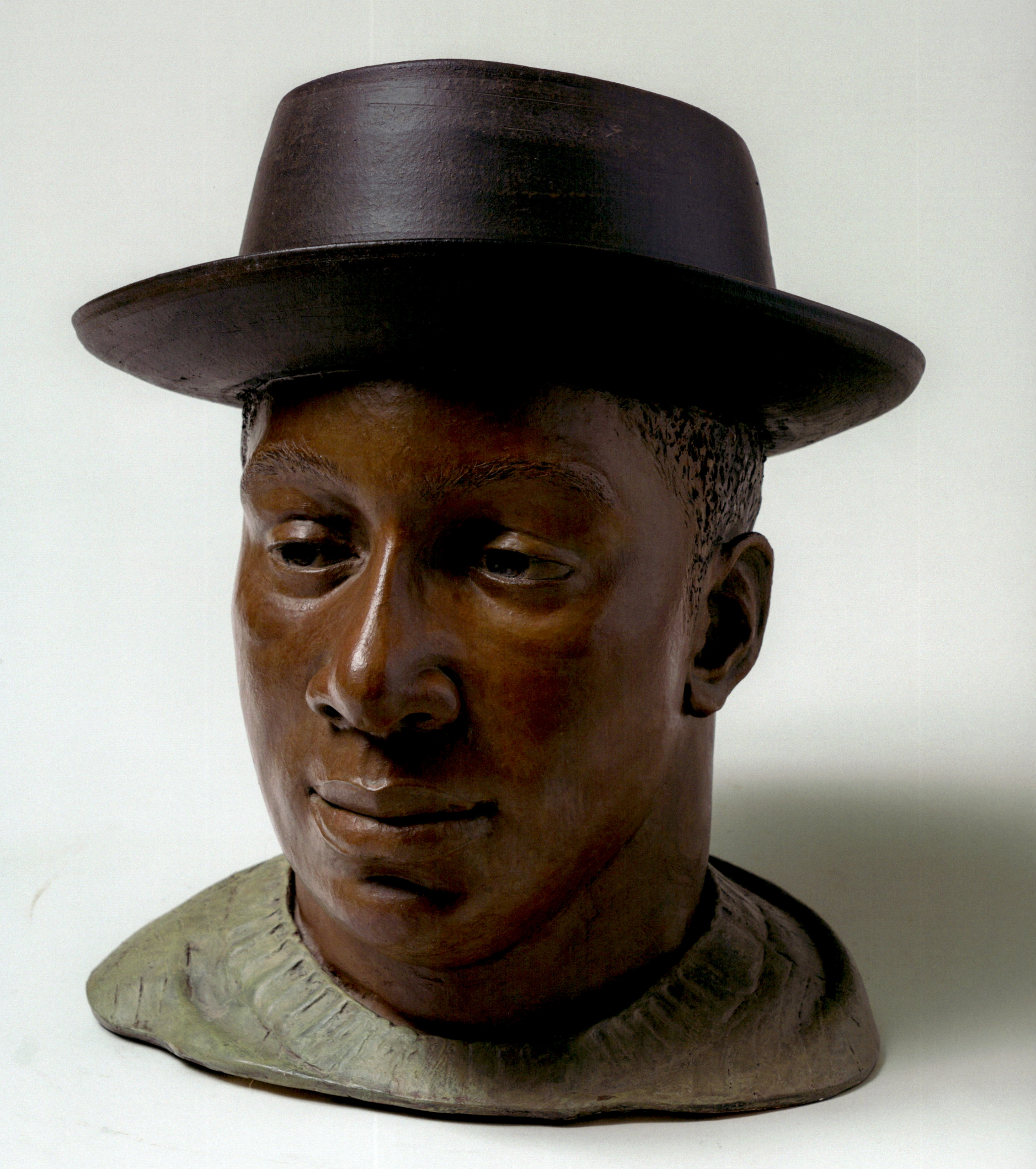

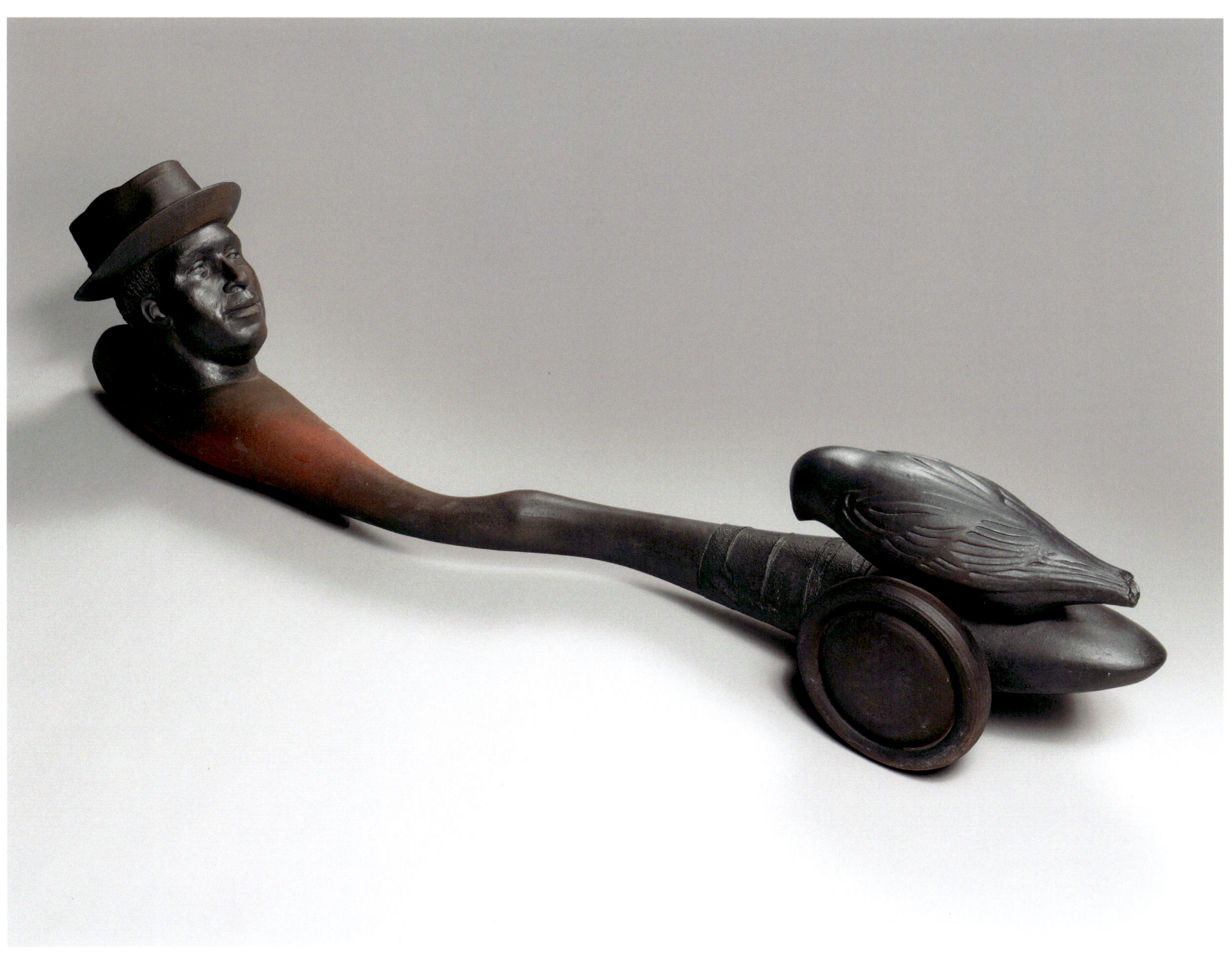

FIG. 2.10   *Frank Portrait*, 2007, clay and watercolor, 15 × 15 × 10 in. (Collection of the artist)

FIG. 2.11   *Frank in Tow*, 2008, graphite on clay, 12 × 52 × 8 in. (Courtesy of the Petrucci Family Foundation Collection of African American Art)

A CONVERSATION WITH SYD CARPENTER

with history, part of a one-time factory, a down-to-earth, industrial element. The hollow of the rectangular pedestal stands in for Frank's body, and it's a reliquary for his boots. Around Frank's head is a halo of symbols: The bird represents my mother again, the stallion is Frank, and there are stars because he was a star.

VALERIO Did he pose for you?

CARPENTER He came to my studio, and I took photographs of him from all different angles. I sculpted it from the photos. There was a level of immortality I was hoping to create for my brother. It's what I needed. I was absorbed by the predicament—and it was a predicament. How could this have happened to him? The suffering was real and there was an intractability, no good way out.

All the works we've discussed have a strong story, a strong narrative. But what was preoccupying me in terms of content was the experience. Everything I did had to move. So the subsequent pieces like these, the three-dimensional leaves, they're a response to Frank because they are alive and on the move. These leaves cannot be static. They're creatures that walk. They shift around: Botanicals become mammals and creatures. The impetus to finally get things off the wall, and out of the wall, is that Frank cannot move, so everything else I make has to move. As with *Breathe*, movement means life. It's the question: How do you find the words that express what it means to be alive? We take so much for granted.

VALERIO Thinking about these works about Frank's life experience takes me back to the story of your journey to your grandmother's farm and garden in Pittsburgh and you looking over the Monongahela River and the steel factories. Again, the art comes out of the unfolding spiritual experience of life and your connection to people you love.

CARPENTER One of the things that's important about my art (or any art) is the unfolding. You can't know it when you first see it. It has to sink in, get in there. I want viewers to experience it over time. If you know the sculpture right away, that doesn't work for me. That's related to the notion that sculpture should compel you to move. I'm talking here about sculpture in the round. You have to engage with the physicality of this thing, so it becomes an experience. It can be spiritual, like my experience at my grandmother's farm site. It's different for the viewer of a sculpture in a gallery or museum, but it's an unfolding experience. It needs to change in space for me. That why I love the work of Richard Serra. It creates an experience that unfolds in space.

VALERIO You started making the farm portraits in 2009, fairly soon after your brother's death. By traveling to see multigenerational Black-owned farms across the country, were you rebuilding your family? Expanding your ancestry?

CARPENTER I was absorbed with gardens, farms, and the people who create them, and that included my family, so it was a wide net. Even as all of these family things happen in my life, as a Black woman, I am still evolving, learning, and finding my voice as an artist. And all these things get stirred into the pot.

VALERIO Your mention of stirring the pot makes me think about the big round farm bowls, like *Albert and Elbert Howard* (see title page). They really do feel like they're moving in a circular way. In videos, the eye of the camera often revolves around them, as if the videographer can't resist the circular movement.

CARPENTER You have to walk around them to see them, and that's what the videographers do. And your mind wants to spin with them. In viewing sculpture, that's the reciprocal physical response I'm looking to create. The experience isn't the same as standing in front of a painting or a sculpture that sits on the wall. Sculpture takes up space. Life affects it. That's just the physical nature of the thing.

VALERIO Many of the farms include mother pins. Let's talk about what they are.

CARPENTER I have in my possession the bag of old-fashioned wooden clothespins that my mother used to hang laundry when I was a child. The shape is beautiful, curvaceous, elegant, and I

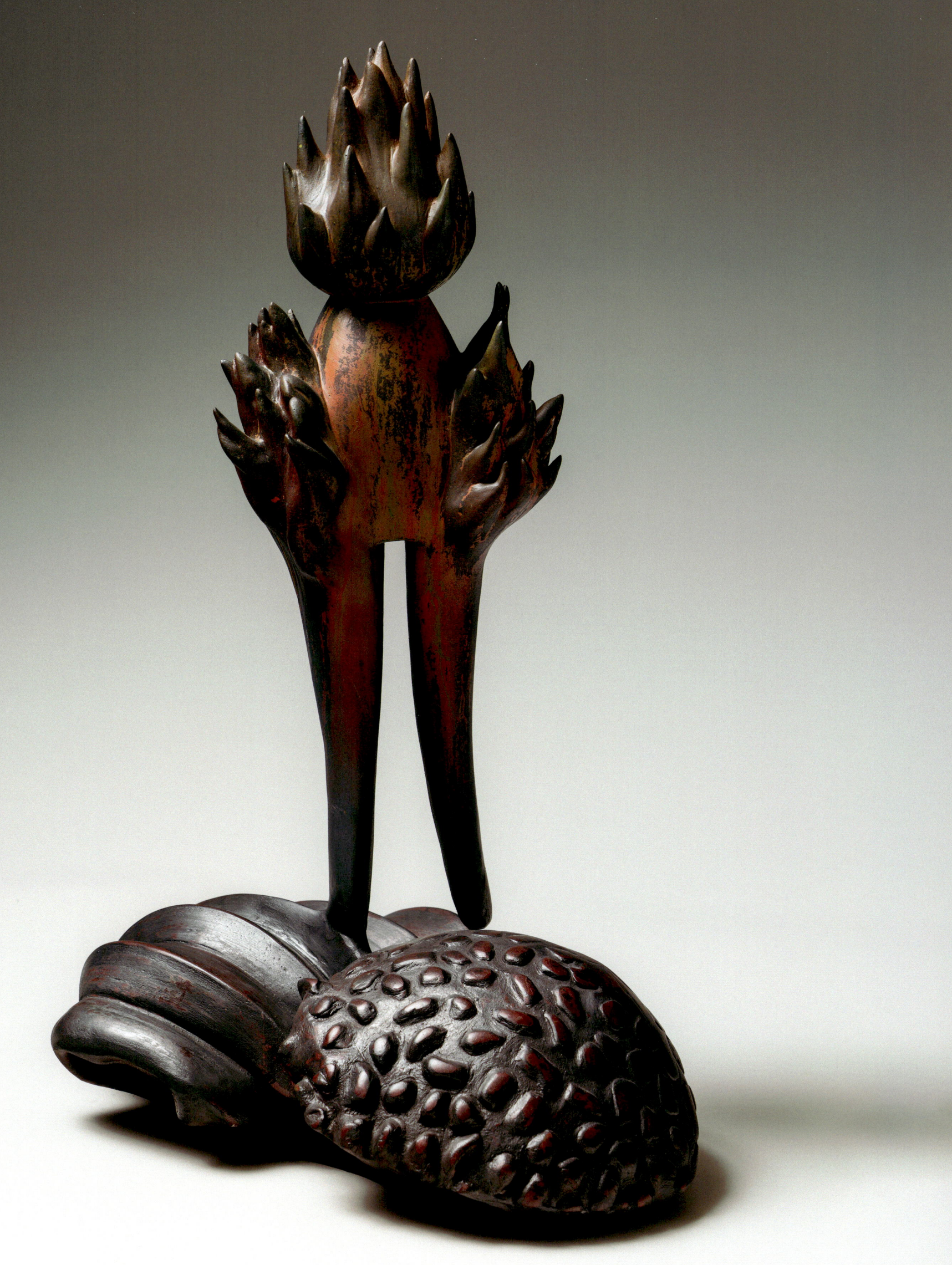

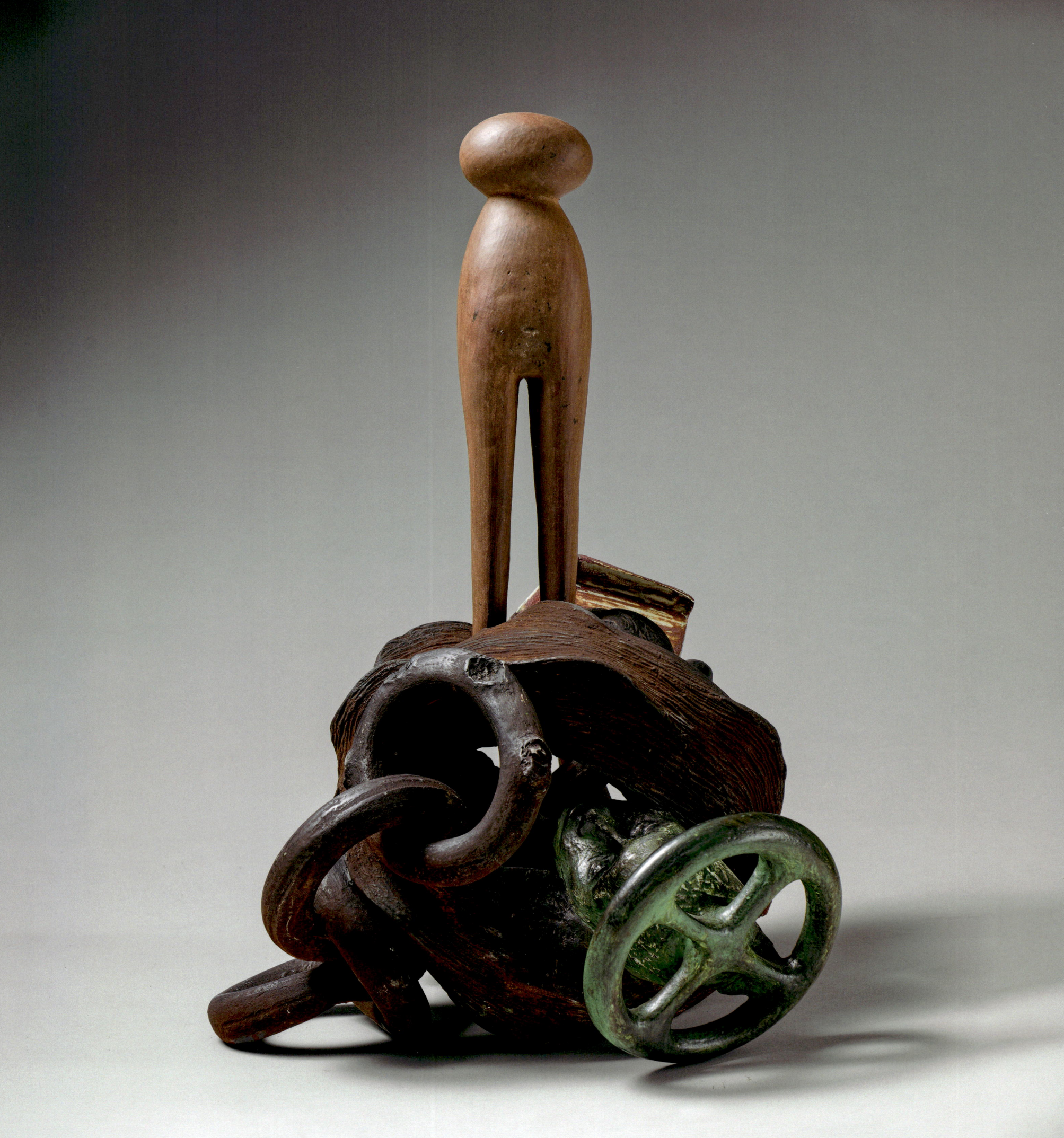

enlarged them to a sculptural scale. They represent my mother across a range of works and contexts. Often she is the main character: *Mother Pin Adrift*, *Mother Pin Arise* (fig. 2.13), *Mother Pin Afire* (fig. 2.12)—all "a" words.

VALERIO   Why *afire*?

CARPENTER   When something is afire, it could be the fire of rage. It could be energized, not passive. For her to be represented on fire is not tragic. It is me acknowledging that, despite all the things that held her down, all the injustices, my mother was afire. There was rage. There was triumph sometimes. Fire is also the energy of life.

VALERIO   Can we talk about the large, six-foot mother pin that's going to be at the Berman Museum? It stands in a large bowl.

CARPENTER   That's *Mother Pin Ascends*. She ascends out of the bowl, another of my farm bowls, but the bowl is the earth. Think of the round form of the hügels at Woodmere as a large bowl of the earth with the growth of plant life. *Mother Pin Ascends* is a spiritual ascension. I want to create a sense of energy rising out of the earth. There's this little house that she's protecting right behind her.

VALERIO   As I'm listening to you, I'm thinking about the birth of Venus, but also the Ascension of Christ (an active rising up to heaven), not so much the Assumption of Mary, mother of God (she is lifted to heaven by angels).

CARPENTER   Rudy Staffel sometimes told me, "You are as original as your sources are obscure."

VALERIO   But it's your own visual language and layers of meaning: a birth, an ascension, a farm, and the clothespin itself. All are evocative of intertwining levels and suggestive of the context that's unique to your life and interests and virtuosity.

CARPENTER   To give you an idea about how my mind works, I'm thinking about a mother pin sculpture inspired by images I've seen in Asian art and pre-Columbian art: rulers vanquishing enemies or gods vanquishing evil spirits. We need that today!

VALERIO   May I ask about your apple sculptures (see p. 41 and fig. 7.1)?

CARPENTER   Those are from a while ago, and I showed them with Sande in the early 1990s. I had given my students at Swarthmore the assignment to select an apple from a big bowl and start eating it. After every bite, they had to draw what was left. I decided to do this assignment myself, and that's how these sculptures came to be.

Sande sold a couple of them. But I decided not to show them again because I liked them too much and didn't want to see them go. They were an academic exercise, a process idea in making sculpture by watching something organic happen. Something important about the apples is that they are my first works painted with no glaze, and no slip. Later on, and many projects later, I would use watercolor for *Breathe* and come back to painting clay again with the farm portraits, the black works like *Everelena Cannon* (fig. 2.14) at Woodmere. Those works are air-sprayed with a graphite paint over a layer of bright orange underpaint. The orange creates a radiant, rich effect; it glows through and brings a richness to the surface that I like.

VALERIO   So that's how you create that smooth, beautiful skin. Am I right in describing it as skin?

CARPENTER   Yes, it's all about black skin. The warmth of it, the smoothness of it, the sensuality of it. They are portraits of people. The landscapes of the places, and portraits of the people. That's why I worked to create an appearance I can equate to black skin.

VALERIO   That's so interesting. Also like *Frank in Tow*, the works can be shown horizontally on their tables and become landscapes. However, they're also set up with the hardware to be displayed on the wall, and when that happens, the piece is definitely figurative.

Everelena Cannon becomes a great torso, but also a belly or a sack-like organ.

CARPENTER Every culture has a symbolic vessel that holds life, holds water. *Everelena Cannon* had this great yoke: an important tool on the farm that seemed unique to her, and her own ramshackle fence.

VALERIO Were you ever tempted to leave the bright orange underpaint?

CARPENTER Bill, you know the piece very well: *Frank as Sun King*. That orange glow—Sun King—was too good to paint over, and it was fitting for Frank, his radiance.

VALERIO Let's also talk about the two other major series of farm portraits: the farm bowls and the farm portraits with steel pedestals.

CARPENTER The bowl is a great format for me in terms of the circular configuration. I can play with it, adding forms, symbols, and elements to the curving surfaces and see how they interact, what they do. I sometimes feel that a piece needs something more, or sometimes I remove objects. If I place a mother pin, I might next look for a place to plant a house, or maybe some kidney beans. I like using those. In one of my shows at Sande's gallery, I hung several hundred clay kidney bean forms on a rope and draped it around the gallery, off the wall, and down onto the floor and back up again. But I had to take it apart, because after a while you make stuff and what are you going to do with it?! You know, what do you do with hundreds of clay kidney beans? I started using them in the farm portraits, and they took on another life. It's a collage process that I orchestrate and edit.

 And then is the moment of truth when I start to ask myself, how am I going to attach that object to that rim without cracking the piece in the firing? So I have to figure out how to engineer it, get it on there, because you're working with clay and you can't push it so far as to throw it off balance. How high are you going to fire it? Or how low? But you have to make sure it's strong enough.

I'm thinking about all of this while I'm composing. It's terrible, but sometimes a work won't make it through the fire and the piece collapses in the kiln.

Animals always attract me too. If I'm on a chicken farm, the bowl gets a chicken, or on a cow farm, you understand. Every bowl also gets a structure of some kind, a house or a shed. I'm also attracted to flowers, and there are a few farm bowls with sunflowers. Fences show up a lot, too, because many farms have improvised fences that serve utilitarian purposes but end up expressing something about the farmer's sensibility. And then the patterns in the earth: Farmers till in different ways, using different machines or tools. And those patterns can make their way into the bowls. There are many special ones. *Thomas Evans* has tilled earth and tools, a very different kind of spirit. *Percy Robinson*'s got some green paint on its surface, and it's unique in the series for that reason.

VALERIO One group of works in the exhibition that we haven't talked about is the farm portraits with legs.

CARPENTER You can call them legs, but I think of them as stems. Those works have a root, a stem, and a flower, and when they're shown together in a group they become a garden. The process is much like the other farm portraits, but they are unique for the three-part structure and what happens when they're shown together.

VALERIO Thank you, Syd. This has been an amazing conversation —I understand so much more about your work than I did at the beginning.

CARPENTER I'm also very pleased to feel so much continuity and so much change.

VALERIO One of the goals of the retrospective is to frame an understanding of your work in your voice and your words, even as there will inevitably be new interpretations that arise over time and in new contexts.

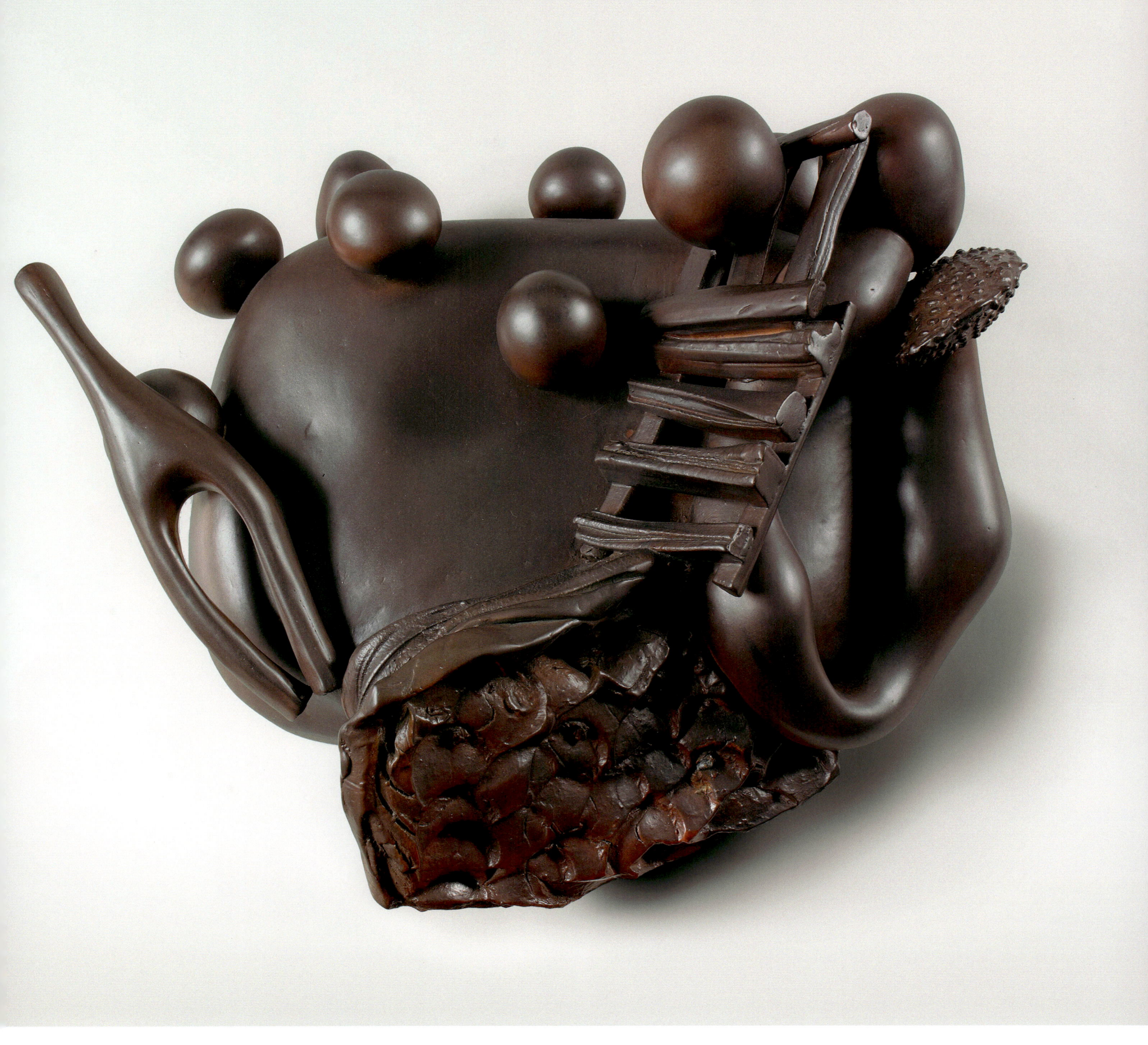

FIG. 2.14 *Everelena Cannon*, 2009, clay, acrylic, and graphite, 41 × 35¾ × 23¾ in. (Woodmere: Museum purchase, 2018)

House for Mr. Biswas

1982, clay with underglazes, 20 × 10 × 10 in. (Collection of James Brantley)

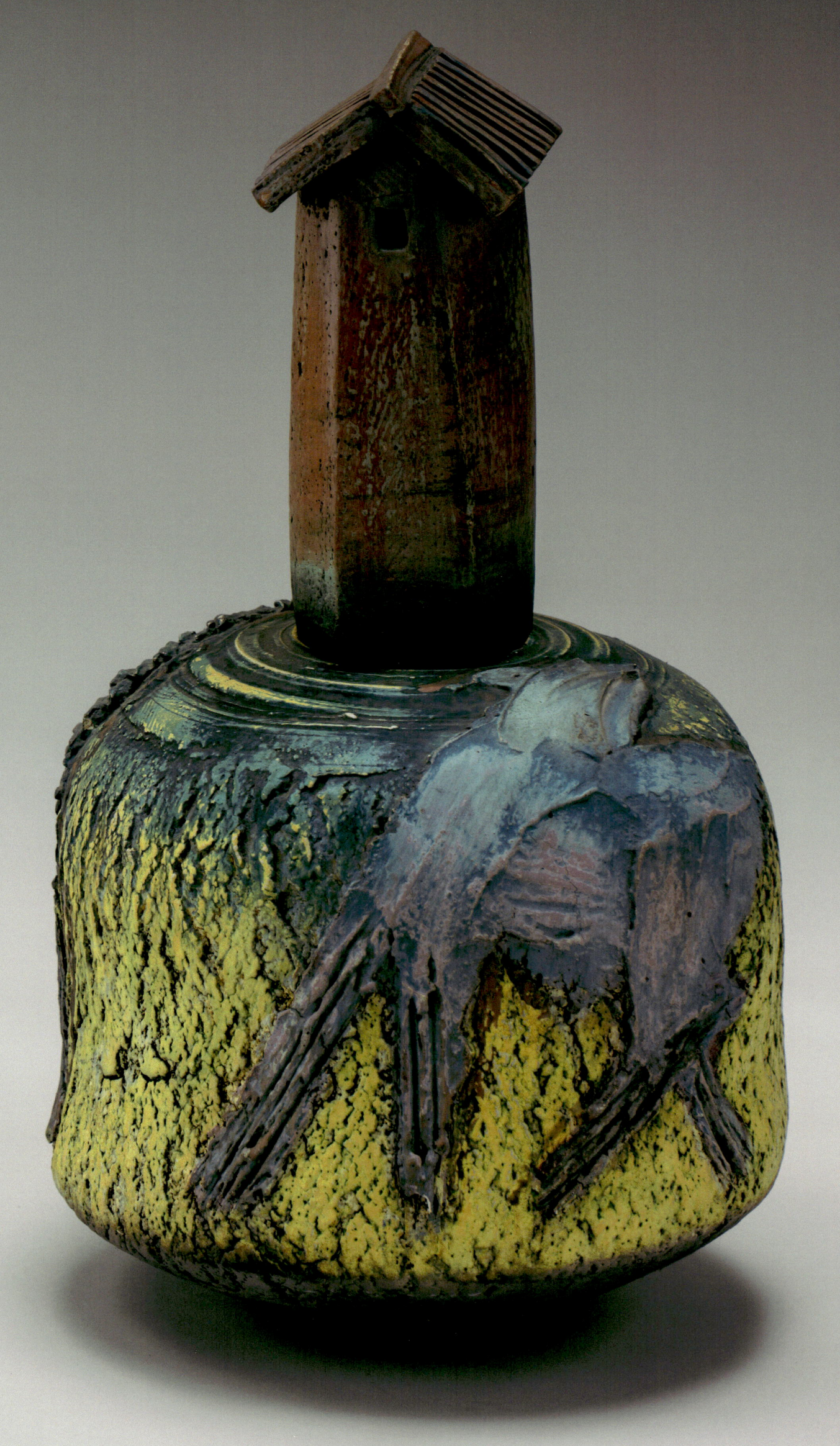

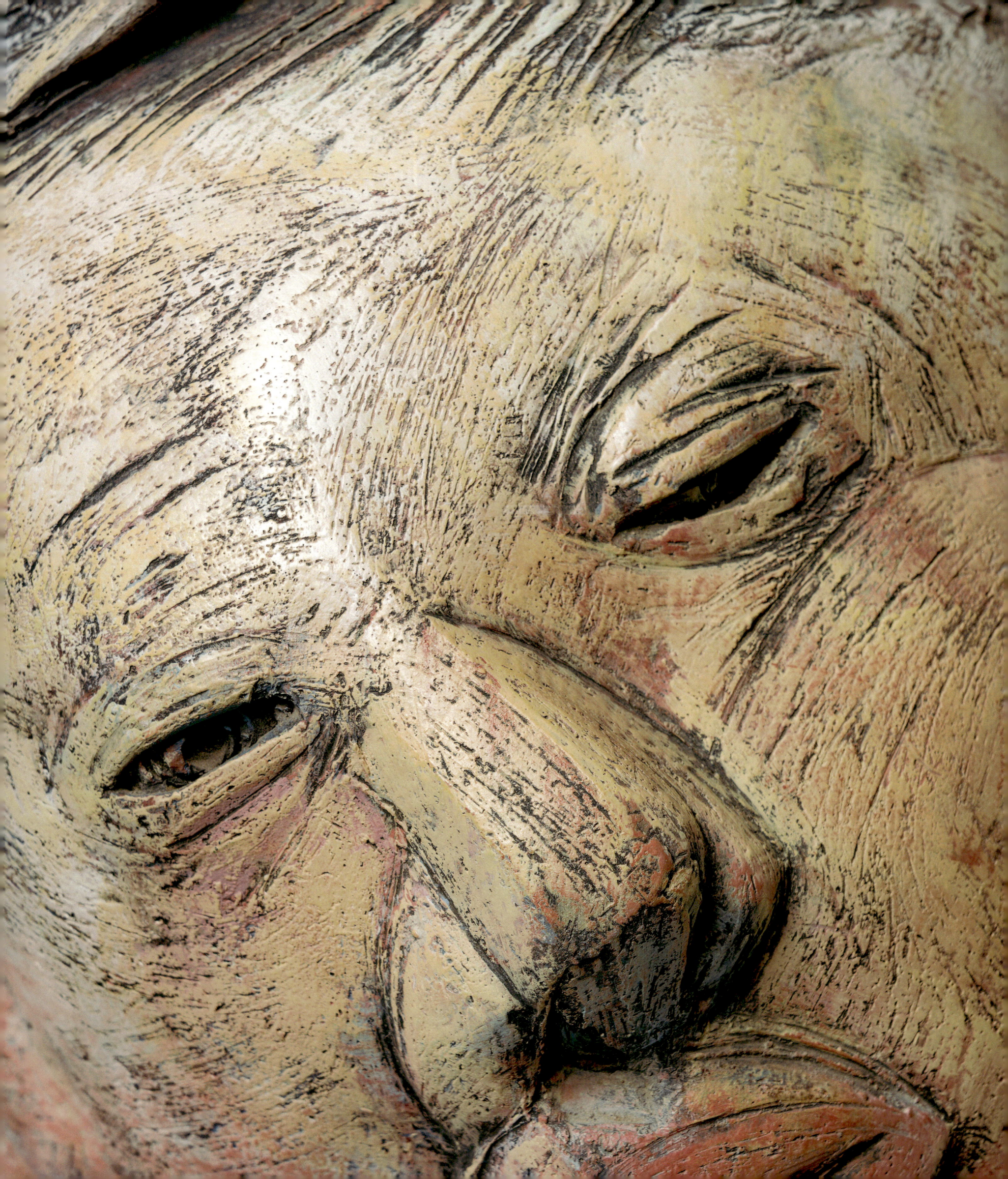

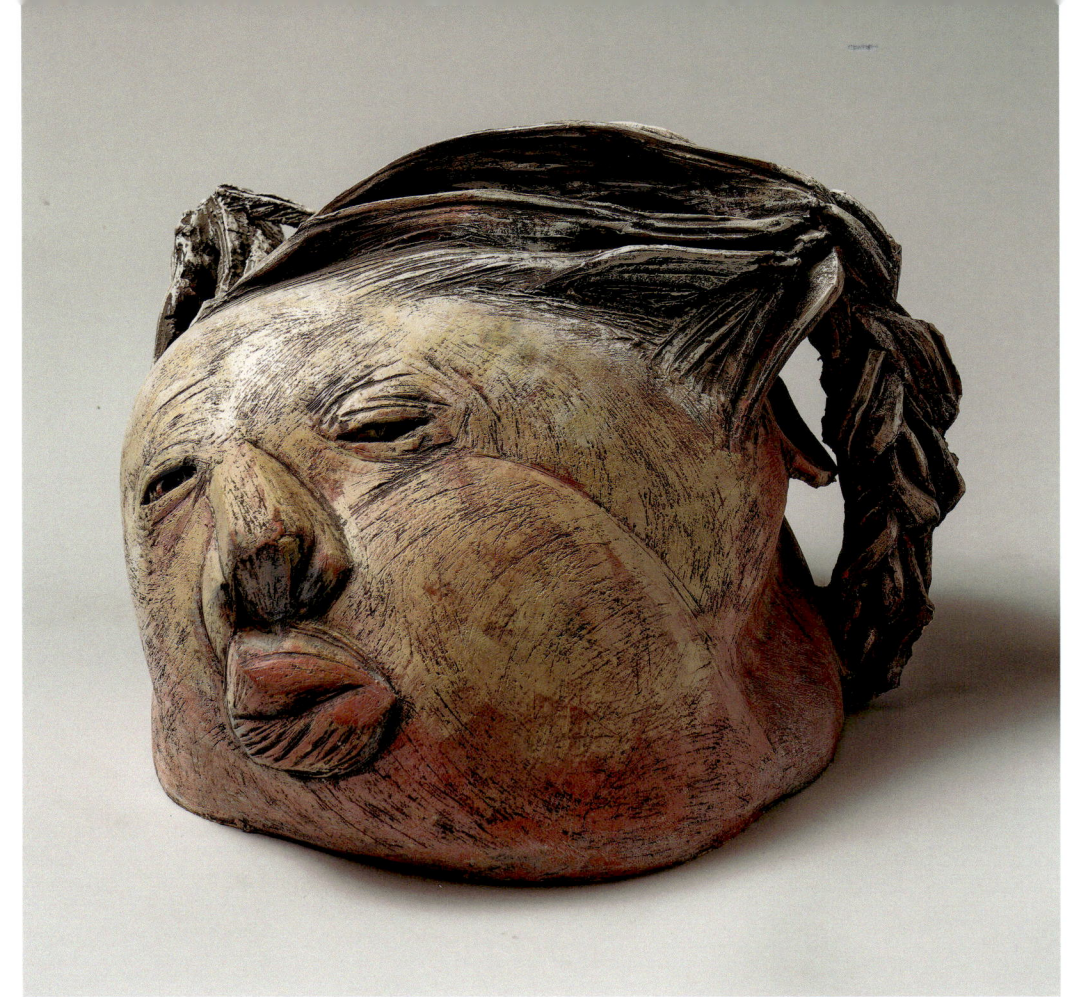

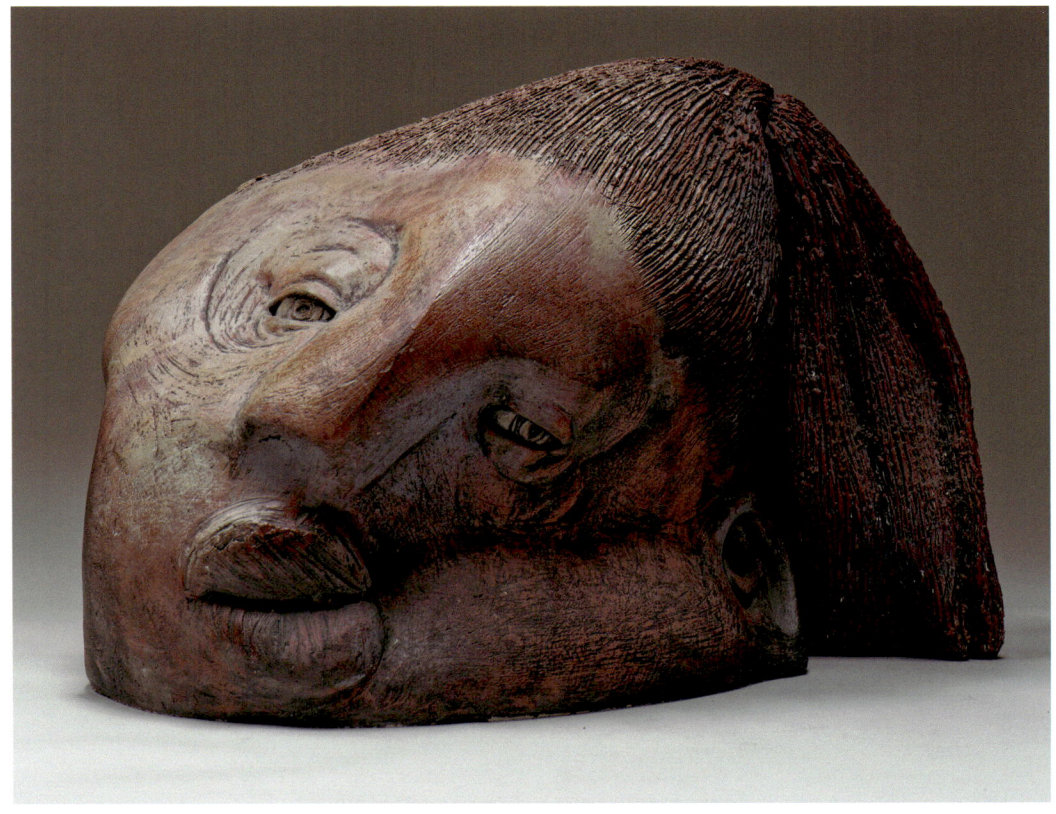

Child 4

1990, clay and terra sigillata, 14½ × 21 × 21 in.
(Collection of the artist)

Child 5

1990, clay and terra sigillata, 15 × 22 × 22 in.
(Collection of James Brantley)

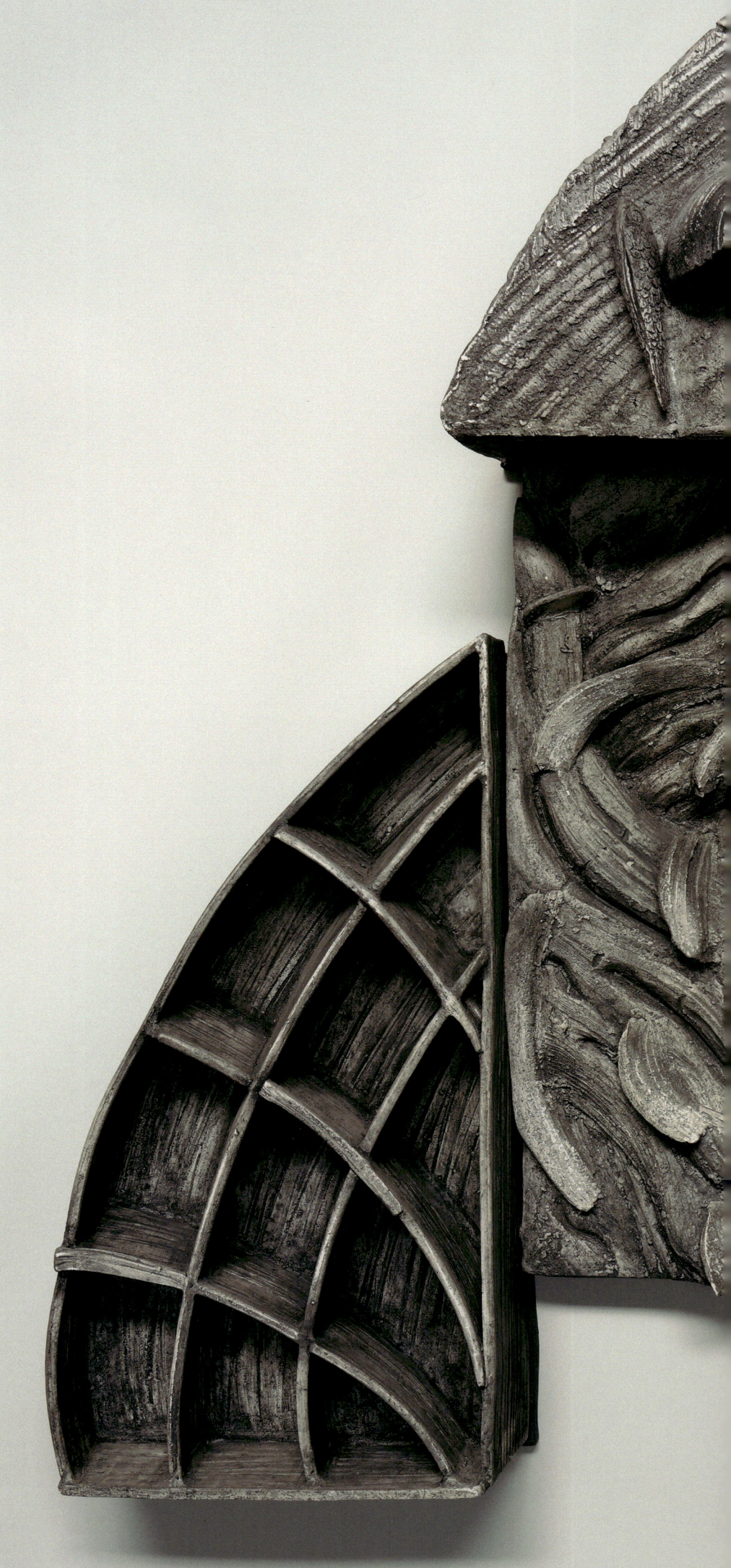

A Part of the Whole

1989, ceramic mounted on plywood, 41 × 64 × 6 in.
(Woodmere: Gift of the Wind Family, 2024)

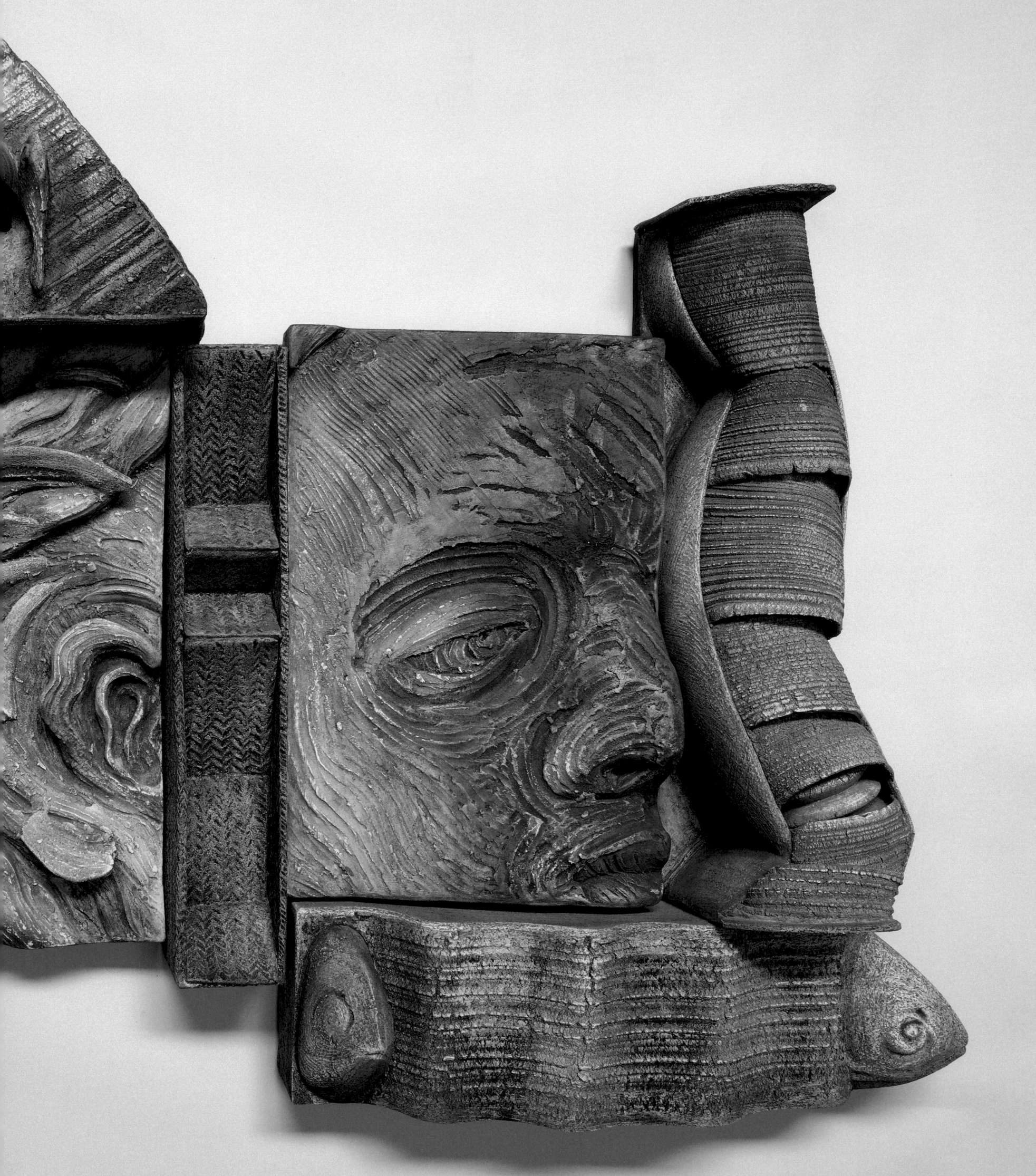

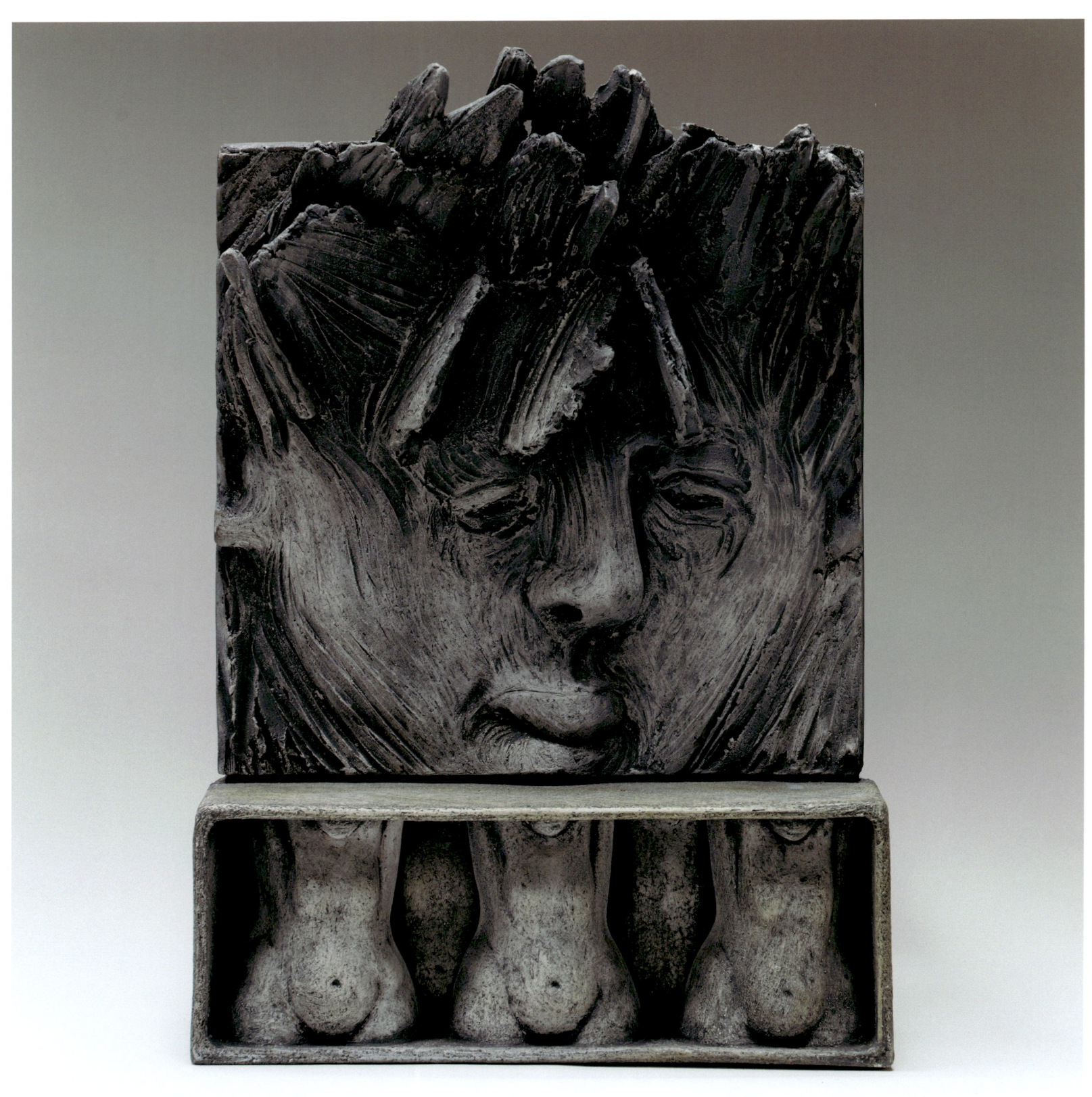

Of a Like Mind

c. 1986–87, ceramic, 26 × 18 × 4 in. (Collection of James Brantley)

Apple 2

1996, clay and acrylic, 10½ × 10 × 12 in. (Collection of the artist)

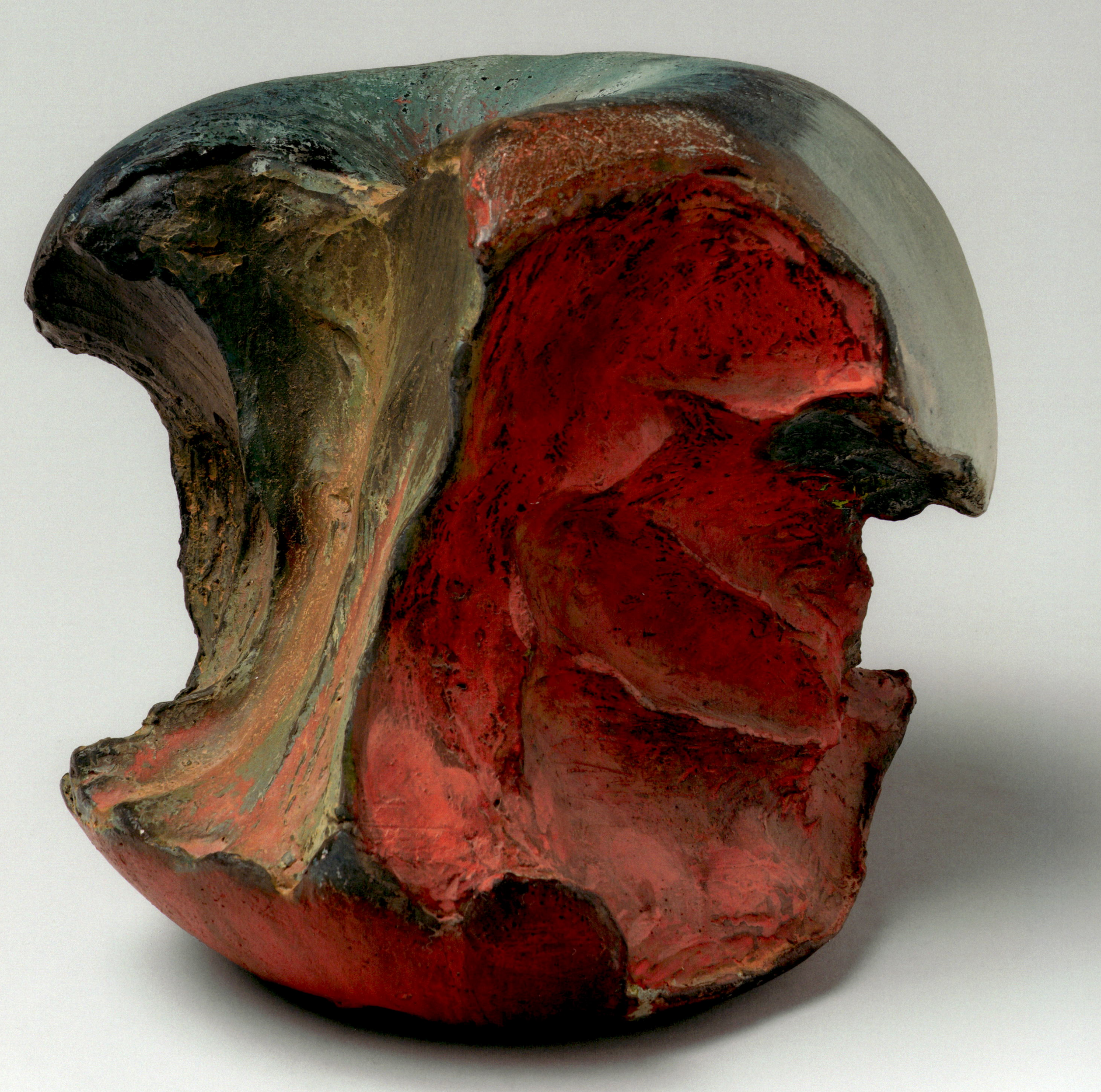

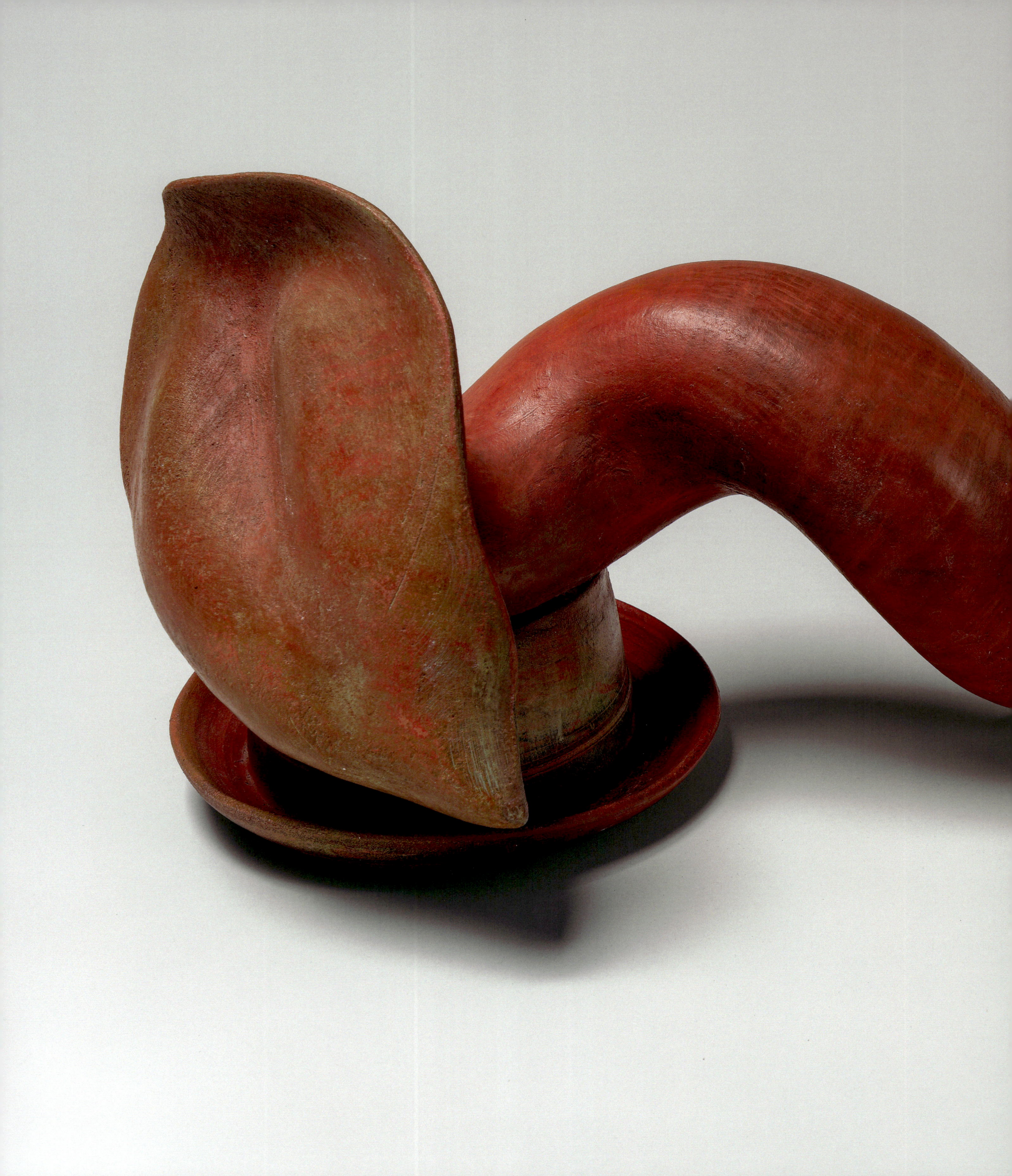

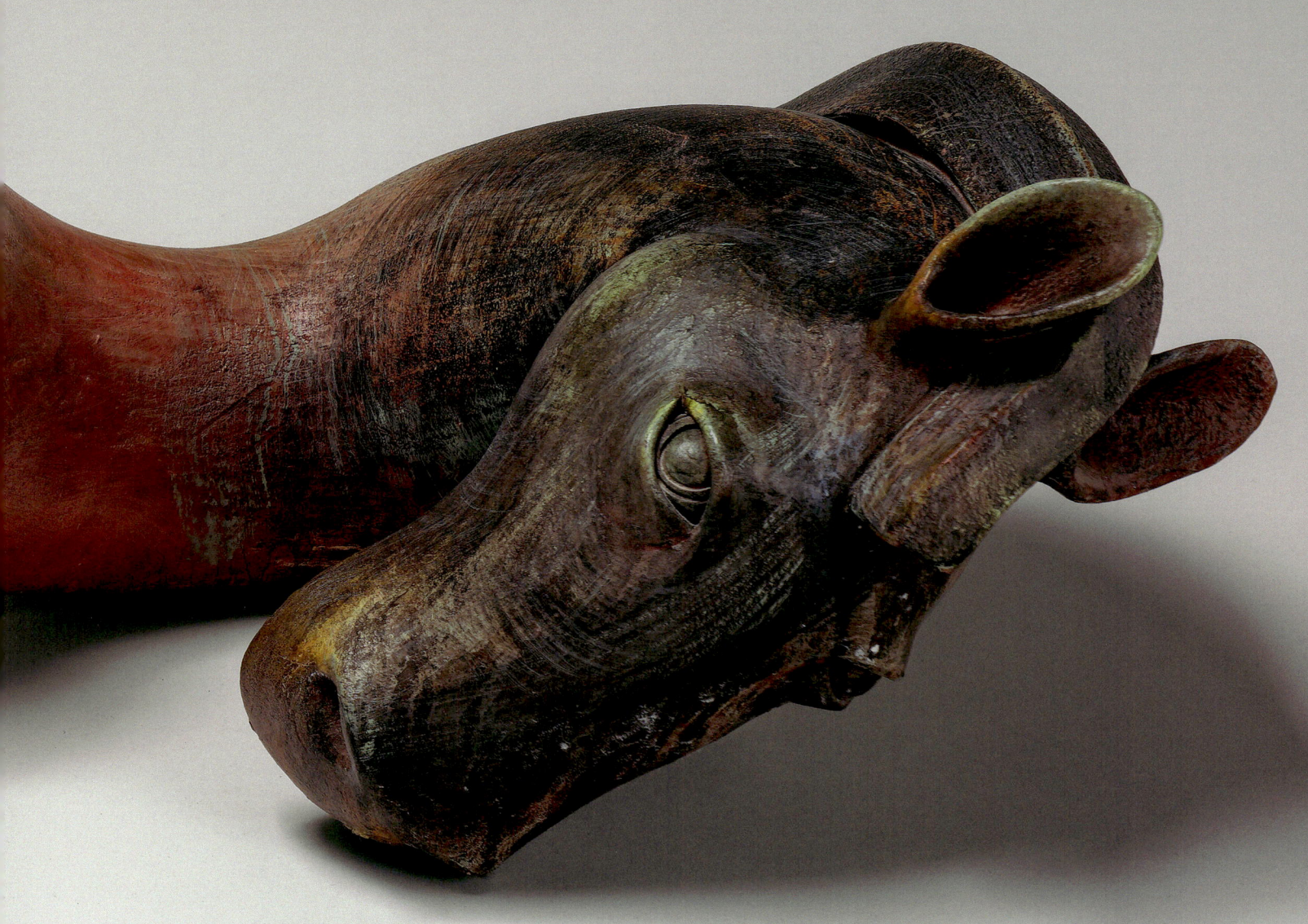

Frank's Peace
2002, paint over clay, 38 × 12 × 12 in. (Collection of the artist)

43

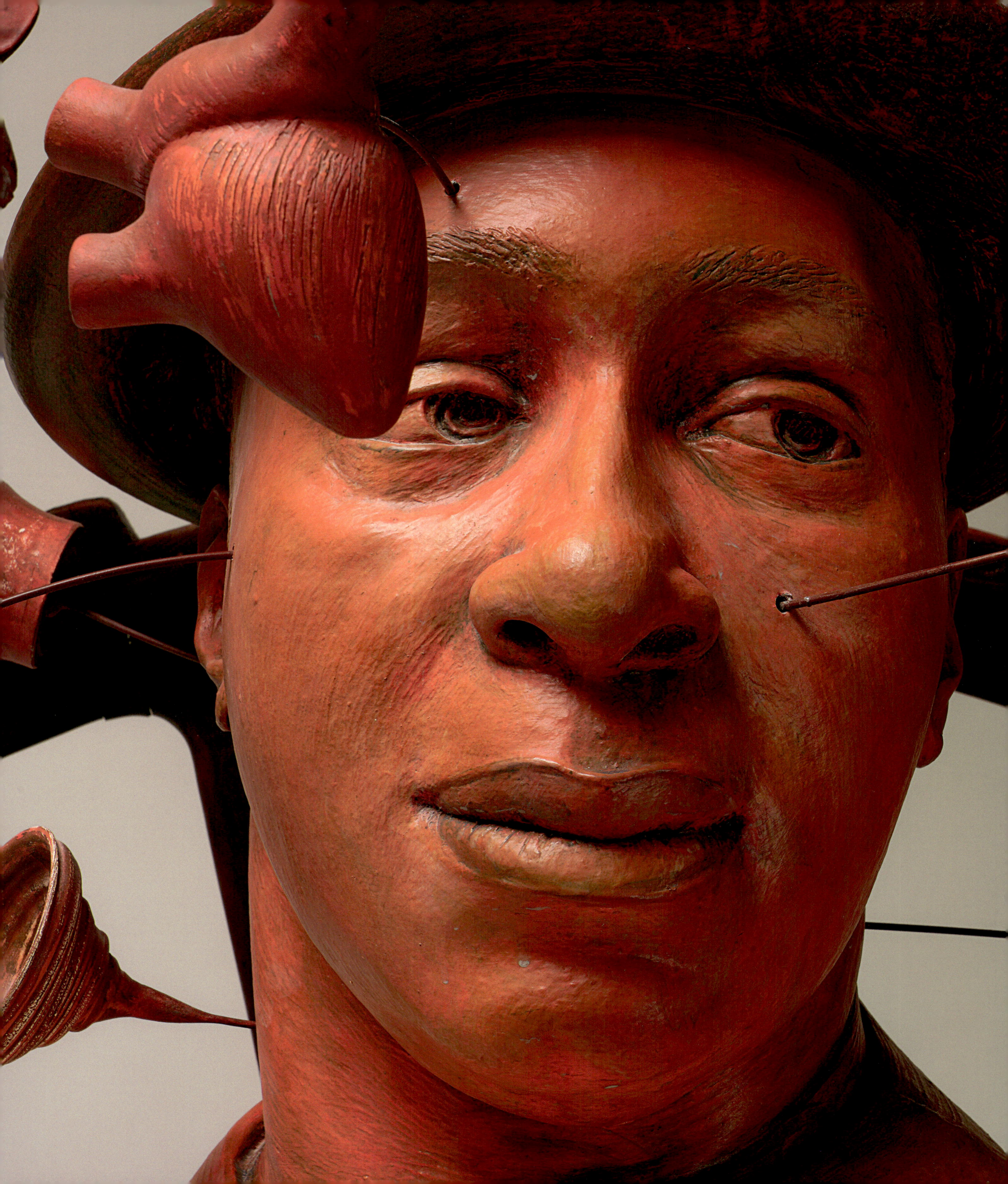

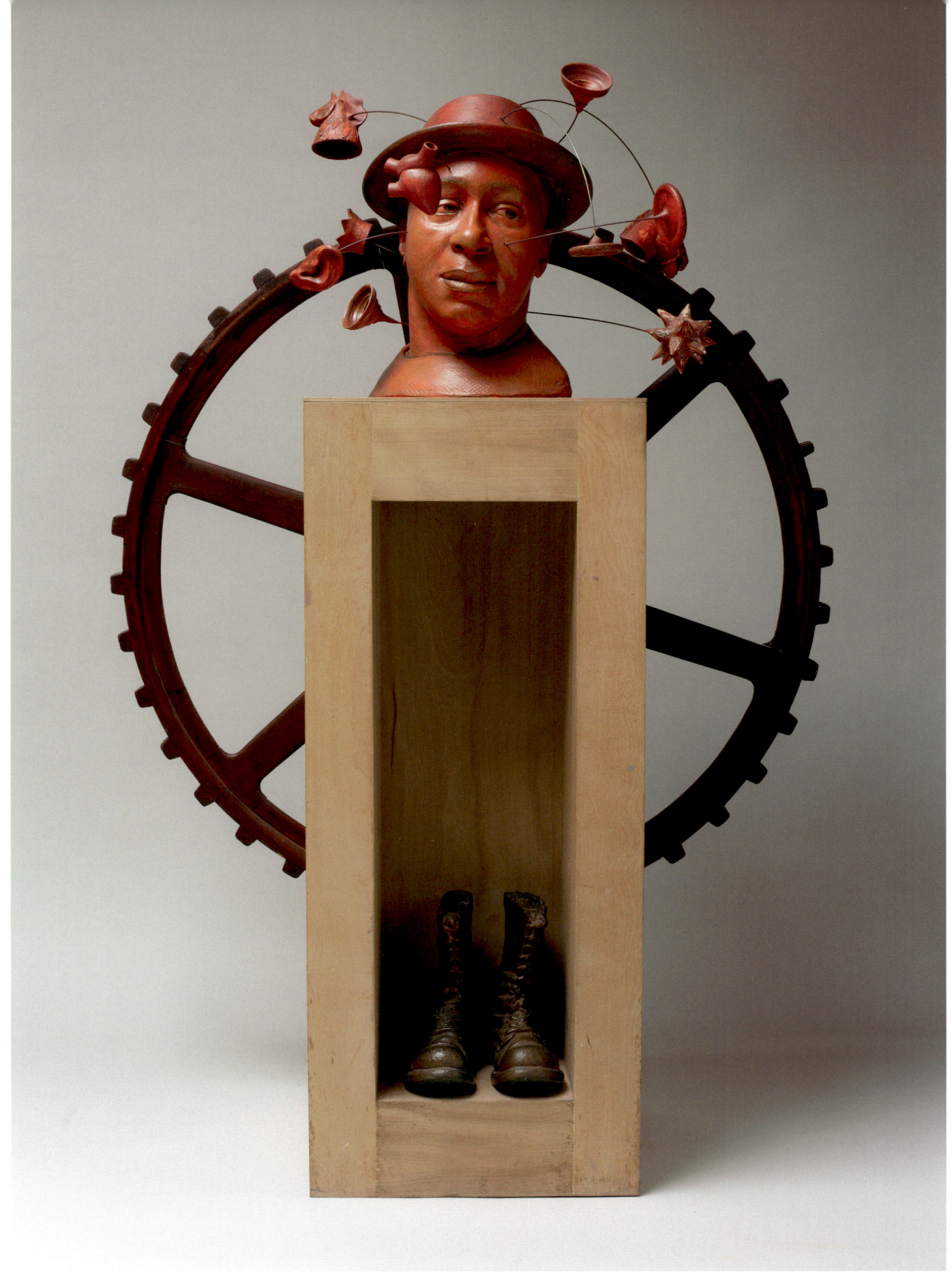

Frank as Sun King

2005, mixed media, 50 × 50 × 20 in. (Promised gift of the artist)

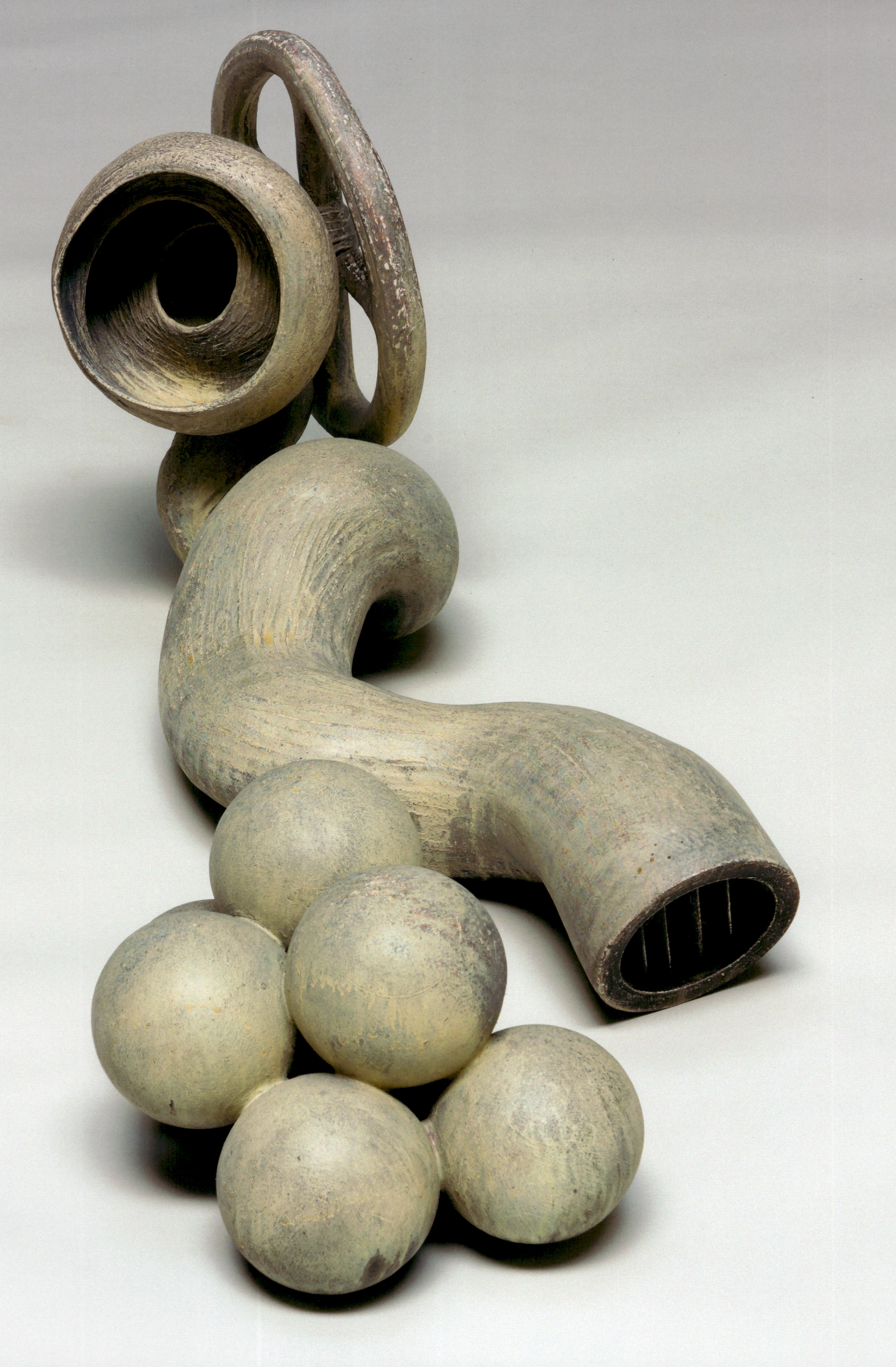

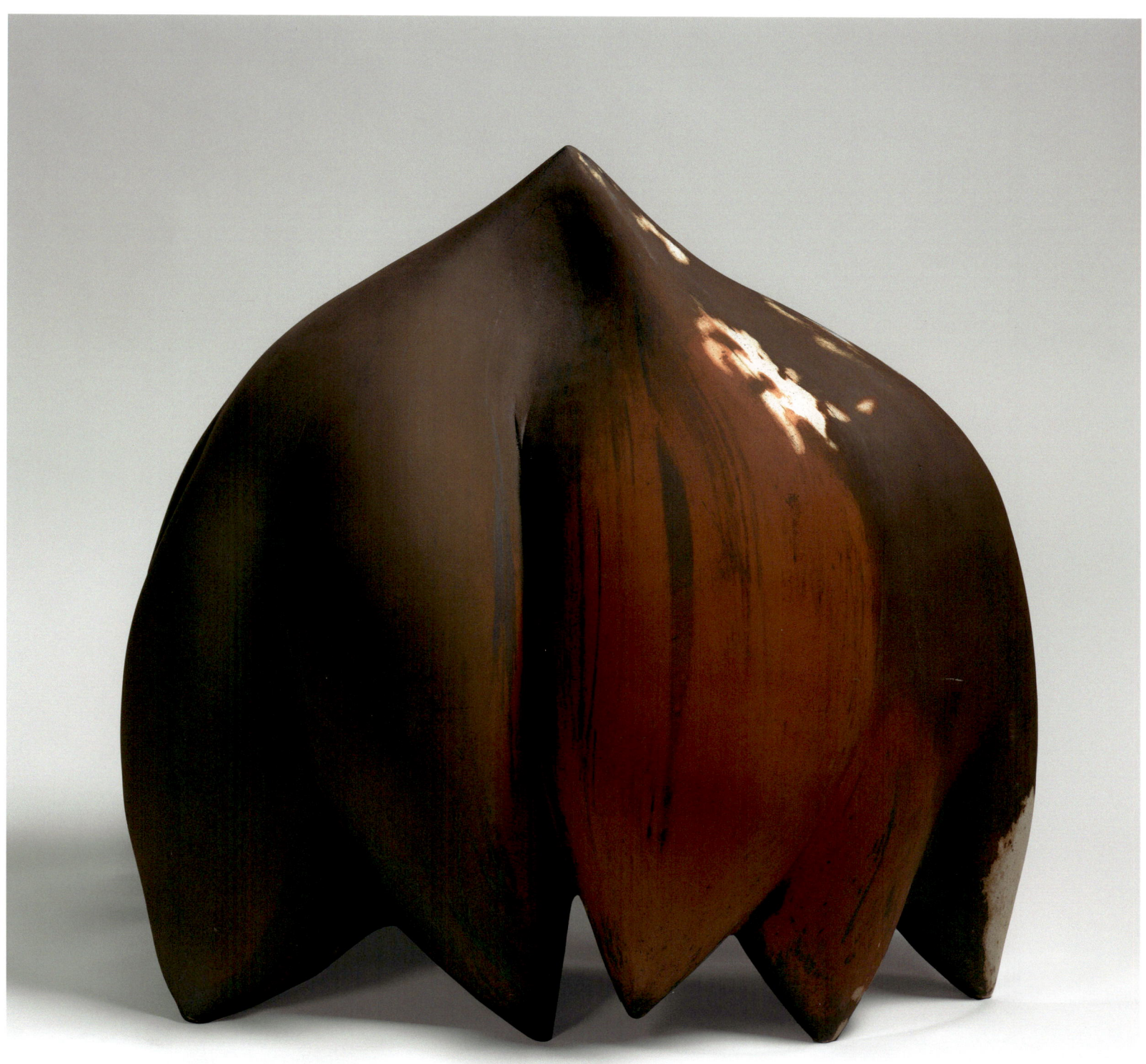

Breathe

2004, watercolor over clay, 20 × 42 × 15 in. (Woodmere: Gift of
the Wind Family, 2024)

Of and About the Skin

2006, clay, underglaze, and oxide, 25 × 25 × 12 in. (Collection of
Sarah Willie-LeBreton and Jonathan LeBreton)

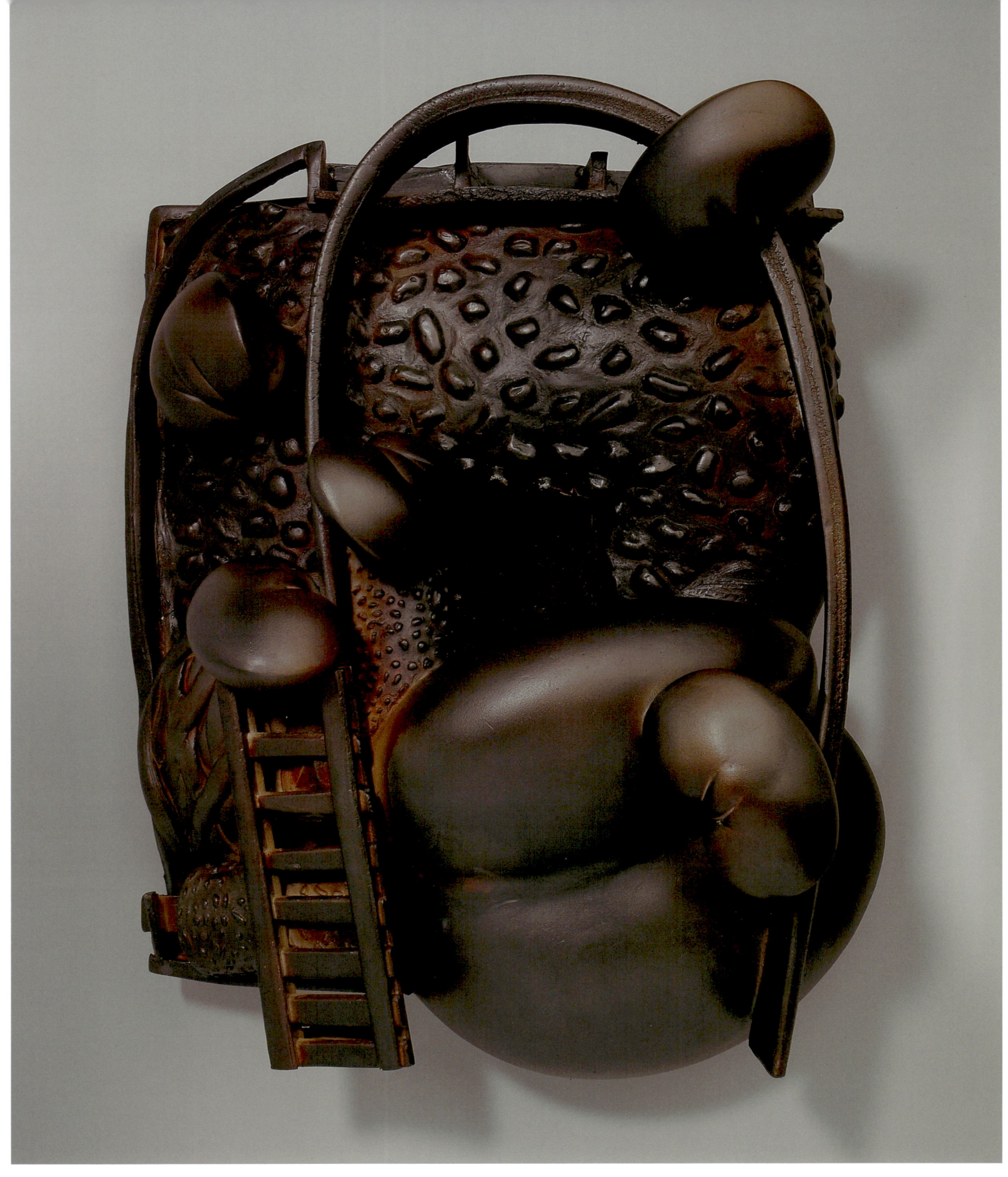

Ervin and Cornelius Hollifield

2009, clay, acrylic, and graphite on wood board, 24 × 24 × 6 in.
(Fuller Craft Museum, 2016.9)

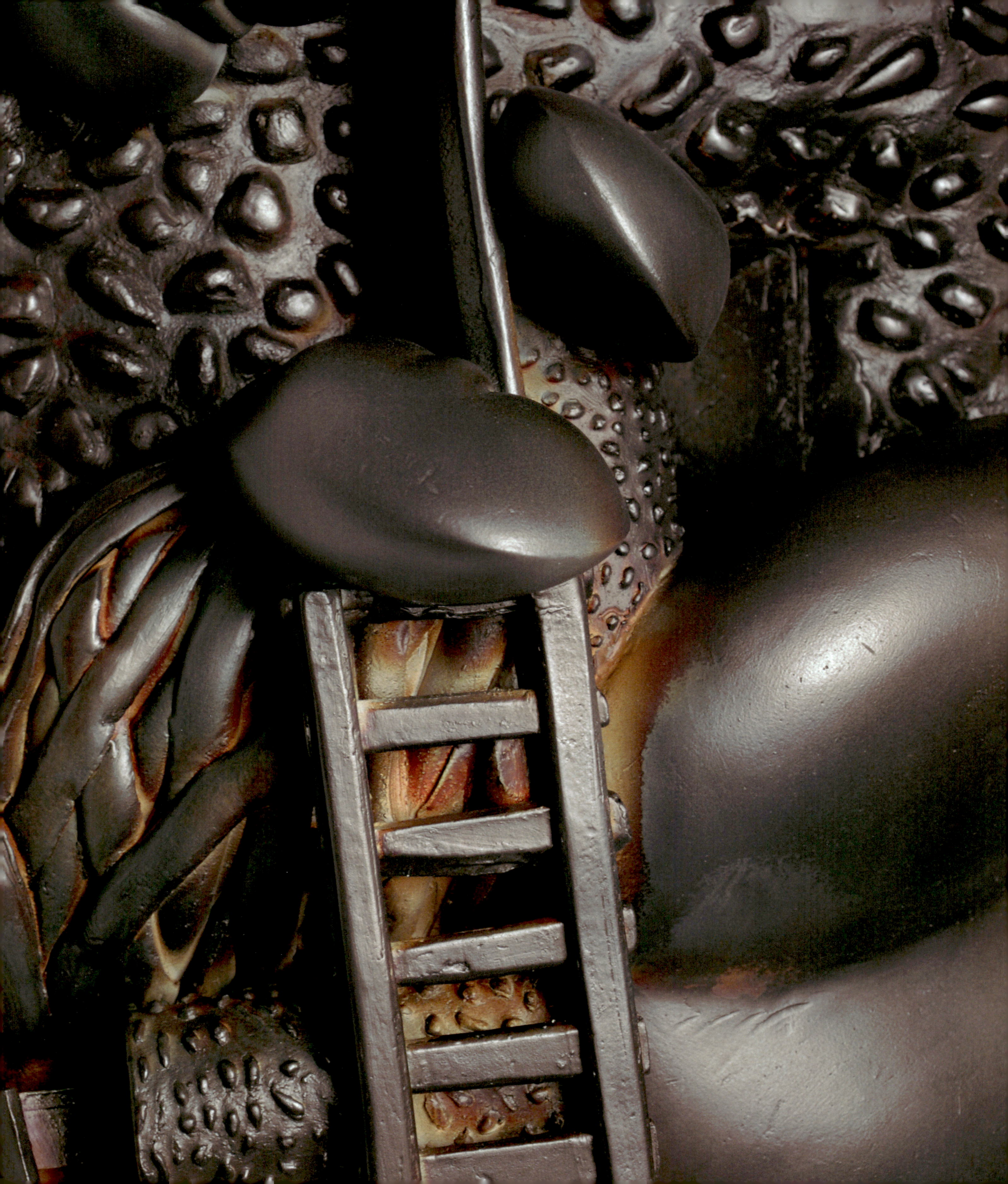

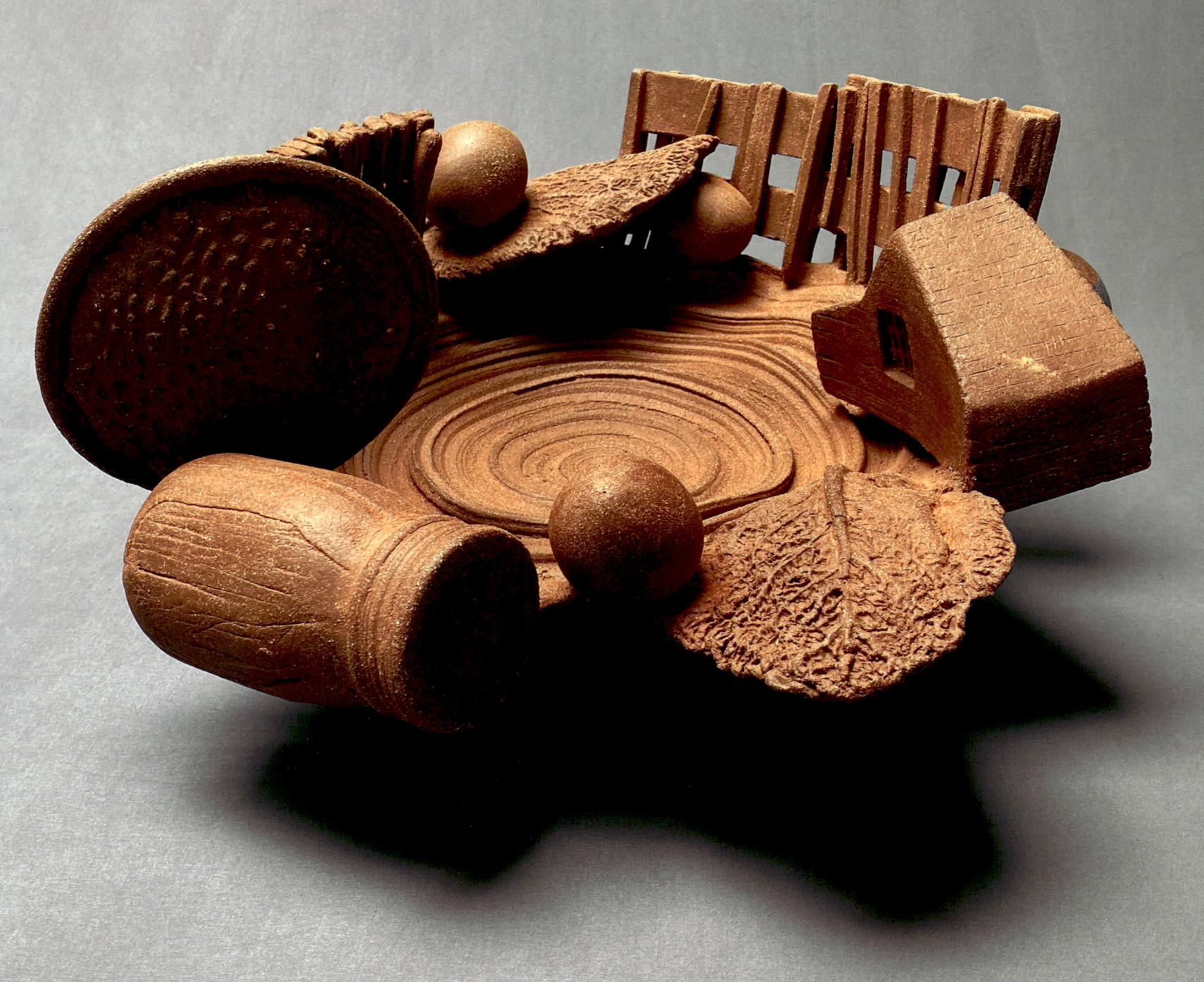

Of Clay, Culture, and Cultivation
The Sculptures of Syd Carpenter

LOWERY STOKES SIMS

I identify with women working the land through my grandmother and mother, a master gardener, in Pittsburgh where I grew up, and it's that line of gardening that I'm continuing in contemporary settings.[1]

—Syd Carpenter

FOR NEARLY TWO DECADES Syd Carpenter has created work inspired by gardening and farming, focusing on the particular experience of African Americans in these horticultural/agricultural activities. She has a deeply personal connection to this subject: During World War II, her grandmother Indiana Hutson cultivated what became a well-known vegetable garden at her home in Pittsburgh to feed her family of seven children. Later, the garden of her mother, Ernestine Carpenter, provided the artist firsthand experience with working the land, and that is actualized today in the elaborate garden at one of Carpenter's homes in Philadelphia.

Carpenter's approach to African American farming and gardening in her work presents agricultural locales and activities in unique and distinctive ways. She eschews the visual tropes one would expect in a presentation of the farm as landscape and locale of labor. Instead she creates forms in clay—utensils, architectural forms, animals, produce, and portions of tilled fields—often in combination with steel, wood, glass, or other materials in formats that include bowl shapes as seen in *Indiana Hutson Farm Bowl* (see facing page), reliefs on the wall as in *Percy Robinson* (fig. 3.4), or on stands or pedestals as seen in *Albert and Elbert Howard* (fig. 3.1). Off-kilter in terms of proportions and spatial placement in relation to one another, they both convey narrative and engage the viewer in particular experiences with form.

THE ARTIST'S WORK IN THE CONTEXT OF AMERICAN ART AND AGRICULTURE

The number of black farmers in America peaked in 1920, when there were 949,889. Today, of the country's 3.4 million total farmers, only 1.3%, or 45,508, are black, according to new figures from the US Department of Agriculture released this month. They own a mere 0.52% of America's farmland. By comparison, 95% of US farmers are white.[2]

—Summer Sewell

One comes away from a conversation with Carpenter with a wealth of facts and stories about Black American farmers, a sector most people—even Black people—don't usually focus on, and may even

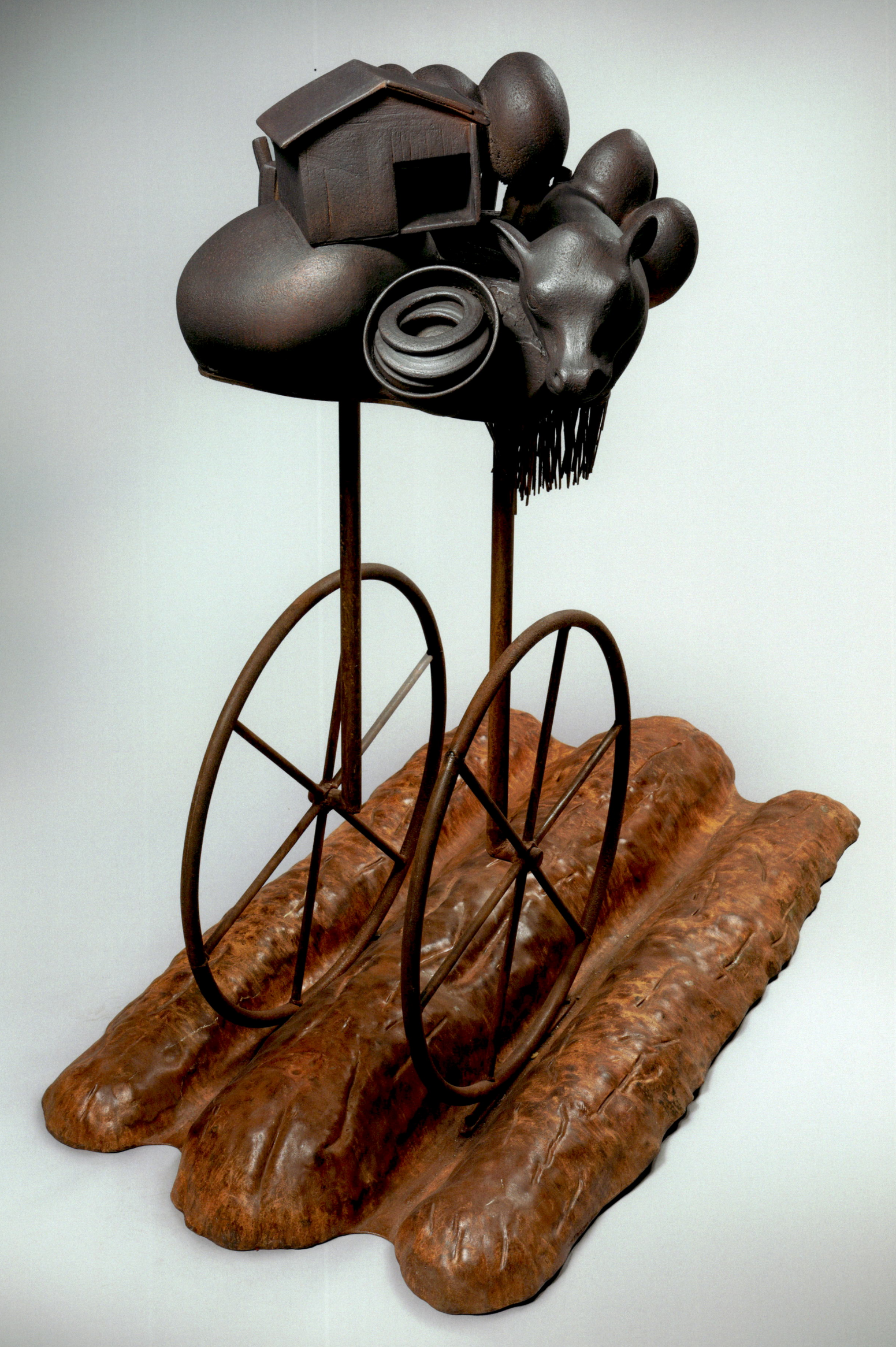

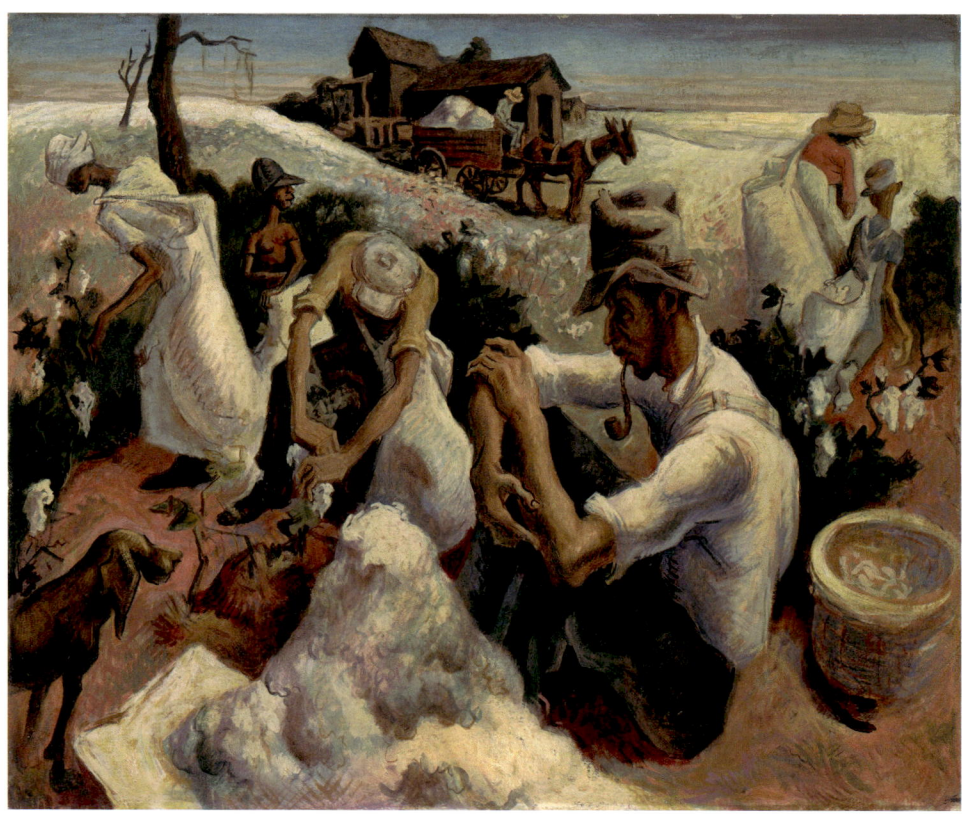

avoid. After all, as the artist observes, most African Americans are descended from enslaved people who did forced agricultural work on plantations primarily in the southern United States.[3] Consequently, African Americans in agriculture would be perceived through that lens. So it is no wonder that after emancipation, when they had the opportunity, they sought to disassociate themselves from that past and the social, economic, and political strictures in the South by seeking relatively more expansive opportunities in urban areas. Indeed depictions of Blacks in farming in American art of the first half of the twentieth century often focus on the cultivation and harvesting of cotton—which, as Carpenter observes, is inevitably associated with the legacy of slavery.[4] In this regard we can consider two iconic paintings: Thomas Hart Benton's *Cotton Pickers* (fig. 3.2) and Earle Richardson's *Employment of Negroes in Agriculture* (fig. 3.3).

The specific nuances of these two representations are striking. Benton's figures are rendered in the artist's characteristic elongated style—influenced by El Greco—and the space is compressed with just a glimpse of a horizon line and a view to the distance at the upper right. The scene is dominated by the male figure, who is undoubtedly a supervisor, sitting leisurely and smoking a pipe while the Black workers toil anonymously, heads down as they hunch into their tasks. This image represents Benton's transition from the abstract work associated with the Synchronist movement that he practiced in the 1910s to his rejection of modernism in the 1920s. He then dedicated himself to working figuratively to highlight the life and customs of rural Americans, as a founding member of the style known as regionalism.

Richardson, on the other hand, produced his painting as one of the very few African American artists employed by the Federal Art Project under the New Deal. It was created for a project specifically conceived to depict the labor of Americans.[5] His Black figures dominate the composition, upright in the performing of their tasks. They wear distinctive clothing in different colors, patterns, and textures, giving us a clear sense of who these figures are as opposed to those dressed in the monotonous homespun attire in Benton's painting. And Richardson provides details of the rows of cultivated cotton and the receptacles that hold the harvest. Especially notable is how Richardson's title affirms that the work in which these African Americans are engaged is a skill-based activity and lends an air of dignity to the drudgery of their labor. As Elizabeth Prelinger notes, Richardson "affirmed his view of rural blacks as young, powerful, and undefeated, a people whose time would come."[6]

The Richardson painting captures the same grit and determination shown by the individuals whom Carpenter celebrates in her farm sculptures. She engages viewers in conversations about the legacy of slavery and the issue of landownership.[7] It is important to recognize that the figures in the paintings by Benton and Richardson represent Black agricultural workers as tenant farmers or sharecroppers. That African Americans did not totally abandon agriculture is evident in the fact that, since the end of slavery, agriculture has been a subject at historically Black colleges

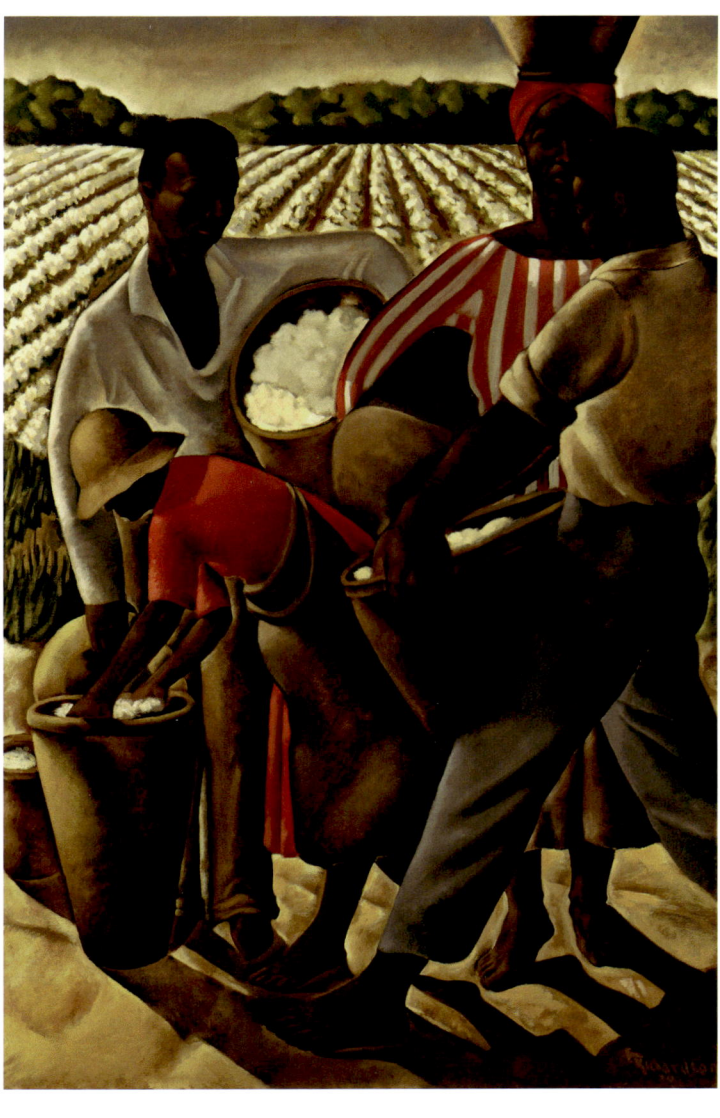

FIG. 3.3 Earle Richardson, *Employment of Negroes in Agriculture*, 1934, oil on canvas, 48 × 32⅛ in. (Smithsonian American Art Museum, Transfer from the US Department of Labor, 1964.1.183)

FIG. 3.4 *Percy Robinson*, 2009, clay, watercolor, and graphite, 24 × 22 × 6 in. (Rhode Island School of Design Museum: Gift of Thomas Daley and Donna Weaverling Daley, 2020)

of HBCUs. When queried, Carpenter doubted that her grandmother would have been aware of that bulletin, but the idea of the Victory garden was widely advertised as a particularly patriotic activity during the war. But even within this nationwide rally, the garden movement separated out African Americans. At harvest shows, separate prizes were awarded to "colored people," in similar categories to those for white people.[11]

In this context it is noteworthy that a 1943 photograph of a Black woman entitled *A Resident of Southwest Washington, DC, and Her Victory Garden* appears in the archives of the Office of War Information, now in the Library of Congress.[12] That photograph is an indication of a point that Carpenter makes that even as Black Americans might have left farms for urban areas, if they had access to a plot of land, they would plant a flower garden or vegetables.[13] This resonates with my own family history. I grew up in Queens in the 1950s and '60s in the home my parents purchased to provide a more bucolic environment for me, my brother, and my sister to grow up in. My father was a scion and descendent of a Black farming family in Tennessee, who after World War II relocated to the Northeast to study architecture at Howard University. He then worked in architectural firms in New York, and ultimately at the Port Authority of New York and New Jersey for over three decades. We visited my father's farm homestead in Humboldt, Tennessee, at least twice in the 1950s, so as a young child I had an immediate sense of the rhythms of cultivation and harvesting, birth and slaughter. When my grandfather died in the late 1960s, the farm was sold, since my father and his three sisters had long since left the farm for city life in Humboldt; Dayton, Ohio; and Queens and Brooklyn, New York.

The issue of land ownership by Black Americans became a central concern for Carpenter when she began her primary research about Black farming in 2012. She noted in a 2023 video interview for Woodmere that after thinking about farms and gardens with regard to her family, she wanted to know more about Black agricultural workers in the United States.[14] Carpenter identified Black farmers through the Southeastern African American Farmers Organic Network, and visited individual sites and several properties in Georgia, South Carolina, and the Gullah Islands. She interviewed the farmers and photographed their farms, yards,

and universities (HBCUs), at times even incorporated into the names of some of the institutions designated as "agricultural and mechanical" (A&M) colleges.[8]

At the forefront of these institutions, of course, was Tuskegee Institute in Alabama, home of eminent scientist, agronomist, and artist George Washington Carver. In connection with the story of Carpenter's grandmother's life-sustaining garden, it is interesting to note that Carver issued a bulletin in 1942 that described resources available to citizens who wished to support efforts to feed the American populace during World War II by planting Victory gardens. Carver imbues the notion of the garden with an expanded repertoire of nature-based vegetation—usually dismissed as "weeds"—with which the American household could supplement their diet.[9] He provides appetizing approaches to dandelion, wild lettuce, chicory, and giant thistle, thus affirming the well-known skill of African Americans to conceive culinary delights out of the "leftovers" of American society.[10] Although Carver's bulletin would have been widely circulated, it is uncertain whether subscriptions sold beyond the immediate audiences

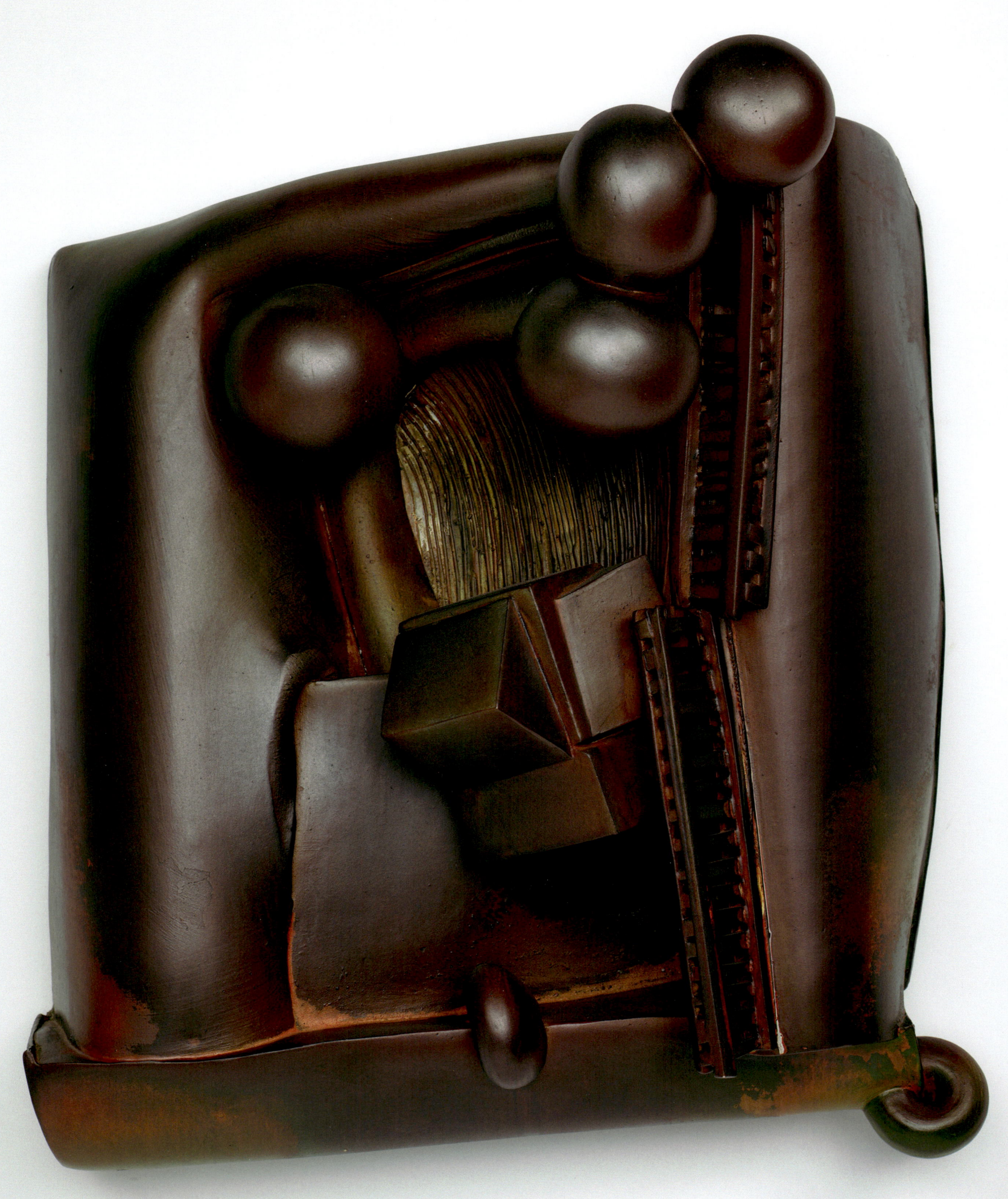

or gardens,[15] and the first question she posed to the various cultivators she met was, "Do you own your land?" The fact that the properties she visited were generationally owned was a key factor for the artist.[16]

Carpenter's research and creativity are both prescient and catalytic. As can be discerned from Mark and Liz Decena's 2023 documentary film *Farming While Black*,[17] a new generation of Black Americans are taking up the work of legacy farms, creating new entities and rejuvenating traditional (that is, remembered African Indigenous) approaches to land stewardship. I absorb the challenges and triumphs of Black farmers with a sense of wistfulness about what might have been in the trajectory of my own family.

PLACES OF OUR OWN

As an artist, you're composing. So I give myself license to improvise.[18]

—Syd Carpenter

After her 2012 research trip, Carpenter returned to her studio to create wall and later freestanding sculptures inspired by her encounters. To map out this series, *Places of Our Own*, she evokes the names of specific cultivators "in order to assert and honor their individuality in the face of historical erasure." She did so by "[c]ombining botanical imagery and vernacular forms like clothespins, tools, fences and sheds," even tillage patterns on the land. "Combined they . . . offer an evocative statement of creativity and resilience . . . of African American stewardship of the land."[19]

But Carpenter had begun creating works on the lore of African American land ownership even before she embarked on her 2012 trip. Her 2010 wall piece, dedicated to Mary Lou Furcron (fig. 3.6), is a case in point. The composition was inspired by a diagram of Furcron's homestead in Vesta, Georgia published in Richard Westmacott's pivotal 1992 publication, *African-American Gardens and Yards in the Rural South*,[20] which has been an important visual source for Carpenter,[21] especially for *Places of Our Own*.[22] Parenthetically, it is interesting that

Carpenter's homage to Mary Lou Furcron is indicative of how Furcron emerged as a star among this community of rural Black cultivators. Just two years after the Westmacott book was published, sculptor Beverly Buchanan, who was engaged in her own survey of shacks in Georgia,[23] produced a number of photographs of Furcron and her shack, which she built herself. As Carpenter noted in 2010:

> *As a gardener myself, the discovery of this study of African American gardeners was revelatory. The gardeners described their relationship to their spaces and the sense of independence derived from providing for themselves and their communities. . . . As fewer and fewer African Americans remain on the land as farmers, their testimony to the value of their way of life appealed to that part of me that also needs the garden as physical and spiritual sustenance.*[24]

Westmacott created diagrams of the sites—"garden surveys" —in which he devised a system of patterns and shapes to indicate various things on the lots.[25] Through these maps, which "documented the location of buildings, roads, fields, trees and animal pens," Carpenter began building the maps, seeing flattened shapes in three dimensions and ultimately digressing from the maps to create her own imagined landscaped farms and gardens. Westmacott also made note in his introduction that, "In the rural south the term 'garden' is used for the place where vegetables are grown. Flowers are grown in the 'yard,' which is often a place for leisure and entertainment."[26] And indeed during the summers of my youth, my mother, Bernice Banks Sims, would tend her hedges of rose bushes and Rose of Sharon trees. Behind the roses each spring, my father cultivated a "garden" where he produced a harvest of greens, tomatoes, lettuce, and string beans. The rest of the "yard" was where we gathered to socialize and enjoy moments of respite.

This linguistic detail reflects Carpenter's own accommodation of a number of sites of varying sizes and scopes in her sculptures. Her interpretation of the graphic forms and notations in the Westmacott diagram of the Furcron homestead, for example, is typical of how she conceives of form moving from two dimensions to three.

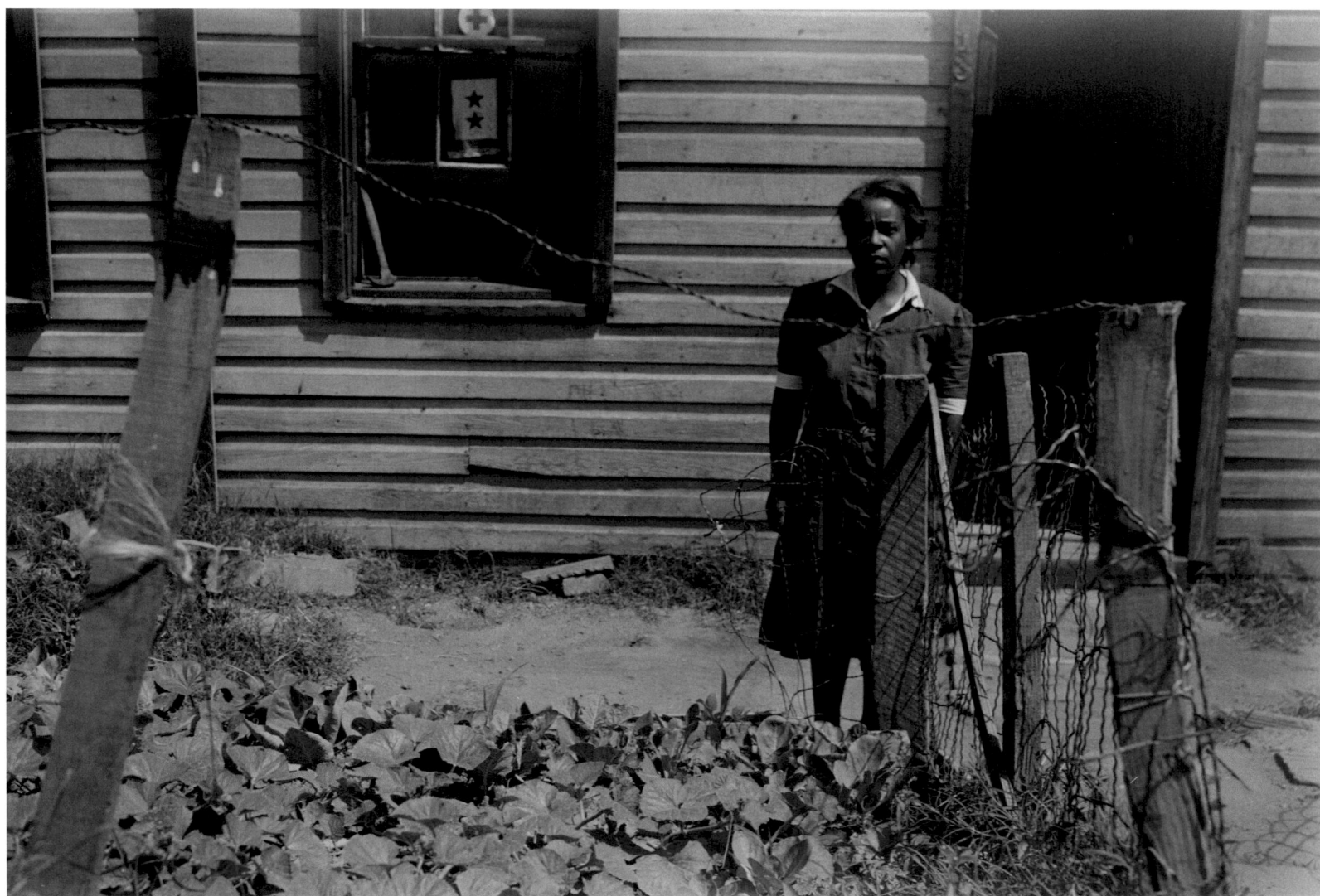

As Carpenter found sculptural equivalents for Westmacott's diagrams, fulsome, bulbous elements seem to vie to crowd each other out of the composition. In this way, Carpenter is always thinking in terms of an integral and satisfying presentation of the precepts of sculpture, as well as the specific character of her primary medium of clay and the other materials she brings to her work. Her goal is to translate narratives and information into forms that exist on their own terms as sculptural clay works as well as within those informational narratives.

There are some provocative visual impressions that come out of Carpenter's approach to form and texture—whether intentional or serendipitous. Her wall translation of Westmacott's diagram of the homestead of *Ellis and Anna Mae Thomas* (fig. 3.7) can be seen as suggesting a female form representing the fertility of the land, as seen in Alexandre Hogue's 1938 painting *Erosion No. 2 Mother Earth Laid Bare*. Hogue's work is intended as a pointed political statement that "testifies to the destructive consequences of poor farming practices, which have stripped away the layer of protective topsoil, but also infers that the disregard for nature's delicate state is a form of sexual violence. . . ."[27] As Hogue was reacting to the specific conditions of the Dust Bowl,

which resulted from poor soil management and land overuse in the devastated Midwestern United States in the 1930s, Carpenter herself has stressed the importance of the relationship of humans to land and our responsibilities with regard to climate change.[28]

This allusive visual relationship between the female body and the landscape, seen in the Hogue paintings and Carpenter's *Ellis and Anna Mae Thomas*, can perhaps also predicate the reading of Carpenter's 1991 wall sculpture *Then, Now, When* (see fig. 2.6). This work shows the evolution of Carpenter's approach to form from the more vessel orientation of *House for Mr. Biswas* (see page 35) and *Untitled (Lorraine's Pot)* (see fig. 2.1), or the more frankly anatomical studies of heads seen in *Child 3* (see fig. 2.5). *Then, Now, When* presents a formal ambiguity where the shape on the left may present Carpenter's three-dimensional transformation of leaves along the same lines as Carpenter interprets the Westmacott diagrams, seen in works like *Merge* of 2006 (fig. 3.8). The figure at right presents as either a female torso with a garment lifted to its shoulders, or perhaps an animal head. Indeed the viewer is subsumed into an experience of visual equivalences familiar in Surrealist artistic practices.

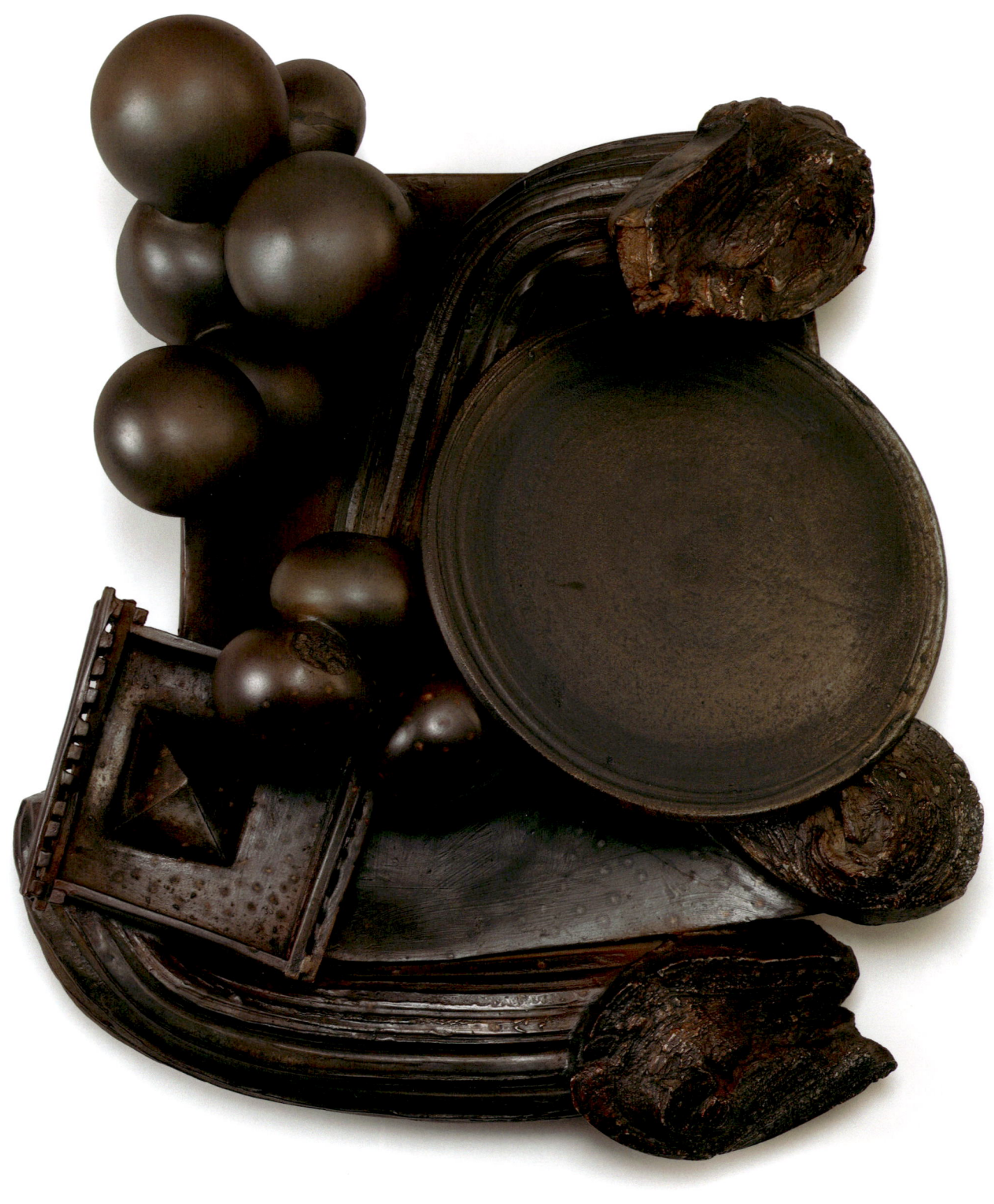

FIG. 3.6   *Mary Lou Furcron*, 2010, terracotta with acrylic paint, graphite, and wood, 25 × 23 × 11 in. (Smithsonian American Art Museum, Museum purchase through the Renwick Acquisitions Fund, 2010.51)

FIG. 3.7   *Ellis and Anna Mae Thomas*, 2009–10, earthenware, acrylic, and graphite, 26 × 20 × 8 in. from the series *Places of Our Own* (Frances Young Tang Teaching Museum and Art Gallery at Skidmore College: Gift of the artist, 2017.30)

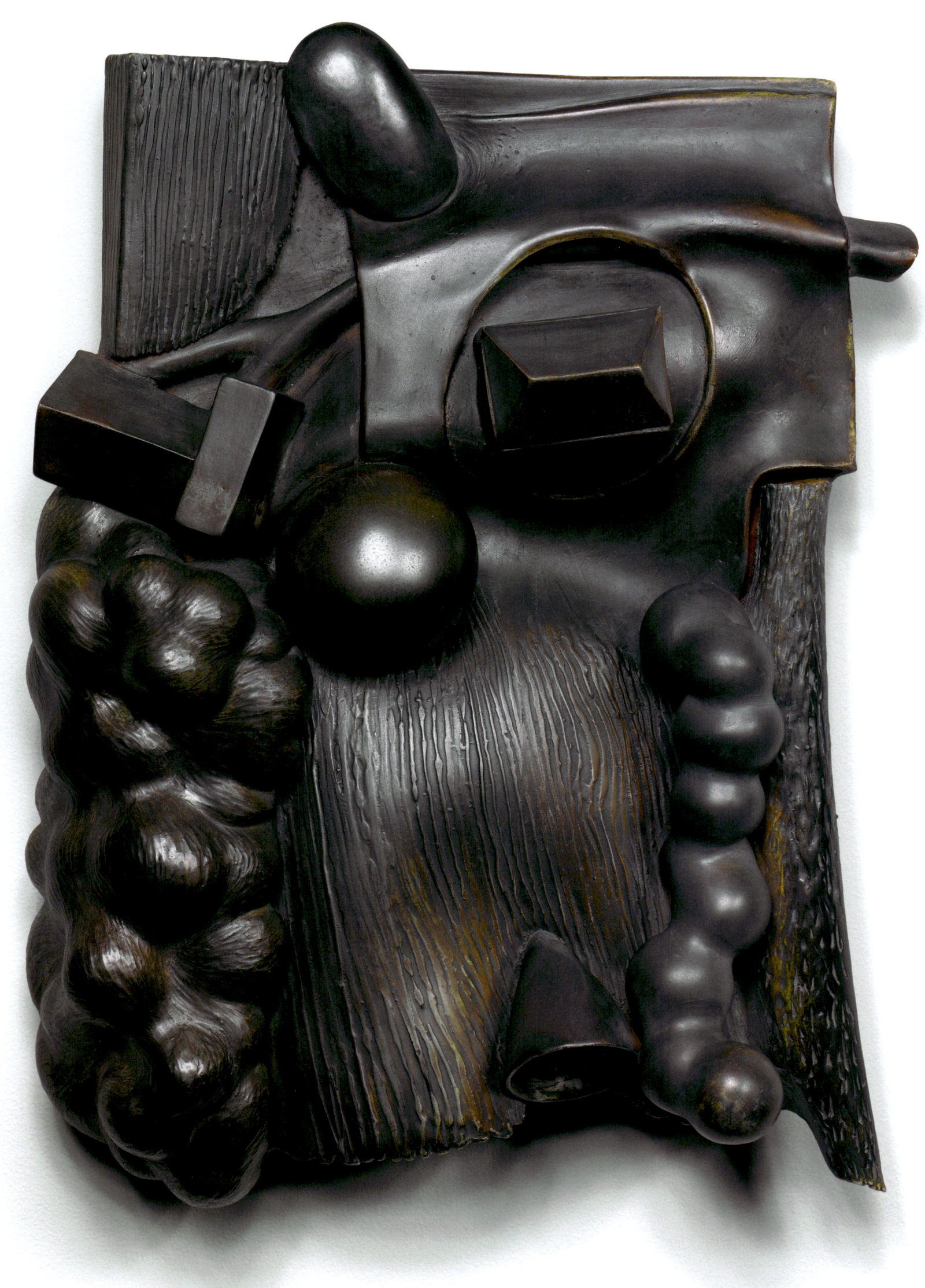

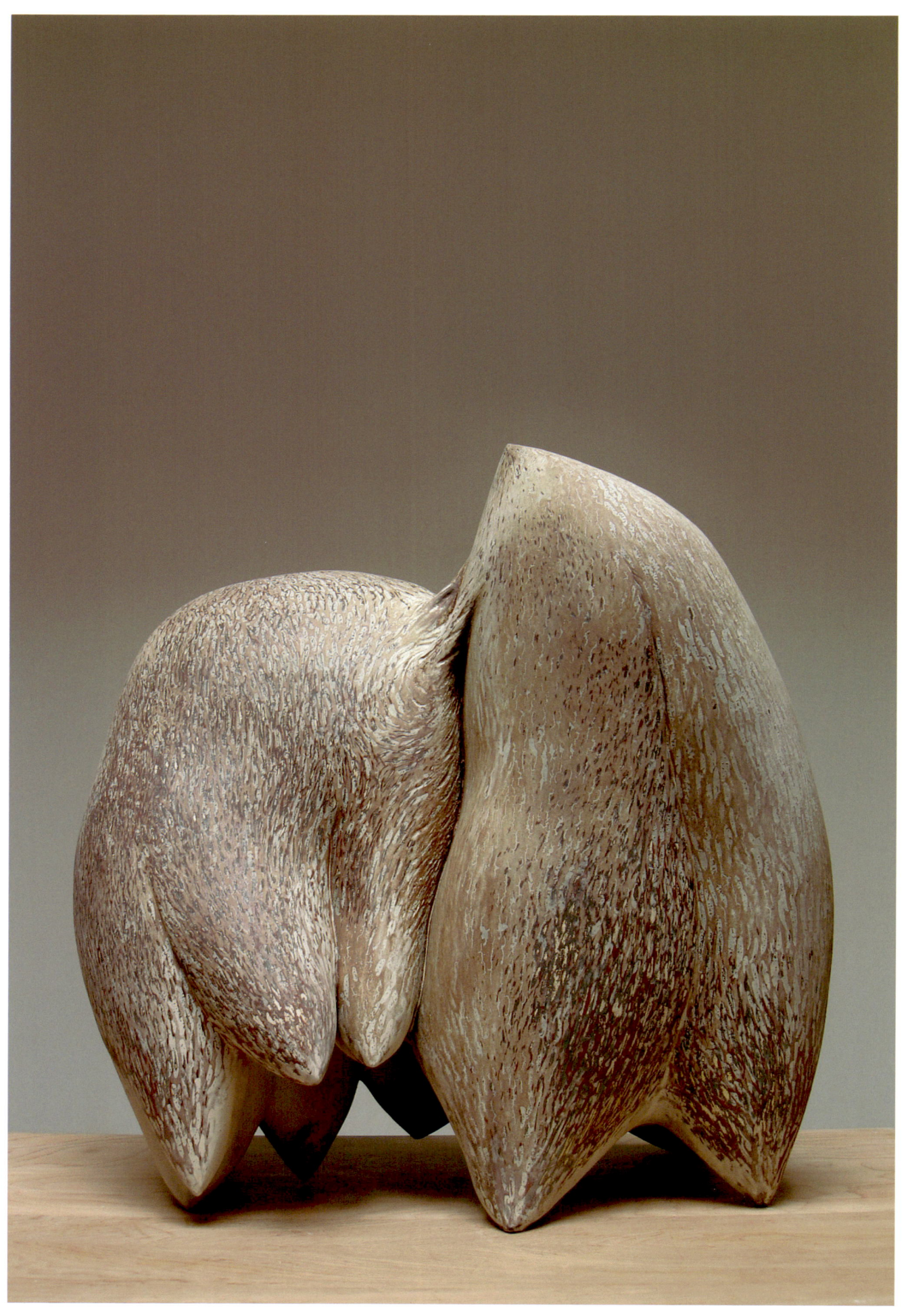

FIG. 3.8 *Merge*, 2006, clay, underglaze, and oxide, 26 × 24 × 15 in. (Courtesy of the Petrucci Family Foundation Collection of African American Art)

What may be seen as a prelude to Carpenter's engagement with growth and change appears in the 1990s in the *Stem* series: tendril-like forms (*A Snake without a Head Is Just a Rope*, see fig. 2.9) with human (*Four Seasons of Interest*, 2004) or animal heads (*Frank's Peace*, see pp. 42–43) intertwined in the composite. These "hybrid shapes . . . combine the natural with the mechanical," and, according to Carpenter, "take their form from what I observed in the garden that I have tended for about thirty years."[29] She notes:

> *Their scale is very close to my own proportions. Those human proportions give them autonomy. Their configurations suggest they could move by themselves. If you turn away and then turn back, they may have changed their position by twisting or sagging. I think of them as physical representations of an active verb: sag, dangle, twist, spiral.*[30]

With the series *More Places of Our Own* and *Farm Bowls*, Carpenter presents more definitively recognizable forms of landscape elements, utensils, animals, or structures. As a consequence, as she noted in the PBS documentary *Craft in America*, slab work in clay became an important component of her working methods in these sculptures.[31] That in combination with her skillful modeling has resulted in the roll call of elements that Carpenter deploys, provided by Jennifer Zarro: "cows, birds, shotguns, wheels, buildings, tools, mason jars, pie pans, and fields . . . each work represents specific individuals and their land." On the sculpture titled *Joseph and Helen Fields* (fig. 3.9), Zarro outlines that specificity: "We see funnels, Jell-O molds, and cake pans hanging like a skirt around a vignette that describes an outsized clothespin, dishes of grain, farm buildings and fences. The whole of this structure is supported by X-shaped steel supports, which in turn rest atop the tin roof of yet another farm building."[32] Zarro concludes, "These items describe the inventories and material cultures of the working life and ways of being of black farmers."[33]

The pedestal piece, *Mary Howard* (fig. 3.10), is another instance of how Carpenter captured the individual character of the locales she visited. The abbreviated site portrait is set atop a metal bench that the artist saw at Howard's place, and chicken wire is wrapped around the pedestal. The clay mason jars that hang off the edges represent Howard's passion for canning. This particular layout demonstrates, according to Carpenter, how her wall pieces migrated onto a pedestal as part of *More Places of Our Own*. Each one is meant to be seen as a plant, with a root, stem, and flower. She calculates how to "load stuff up" according to how she conceives of these works along those lines.[34]

When Carpenter shifted to the bowl shape as the support for her landscape portraits of the various growers and different plots of land she visited, she investigated the almost innate cultural meaning of the bowl in human history. She was interested in how it was "emblematic of a way of life and history and a type of present—importance of relationship of ourselves to land and climate change and—again—how we need to reconnect with the land."[35] This was also her way of moving beyond the typical view of this utilitarian object that has been a staple of pottery production. So the bowl is not merely about containment: It can have ceremonial functions. The inclusion of a brain shape as the foot of certain of these sculptures represents a more cerebral aspect of the bowl, and the shape can conjure cosmological associations and references to pre-Galilean concepts of the universe and the shape of planet earth.[36]

For Carpenter the choice of motifs for each sculpture is not calculated beforehand: That evolves in the process of the making. The various objects are specific to the farms, idiosyncratic to places as she experienced them in her travels to various sites. She starts each sculpture with her repertory of forms, responding to what they represent to her—tantamount to conveying her own language—and how we perceive the forms and assign identity and associations to them.[37] So a mule's foot indicated the lack of mechanized machinery on one of the first Black farming co-ops she visited. A rifle on the same sculpture was stored over the door in a building on the site to "deal with vermin and hostile neighbors."[38] There are additional reminders of some of the farm depictions of the 1930s and '40s in American art: The structure and mule in a work such as *O'Neal Smalls* (fig. 3.11) can be seen alongside those elements in William H. Johnson's *Sowing* (fig. 3.12). And in line with Carpenter's assertion that "family is

OF CLAY, CULTURE, AND CULTIVATION

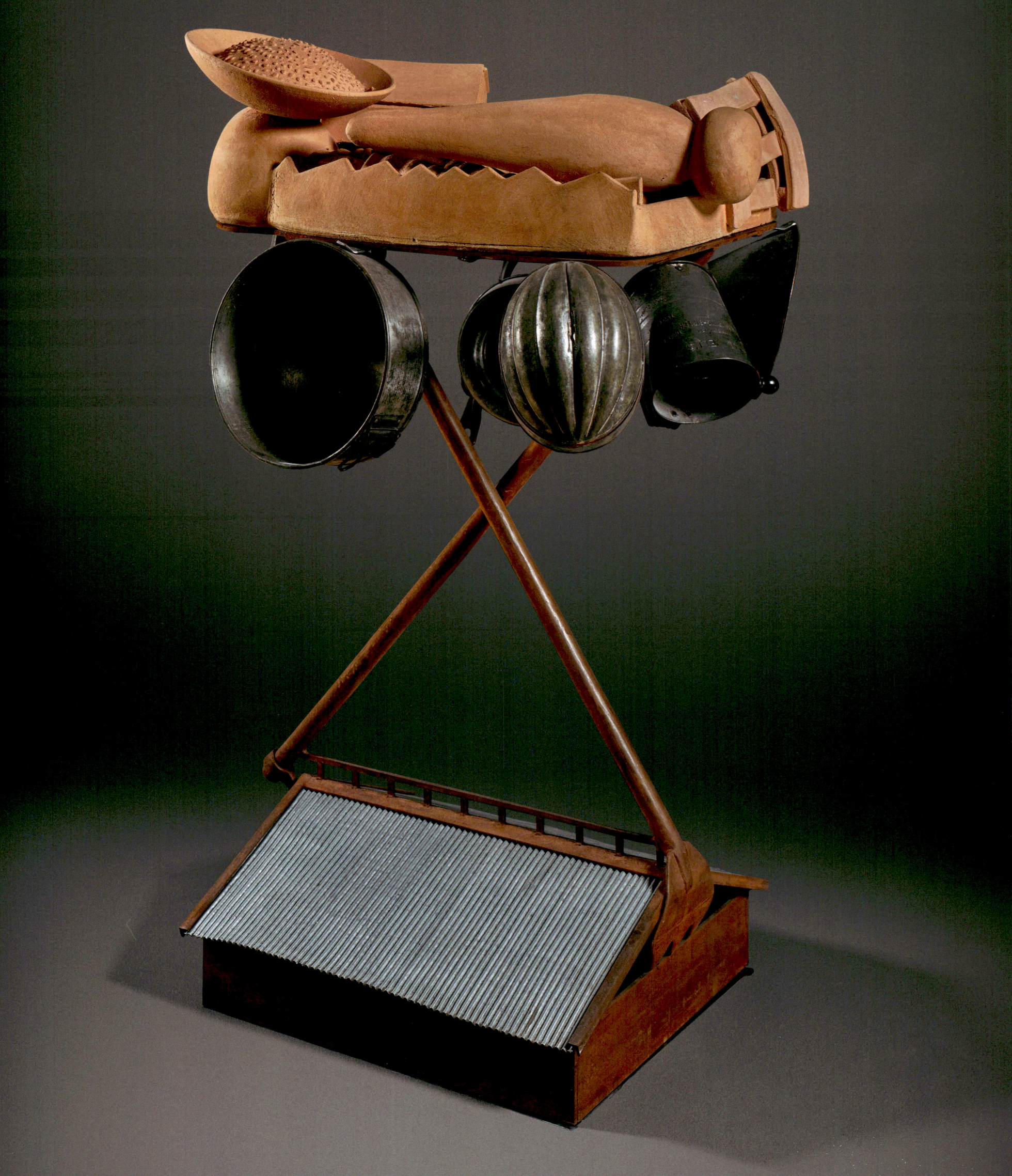

FIG. 3.9 (FACING PAGE) *Joseph and Helen Fields*, 2014, clay, found objects, and steel, 43 × 27 × 27 in. (James A. Michener Art Museum: Gift of the artist, 2021.1.2ab)

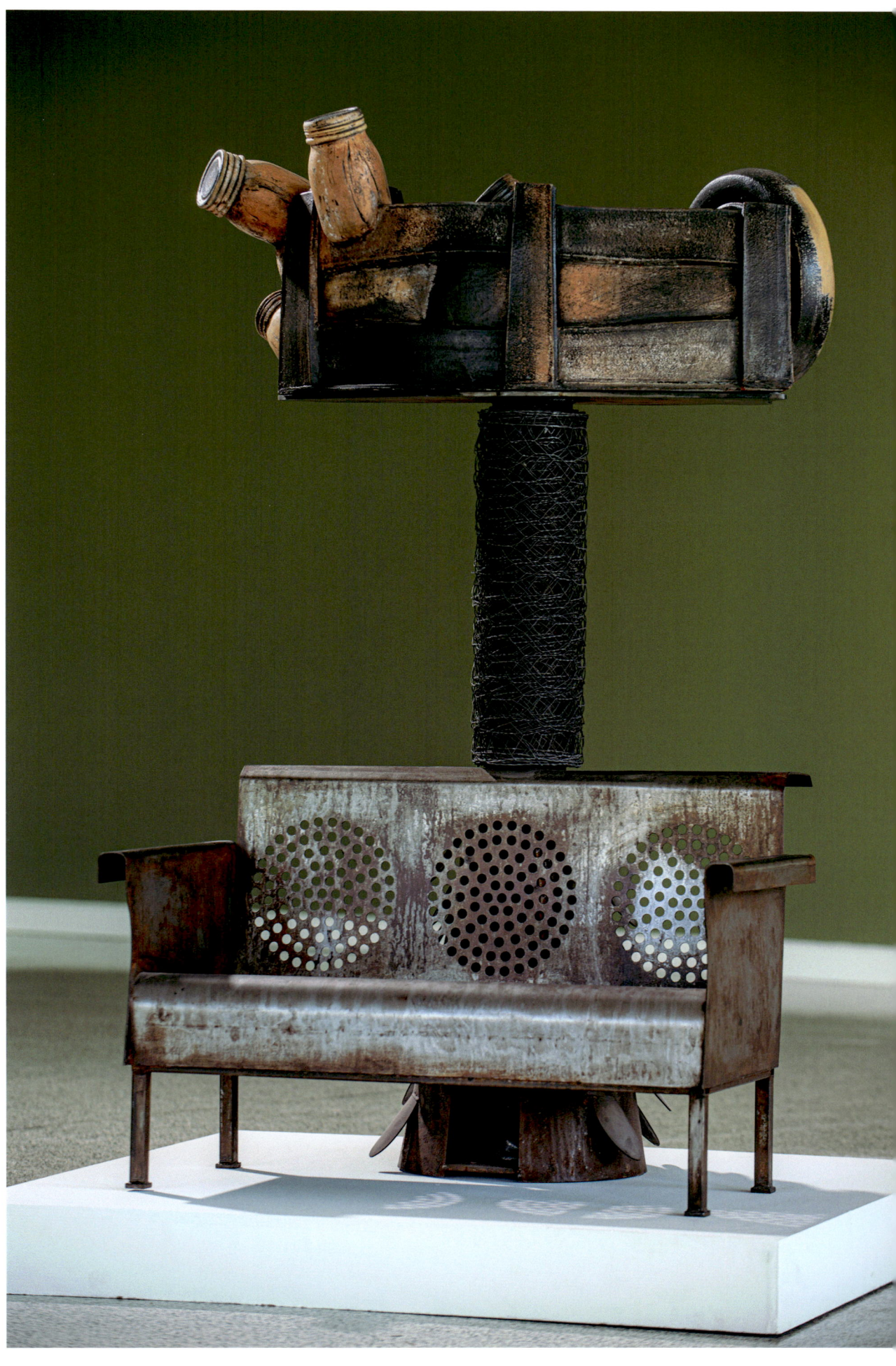

FIG. 3.10 *Mary Howard*, 2014, ceramic and steel, 53 × 35 × 24 in. (Collection of the artist)

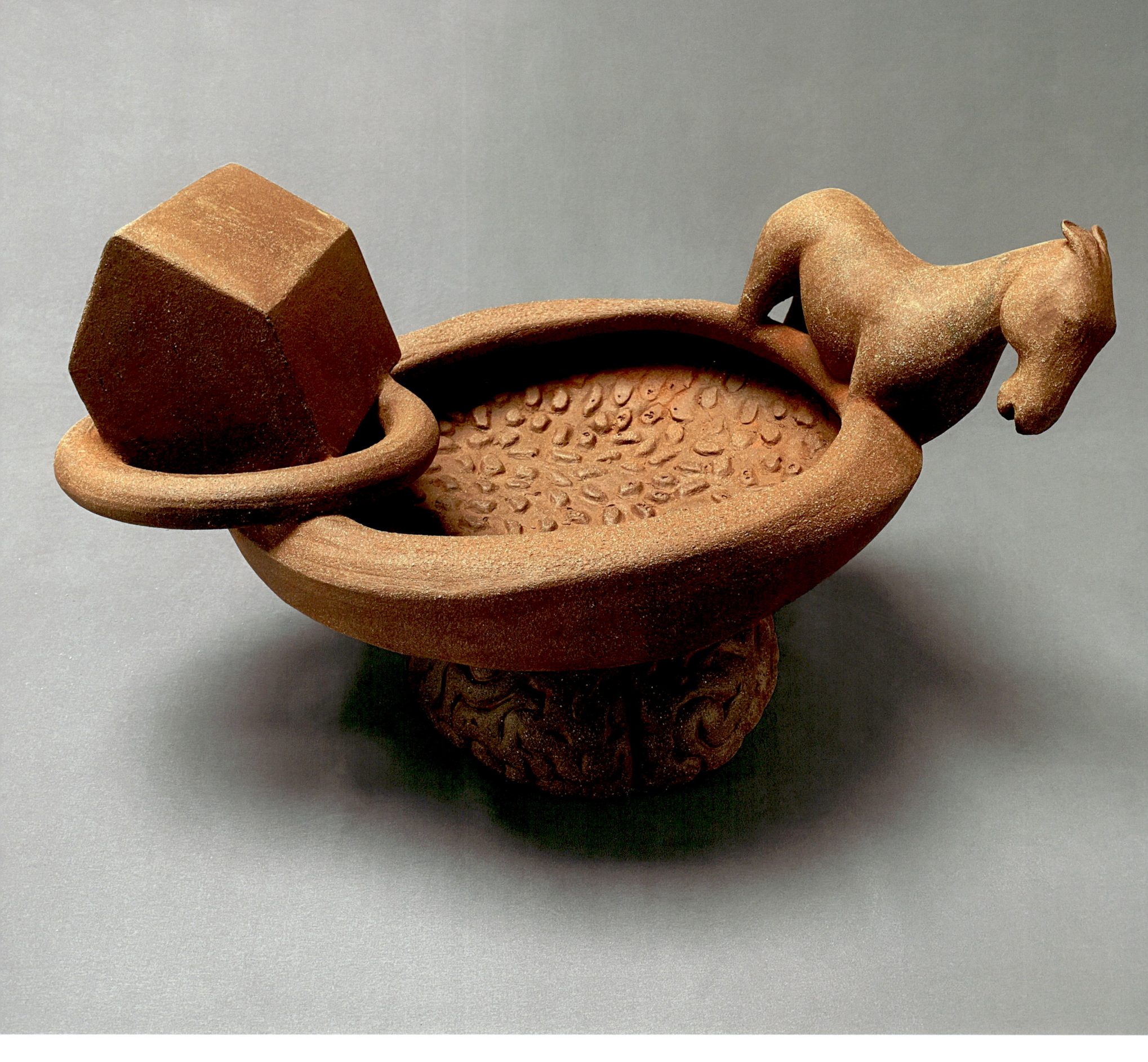

FIG. 3.11 *O'Neal Smalls*, 2021, stoneware, 13½ × 23 × 17 in. (Collection of the artist)

a constant source of inspiration both as image and encouragement,"[39] we can consider the farm bowl that Carpenter created to honor her grandmother, *Indiana Hutson* (see p. 50). The rim is enclosed by sections of a fence, and within impressions of leaves, circular egg shapes, a miniaturized house, and an outsized sieve surround a circular track of tillage.

With its plethora of objects, fragments, and landscape elements, Carpenter's farm works beg the question of formal and thematic relationships to the work of her contemporaries. Take, for example, *Ramshackle Fence* (see fig. 2.3), which is distinctive in the artist's oeuvre with its presentation of what Andrea Kirsh describes as "a range of worn, everyday items that sit in front of and are suspended from the fence, the debris awaiting reuse: bottles, tools, barrels, clothing. An oversized clothespin is nestled among the other objects. The fence itself is missing some of its upright sections and is partially held together with string."[40]

This conglomeration of individual elements from the dictionary of forms that Carpenter inserts on the individual landscape "portraits" can be seen in dialogue with the assemblagist impulse found in the work of Carpenter's slightly older contemporary, sculptor Melvin Edwards. Indeed one can isolate comparable shapes of individual utensils that have appeared in the wall pieces of Edwards's *Lynch Fragment* series since the 1960s.

So the hoe projecting prominently from the conglomeration of Edwards's *Ready Now Now* (1988); the ax, whose handle curves around the composition of *Weapon of Freedom* (1986); and the trowel and blade thrusting upward from *Tambo* (fig. 3.13) assume a fascinating congruence in conversation with Carpenter's deployment of objects. Less biographical in nature, they are certainly auto-expressive in a manner that allows for an open-ended response to Edwards's work. These works are prominent in his oeuvre and ". . .have been vehicles for Edwards to respond to racial violence in the United States, the Vietnam War, and, since the late 1970s, to honor individuals, explore notions of nostalgia, and investigate his personal interest in African culture."[41]

Additionally, "Edwards looked to the use of these steel industrial and agricultural objects to lend varying cultural, social, and political connotations to his sculptures' modernist structures."[42] In that context he views his work in relation to the traditions of

blacksmiths in West Africa, and, as he notes, his work has been associated with Yoruba orisha Ogun, who protects warriors, hunters, and blacksmiths.[43] Carpenter and Westmacott have recorded the deliberate accumulation of metal objects such as hubcaps, and other cast-offs, such as "railroad ties, granite block from local quarries, cable reels, auto tires, etc.,"[44] recast in specific arrangements on the properties of Black gardeners and farmers in the South, such as *Albert and Elbert Howard* (see fig. 3.1). As evidenced in the biographical objects Carpenter adheres to her own work, she is certainly recording such an impulse related to African retentions that now are recognized as prevalent in Black life in the United States. And as Westmacott opines, the presence of these elements in African American yards and gardens demonstrates the "resourcefulness" of the growers he examined in his book,[45] in the face of reduced material resources.

An important aspect of Carpenter's shapes is based on evoking a sense of intimate familiarity, as well as inspiring a recognition of our relationships to the objects we use in daily life. This is especially exemplified by the *Mother Pin* figures based on the form of the doll clothespins. For the artist they evoke memories and associations with her mother, Ernestine Carpenter; she still has the bag of clothespins that her mother used. Seen as a feminine form, and enlarged and in charge, these figures ascend to the mystical status of goddesses who reign over domesticity, nature, and nourishment[46]—replete in the version fashioned out of glass and filled with beans seen in *Storage Jar 2* (2017).[47] This is how she remembers her mother, to whom she paid special homage in *Mother Pin with House* (2018). Here the pin form presides over a woman's profile, from whose head a house projects out into space, while the kidney beans—at monumental scale—cluster around the base of the sculpture. The clothespin appears in a myriad of other guises: with a shirt (*Mother Pin with Shirt*, 2017), or standing in waves of water, with a chain and bottle encased in twine (*Mother Pin Awash*, 2016), and with an elongated body and wheel head in the trio seen in *Three Mother Pins on a Vine* (fig. 4.10).

The origins of Carpenter's extraordinarily integral and personal approach to clay may be glimpsed in the facts of her education and early associations in the field. She received her BFA and MFA from Temple University's Tyler School of Art and

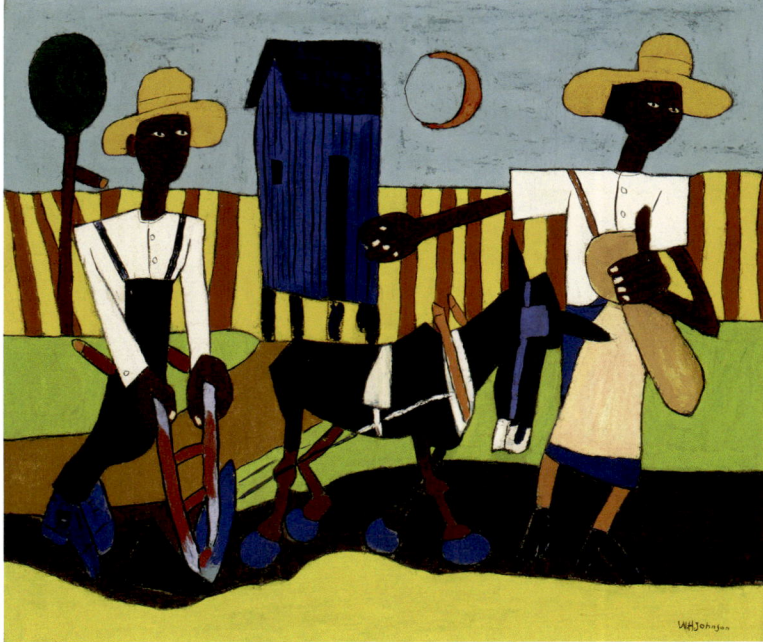

FIG. 3.12 William H. Johnson, *Sowing*, c. 1940, oil on burlap, 38½ × 45¾ in. (Smithsonian American Art Museum: Gift of the Harmon Foundation, 1967.59.1002)

Architecture in the 1970s, having trained in ceramics with the late Rudolf Staffel and Robert Winokur. Importantly, she forged lasting friendships with a cohort of women artists who came through Tyler or whom she learned about as she sought to familiarize herself with the field: Martha Jackson Jarvis, Sana Musasama, Judy Moonelis, and Winnie Owens-Hart. As can be read in the interview conducted by Dr. Leslie King-Hammond in this catalogue, this group of women, who forged their artistic identities through clay, have maintained a strong, supportive network since the 1970s.

Carpenter and several others in her cohort came to pottery after entering Tyler with the intention of being painters. These women emerged as a generation of ceramic artists who were committed to "getting past the usual associations with pottery," by getting beyond functionality.[48] By her own admission, at the beginning of her career as an artist, she eschewed the macho approaches of Peter Voulkos and the like, in favor of creating what she has described as "pretty pots."[49] These are exemplified by *Late Season* (see fig. 2.4) or *Untitled* (see fig. 2.1). In terms of their development within the medium, Carpenter and her fellow Tyler artists all acknowledge the particularly supportive presence of Staffel, which was exceptional in an environment that dismissed the efforts of women. Carpenter observes that support also included allowing students to be "turned loose in the studio to figure things out."[50]

Despite this seemingly laissez-faire approach, which allowed for the development of greater individual expression, one can't help but take note of Staffel's evocative vessels and Winokur's architectural forms in relationship to Carpenter's own work. Carpenter continues to be engaged with how "profound" a material clay is and "what it allows her to do." She notes that along the way to finding the "language" of clay, she gradually figured out how that language could allow her to develop content about the issues that were important to her.[51] Additionally, her method

of working in steel, wood, paper, glass, and foodstuffs like beans, often in collaboration with artisans in these different media, allows her to extend the capacity of her work to communicate meaning to the viewer.[52]

The relationship of Carpenter's work to American art in the 1930s and '40s, as well as assemblagist trends that have emerged at various moments in the twentieth and twenty-first centuries, has already been referred to earlier. But it is clear that her practice must also be considered in the context of the varied artistic practices chronicled by Silvia Bottinelli in *Artists and the Practice of Agriculture: Politics and Aesthetics of Food Sovereignty in Art Since 1960*.[53] Bottinelli surveys artistic nuances of agriculture in the context of transformations in the global art world in the 1960s and '70s that began to accommodate "connections with sites and communities" and "the multisensorial perception of material and environments."[54] Her observations that "artists who engage with agriculture embrace it as a tool for both political critique and aesthetic expression"[55] are certainly in sync with Carpenter's goals and philosophy. Bottinelli identifies a number of practices that parse the nature of the relationship of humans to the land in the modern context, which challenge the determinist mindset of humans to dominate elements that are unpredictable: "soil, light, seeds, pollinators . . ."[56]

Among the practices featured by Bottinelli is the mound planting of the Tuscarora Nation. This was the inspiration for the 2016 installation *Ah-Theuh-Nyeh-Hah (The Planting Moon)* by the Tuscarora artist and Cornell professor Jolene Rickard in the Pounder Vegetable Garden at Cornell University. Rickard created thirteen mounds of soil planted with seeds integral to Haudenosaunee culture, which include the "three sisters" (corn, beans, and squash), along with tobacco, sunflower, and wild strawberry.[57] The mound formation "facilitates the growth of crops with different root depth and fosters both symbiosis among different plants and easier care from humans."[58] Carpenter adapted this

FIG. 3.13 Melvin Edwards, *Tambo*, 1993, welded steel, 28⅛ × 25¼ × 22 in. (Smithsonian American Art Museum: Museum purchase through the Luisita L. and Franz H. Denghausen Endowment and the Smithsonian Institution Collections Acquisition Program, 1994.55)

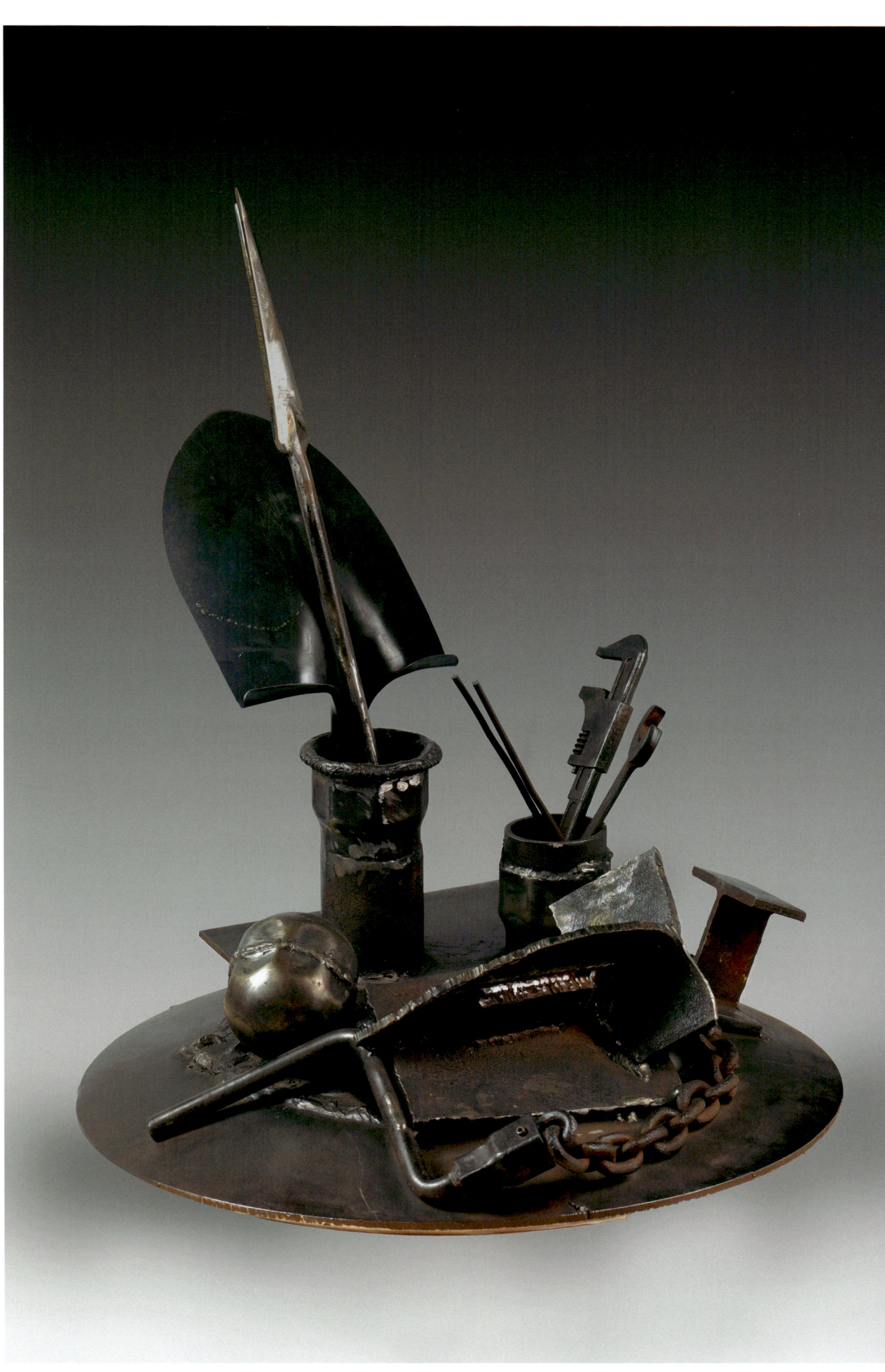

planting method when she collaborated with her husband, artist Steve Donegan, to create two hügel mounds, *La Cresta* (2021) at Woodmere[59] and *The Instrument* (2024) at the Berman Museum at Ursinus College, which likewise "blur the line between creativity and horticultural practice."[60]

Carpenter's Woodmere installation includes "two curving hügels...[e]ach...about forty-five feet in length, with a maximum height of just under six feet at the highest point."[61] Their structures highlight the specific elements of hügel mounds, which were originally conceived in Germany and Eastern Europe: "logs and other disposable materials" which over time "decompose ...to create rich, nutrient-dense soil" and a fertile soil bed.[62] The resulting "improved drainage and water conservation...reduces the need for fertilizers and pesticides, and require[s] less maintenance."[63] This serves the needs and purposes of Carpenter's installations. As she observes about the Woodmere hügel: "The emphasis...was on sustainability, with use of on-site materials a priority" including "several fallen trees available for the project." Additionally, "The plants...selected are drought tolerant, deer and rabbit resistant, and have four seasons of interest."[64]

Carpenter's land installations find synchronicity with the symbolic import of the famed mounds created by Native American peoples in the Midwestern United States that served variously as burial sites and locations for ritual structures.[65] They also place her in the company of artists such as Robert Smithson, Michael Heizer, and Maya Lin, whose *Storm King Wavefield* (2009) features an undulating character similar to Jolene Rickard's mounds and Carpenter's hügels. Carpenter actuates planting practices that complement those of her own family, as well as the farmer/growers she met in 2012, and her hügel installations also share the somewhat defiant purpose and spirit of Agnes Denes's *Wheatfield—A Confrontation* (1982).[66] This urban farming project on a two-acre swath of the Battery Park landfill on Manhattan's west side, in the shadow of the World Trade Center, reflects an issue Carpenter emphasizes again and again in her chronicling of the precariousness and risks of African Americans and the land. Denes risked initiating farming on land that has a high commercial value, and risked initiating this project as a non-farmer unfamiliar with what Silvia Bottinelli

notes are the "unpredictable" elements of agriculture.[67] But as with Carpenter's hügels, Denes's project proved to be viable, and over one thousand pounds of viable wheat was harvested after four months.[68]

CONCLUSION

Everything was done to get us off the land. So generations faced a sense of threat. But they stayed and Black churches were the focal points of unity.[69]

—Syd Carpenter

The persistent themes that come up as Carpenter talks about the farmers, gardeners, and growers she is related to, has known and met is the courage and tenacity that Black Americans have faced to pursue growing, and keep land in families. Since the late twentieth century, the pressures on small farms have been relentless given the capriciousness of financial resources.[70] As this exhibition opens in 2026, a new challenge has presented itself as the Trump administration suspended the USDA 1890 National Scholars Program that supports Black students in the various land grant schools, many of which provided coursework in agriculture.[71] Competition from food imports, the imposition of tariffs on machinery, and other factors are a challenge for Black Americans. In urban areas, the mechanisms of gentrification are a constant threat, even in cases where Black growers set up in lots that are deemed less desirable or ideal. In *More Places of Our Own*, Carpenter dedicated a sculpture to Rashid Nuri (2014), who started a garden in an abandoned plot in Atlanta. The work features the back of a ubiquitous resin chair and a set of stairs "to nowhere," remnants of the foundation of a demolished high-rise.

As noted in the *Artblog* feature on the exhibition of *More Places of Our Own* at the Philadelphia African American Museum in 2023:

Farmers and their families have built their own geographies and traditions—which may have roots reaching back to the agrarian ways of life in West Africa, as the

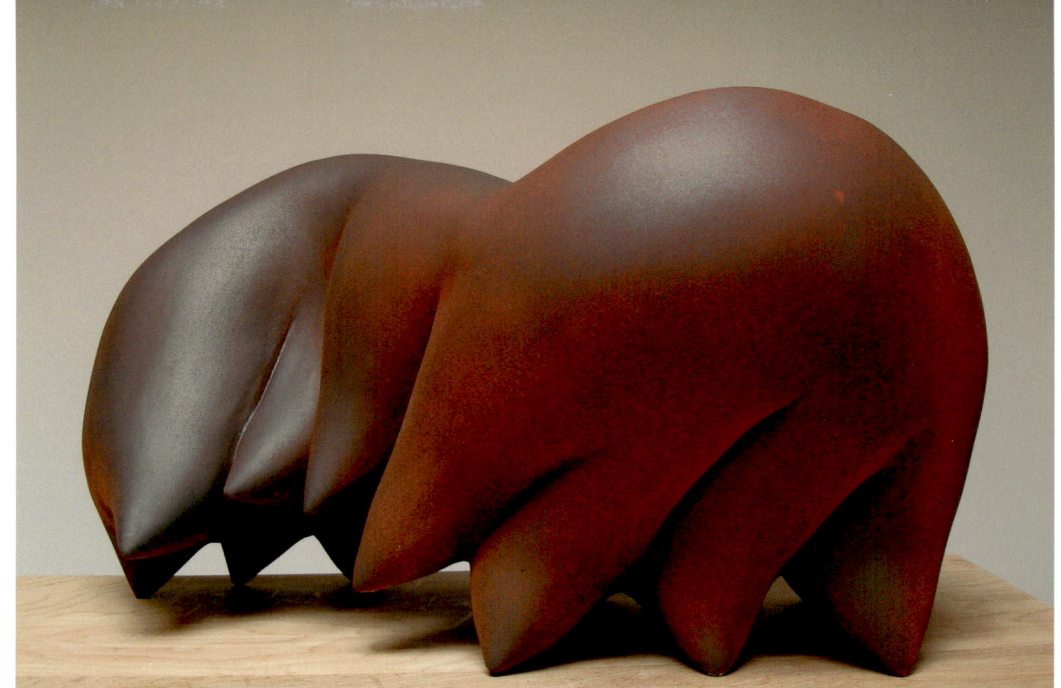

video outlines. Cultural events and gatherings are often celebrated in local churches built from timber taken from the cleared areas of black-owned farms. Losing these farms could mean the loss of an immeasurable history.[72]

Naima Penniman, who is featured in the documentary *Farming While Black*, is part of the new generation of Black farmers who are determined to reclaim and maintain that history. She speaks to the "regenerative farming" they are involved in with her sister on their family farm in Upstate New York

that helps to heal the land, the soil, the climate and the ecosystem as opposed to extracting it.…[U]nfortunately, the majority of the agriculture in this country is really rooted in an ethos of exploitation and extraction. The practices that we use at Soul Fire are really rooted in the African diasporic traditions of farming in a way that creates really life-giving food while also giving back to the land that feeds us.[73]

Carpenter has also heralded the fact that Black farmers, growers, and gardeners are at the forefront of ideas about recycling and soil conservation. Penniman emphasizes how

Black farmers are really innovating on, what are the ways we can reclaim these ancestral technologies to support in not losing precious topsoil and precious crops in times of climate emergency? It's really important we use our both personal and institutional purchasing power to support Black farmers and operations instead of investing our money into fast food and commodified and corporate foods that are rooted in this lineage of industrial agriculture. That is not fair to the farmers; it's not fair to the earth.[74]

Carpenter has therefore emphasized the fact that farms and land ownership are crucial to building intergenerational wealth for African Americans. Through her work she seeks to name people, who would otherwise be anonymous, because their survival is

foundational to ours. This exhibition includes her newest installation work at the Berman Museum of Art at Ursinus College, Collegeville, Pennsylvania: a stainless-steel barn (2026) that the viewer can enter and take in projections of Carpenter's photographs of the people and sites she visited in 2012. As Naima Penniman's sister Leah noted in a conversation with Carpenter at the Tang Museum in 2017:

In my experience of farming in the past twenty years, when black folks come back to land and experience the tilling, the harvesting, the reaping, the sharing food, that unnamable emptiness, which has been empty for generations, is filled.…But to see a deeper healing, a reclamation of our ancestral right to belong to the land and have agency when it comes to food and land is profound.[75]

In response, Carpenter affirms her commitment to her artistic goals and advocacy:

There is a need for the word to get out. What are the ways that the word can get out? It's through art making and interdisciplinary conversations between a farmer and a poet and a musician and an engineer. All of that, to me, is another form of art making. At a certain point, truth has to emerge. Those varied and imaginative possibilities that come from these intersections of knowledge that include artists, to me, that's the hope. That's my hope.[76]

If the gestures of recognition that Carpenter creates through her work mean that African American cultivators will achieve recognition, and help the Black community as a whole transcend the generational disconnect with the land, then she will have achieved her goal of encouraging African Americans to reclaim their relationship to the land and to conceive "different ways to be present on the land."[77]

NOTES

1. Laura Feragen, "PHL Airport Exhibitions Program 25 Anniversary," PHL, June 1, 2023, https://www.phl.org/newsroom/profile-SydCarpenter.

2. Summer Sewell, "There Were Nearly a Million Black Farmers in 1920—Why Have They Disappeared?" *Guardian*, April 29, 2019, https://www.theguardian.com/environment/2019/apr/29/why-have-americas-black-farmers-disappeared.

3. Syd Carpenter, in conversation with Leslie King-Hammond and the author, the artist's studio, Philadelphia, January 29, 2025.

4. Carpenter, King-Hammond, and the author, January 29, 2025.

5. "Earle Richardson," Smithsonian American Art Museum, https://americanart.si.edu/artist/earle-richardson-4035.

6. Elizabeth Prelinger, *Scenes of American Life: Treasures from the Smithsonian American Art Museum* (Watson-Guptill Publications, in cooperation with the Smithsonian American Art Museum, 2001).

7. Carpenter, King-Hammond, and the author, January 29, 2025.

8. See "Historically Black Colleges (HBCUs) Offering Agricultural Programs," Entomological Society of America, https://www.entsoc.org/historically-black-colleges-and-universities-hbcus-offering-agricultural-programs.

9. See George Washington Carver, "Nature's Garden for Victory and Peace," https://archive.org/details/CAT31355423/page/n1/mode/2up.

10. See, for example, "Rooted in a Zero Waste Culture: Celebrating Black History Through Food and Ingenuity," ReFED, February 1, 2023, https://refed.org/articles/rooted-in-a-zero-waste-culture-celebrating-black-history-through-food-and-ingenuity/.

11. Amy Bentley, *Eating for Victory: Food Rationing and the Politics of Domesticity* (University of Illinois Press, 1998).

12. See "Victory Gardens on the World War II Home Front," National Park Service, https://www.nps.gov/articles/000/victory-gardens-on-the-world-war-ii-home-front.htm.

13. Syd Carpenter, Martha Jackson Jarvis, Sana Musasama, Winnie Owens-Hart, and Judy Moonelis, Maguire Art Museum, St. Joseph's University, Philadelphia, February 27, 2025. This exchange forms the interview edited by Dr. Leslie King-Hammond in this publication. Notes taken by the author.

14. "Syd Carpenter: Places of Our Own," Woodmere, 2024, https://www.youtube.com/watch?v=GYiRq5T5poI.

15. See *Syd Carpenter: Portraits of Our Places*, Michener Art Museum, October 16, 2020–February 28, 2021, https://michenerartmuseum.org/exhibition/syd-carpenter-portraits-of-our-places/.

16. Carpenter, King-Hammond, and the author, January 29, 2025.

17. See Mark Decena, *Farming While Black*, 2023, https://www.farmingwhileblackfilm.com.

18. "Syd Carpenter Segment from the Home Episode," *Craft in America*, 2022, https://www.youtube.com/watch?v=xSpVxbgjVNY.

19. *Syd Carpenter: Portraits of Our Places*.

20. Richard Westmacott, *African-American Gardens and Yards in the Rural South* (University of Tennessee Press, 1992).

21. "Places of Our Own," Woodmere.

22. *Craft in America*.

23. Eleanor Flomenhaft, ed. *Beverly Buchanan: Shackworks, A 16-Year Survey*, exh. cat. with essays by Lowery Stokes Sims and Trinkett Clark (Montclair Art Museum, 1994).

24. "Artist Statement," 2010, Syd Carpenter, https://syd-carpenter.swarthmore.edu/artist-statement/.

25. Westmacott, 128.

26. Artist statement.

27. Mark Andrew White, "Alexandre Hogue's Passion: Ecology and Agribusiness in the Crucified Land," *Great Plains Quarterly* 26, no. 2 (spring 2008), 72. https://www.jstor.org/stable/23533712.

28. "Places of Our Own," Woodmere.

29. Syd Carpenter, email to the author, March 1, 2025.

30. Syd Carpenter, email to the author, March 1, 2025.

31. *Craft in America*.

32. Jennifer Zarro, "Syd Carpenter's *Places of Our Own* at the African American Museum in Philadelphia," *Artblog,* May 16, 2014, https://www.theartblog.org/2014/05/syd-carpenters-more-places-of-our-own-at-the-african-american-museum-in-philadelphia/.

33. Zarro.

34. Carpenter, King-Hammond, and the author, January 29, 2025.

35. "Places of Our Own," Woodmere.

36. Carpenter, King-Hammond, and the author, January 29, 2025.

37. Carpenter, King-Hammond, and the author, January 29, 2025.

38. Carpenter, King-Hammond, and the author, January 29, 2025.

39. Syd Carpenter website.

40. Andrea Kirsh, "Syd Carpenter's Ode to Women and Black-Owned Family Farms," *Artblog,* March 15, 2022, https://www.theartblog.org/2022 /03/syd-carpenters-ode-to-women-and-black -owned-family-farms/.

41. See "Melvin Edwards: Lynch Fragments, 1960s– Present," Alexander Gray Associates, https://www .alexandergray.com/series/melvin-edwards/melvin -edwards-lynch-fragments/.

42. "Lynch Fragments."

43. Michael Brenson, "An Oral History with Melvin Edwards," *BOMB Magazine*, November 24, 2014, https://bombmagazine.org/articles/melvin -edwards/.

44. Westmacott, 109–10.

45. Westmacott.

46. *Craft in America*; and Carpenter, King- Hammond, and the author, January 29, 2025.

47. Carpenter, King-Hammond, and the author, January 29, 2025.

48. Carpenter, King-Hammond, and the author, January 29, 2025.

49. Carpenter, Jackson Jarvis, Musasama, Owens- Hart, and Moonelis, February 27, 2025.

50. Carpenter, King-Hammond, and the author, January 29, 2025.

51. Carpenter, Jackson Jarvis, Musasama, Owens- Hart, and Moonelis, February 27, 2025.

52. Carpenter, King-Hammond, and the author, January 29, 2025.

53. Silvia Bottinelli, *Artists and the Practice of Agri- culture: Politics and Aesthetics of Food Sovereignty in Art Since 1960* (Routledge, 2004).

54. Bottinelli, 1.

55. Bottinelli, 1.

56. Bottinelli, 17.

57. Bottinelli, 34.

58. Bottinelli, 34.

59. "La Cresta" is a reference to nearby Ridge Ave- nue, one of the longest streets in Philadelphia and a Lenape byway established before European set- tlers arrived in the area in the 1600s. "*La Cresta: A Land-Sculpting Installation by Syd Carpenter and Steve Donegan*," Woodmere, April 17, 2021, https:// woodmereartmuseum.org/experience /exhibitions/la-cresta.

60. "La Cresta," Woodmere.

61. "La Cresta," Woodmere.

62. See "Hügelkultur," Wikipedia, https://en .wikipedia.org/wiki/Hügelkultur.

63. "Community Planting: The Berman Hügel Garden," Ursinus College, April 27, 2024, https:// ursinus-archive.livewhale.net/live/events /community-planting.

64. Garden Photo of the Day Contributor, "Syd's Hügel Garden," *Fine Gardening*, https://www .finegardening.com/article/syds-hugel-garden ?srsltid=AfmBOooejg3DAbWuBjDYsyckkk -2KMQnZ94QRSjZFd4PK5rKHhW7KTiS.

65. See "Indian Mounds," Natural Resources Con- servation Service, https://www.nrcs.usda.gov/sites /default/files/2023-08/Indian-Mounds.pdf.

66. See "Works," Agnes Denes, http://www .agnesdenesstudio.com/works7.html.

67. Bottinelli, 17.

68. For details about *Wheatfield*, see "Works," Agnes Denes, http://www.agnesdenesstudio.com /works7.html.

69. Carpenter, King-Hammond, and the author, January 29, 2025.

70. Carpenter, King-Hammond, and the author, January 29, 2025.

71. Walter Hudson, "CBC Calls on Trump to Rein- state HBCU Agriculture Program," *Diverse: Issues in Higher Education*, February 24, 2025, https://www .diverseeducation.com/institutions/hbcus/article /15738200/cbc-calls-on-trump-to-reinstate-hbcu -agriculture-scholarship-program.

72. Zarro.

73. Lola Fadulu, "New York Today," *New York Times*, April 19, 2024, https://www.nytimes.com /2024/04/18/nyregion/nigerian-chess-master -tunde-onakoya.html.

74. Fadulu.

75. "Syd Carpenter and Leah Penniman: Uplifting Truth Through Making," Tang Museum, https:// tang.skidmore.edu/collection/explore/140-syd -carpenter-leah-penniman.

76. Tang Museum.

77. Carpenter, Jackson Jarvis, Musasama, Owens- Hart, and Moonelis, February 27, 2025.

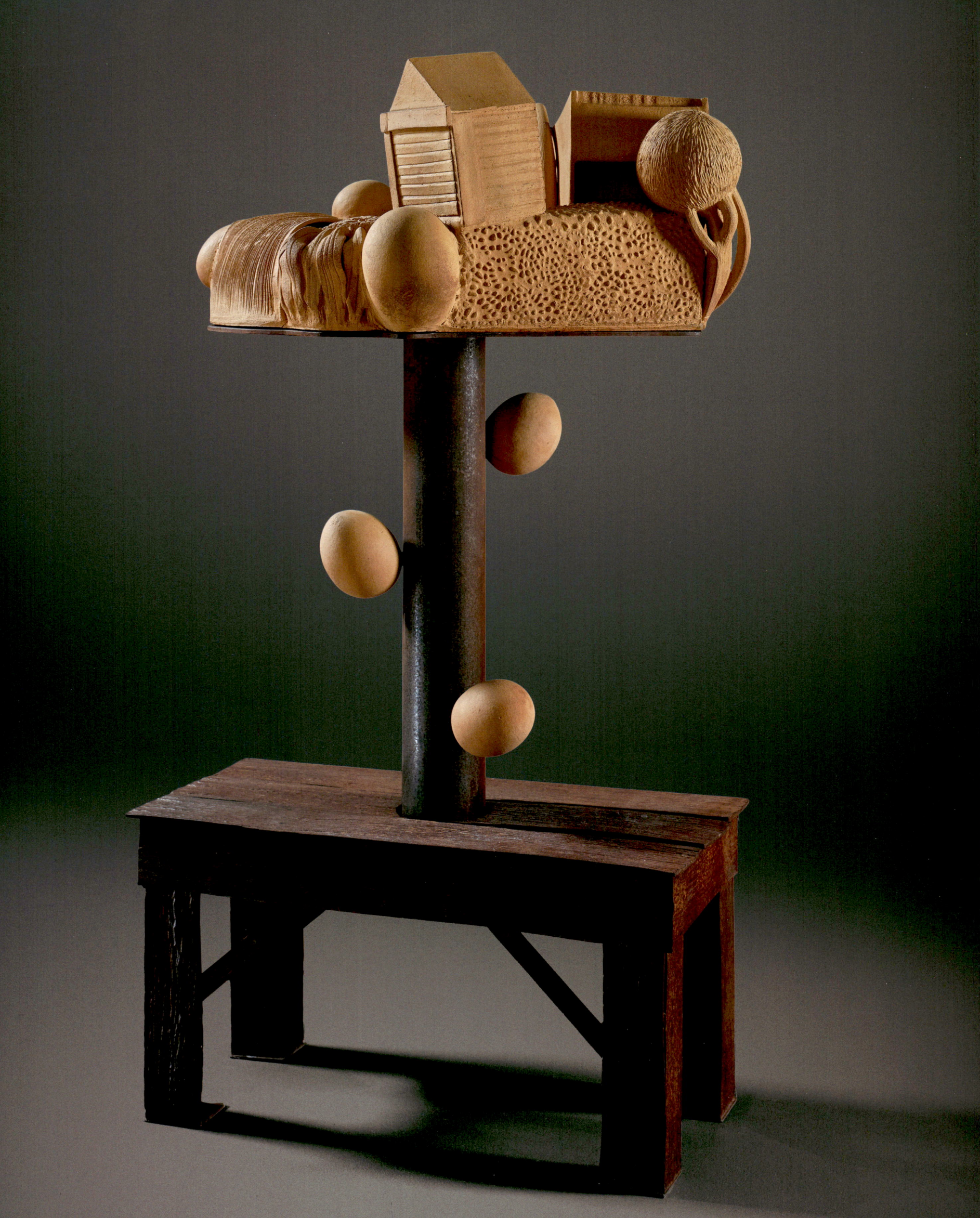

A Conversation with
Syd Carpenter, Sana Musasama, Winnie Owens-Hart, Martha Jackson Jarvis, and Judy Moonelis

MODERATED BY LESLIE KING-HAMMOND

Creativity takes courage. Whatever the mind can conceive and believe, it can achieve.
—Anderson Sunda-Meya

LESLIE KING-HAMMOND Welcome, everyone. This is a very exciting moment for us to have a conversation with such esteemed artists, who will be exhibiting simultaneously with the virtuoso works of Syd Carpenter. I want to take advantage of the time, because Sana is in Cambodia, in the wee hours of the morning, and Winnie Owens-Hart is here with us on audio from Virginia. This interview will be more akin to a conversation with artists who have very special kinship and have not seen each other in a long time. This is an opportunity to reconnect, share, and most importantly, explore the sense of who we are, why we're here, and what needs to be addressed at this point in your lives as artists and as women. Let's start with some introductions from each artist because this conversation will augment the exhibition at the Woodmere and its audience needs to know each artist.

SYD CARPENTER Hi, everyone. I'm Syd Carpenter (fig. 4.1). I want to say just up front how honored I am to have this sequence, this gathering of women who have just been so integral to my awareness of myself as an artist. I live in Philadelphia, have lived here for many, many years, have a studio here, of course, I've taught here for thirty years at Swarthmore College, but always in the background has been this awareness of these women who have been so important to me as I watched them grow.

It gave me confidence, it helped propel me, to see them moving along into spaces that women were not welcomed in, have not been known to be in, and see them intrude in these wonderful ways. This is really an important event for me, a once-in-a-lifetime situation for me, to be able to show my work at these prestigious institutions, and to have these women, Lowery and Leslie, write about me. This is an important, amazing experience for me. I thank all of you. I thank the Frances M. Maguire Art Museum, I thank the Berman Museum of Art, and I thank Woodmere.

KING-HAMMOND Too wonderful. Thank you. Sana, let's hear from you.

SANA MUSASAMA Wow, did I have to go behind you? [LAUGHTER]

CARPENTER Girl, you've gone beside me, always.

MUSASAMA I like that. I like that. Well, I'm Sana Musasama (fig. 4.2). I'm from New York City area, and currently, I'm in Cambodia, where I do my activism work with girls who I've helped rescue from the sex industry. This is my seventeenth year, and I've recently retired from being an adjunct professor at Hunter College, Queens College, and John Jay College, and a host of other jobs to supplement a very low income.

In terms of Syd, I don't know when I met Syd, but I know that she entered my life very, very easily. I think probably with many of us, we know each other by our work first, and we see it in different exhibitions. I remember early in my career, looking at her work and being mesmerized in wanting to know whose it was. I'm not sure when we did meet, but when we did, we made a link for a lifetime. Syd has been almost the wind beneath my wings and my career. Every place that she's gone, every institution she's taught in, she's weaved me into her life. She's been monumental, and a lot of my successes I hand over to Syd. A very, very, very special human being to me, and probably to a lot of other people as well. I'm so lucky, Syd, to be loved by you.

CARPENTER Oh. I knew this was going to happen. Where are the Kleenex? [LAUGHTER]

KING-HAMMOND I think that the next one we should hear from is Winnie Owens-Hart.

WINNIE OWENS-HART Hi, guys (fig. 4.3). I'm so sorry I couldn't make this work, but anyway. I've known everybody in that room for a long, long time. Sana and I met when we were working at Baltimore Clayworks.

It's just an amazing thing that this convening was even thought about, and I am so happy because the only time we used to see each other was at the NCECA (National Council on Education for the Ceramic Arts) meetings—it would be all the girls together. I was born in Washington, DC, I'm a freedman's baby, so I grew under a lot of segregation. I lived in Philly for a while. Met my sweetie, then came back to my home place. I am always interested in traditional work, and everybody that I know in this group also used that as a beginning or a platform for their work. So I hope to see you one day, and thank you for inviting me.

KING-HAMMOND Thank you, Winnie. Wow, it's been decades since I've seen you, but it's so good to hear your voice. Martha, tell us what this moment feels like in the creation of these inspired exhibitions in honor of Syd's career and the critical relationships you have each nurtured and mentored for decades.

MARTHA JACKSON JARVIS Well, I have to echo what's already been said (fig. 4.4). The energy that surrounds this table and this event is awe inspiring. I met each of these individual people during the course of my life's journey, and each of you have impacted that work. For me, that's extraordinary! I'm not a joiner kind of person, but there's something about, as you move through space and time in your life, you meet individuals who record something into you, and you into them.

In this room, these individuals here, the scholarship, the work ethic, the energy, the beauty, the camaraderie, the ability to not only succeed for themselves at their personal levels and professional levels, but to share in that and to find and invent ways to bring in other artists. I view this as another step in that process. As we mature in our work and our growth, it just gets to be more precious.

I think we're living in a complex time now, an era where this sort of bond that we all experience and we've nurtured in our lifetimes as creatives becomes really paramount, because it speaks in a loud voice to the larger community, that there are multiple ways of communicating and connecting and knowing. As artists, we have a special place, a gift, how to wield that, and it needs to be wielded mightily as we sit here. So I'm so thankful to be part of this gathering.

KING-HAMMOND Should we all say Amen? [LAUGHTER]

JUDY MOONELIS Well, hello, I'm Judy Moonelis, and you guys all said such great things (fig. 4.5). I just feel like wanting to say ditto, you know? [LAUGHTER]

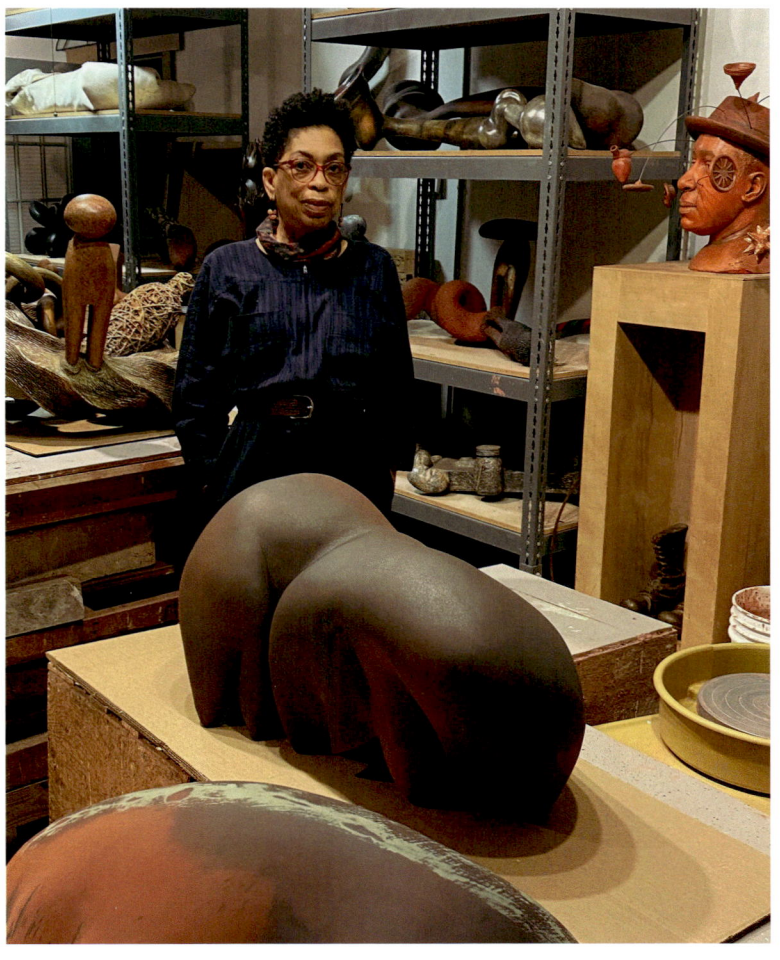

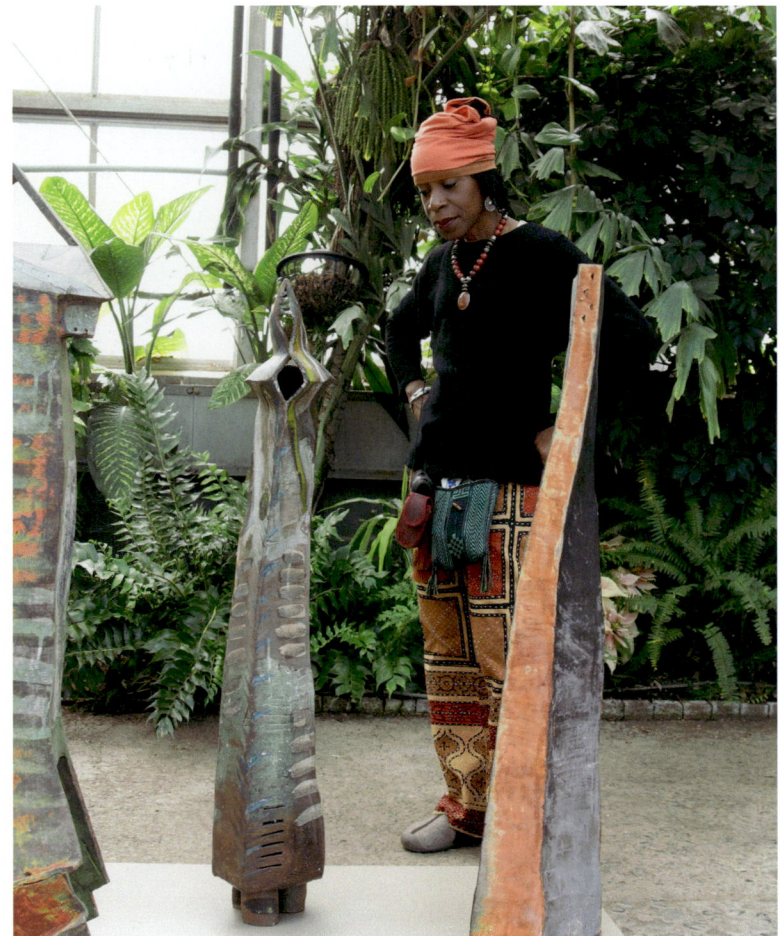

FIG. 4.1   Syd Carpenter in her studio

FIG. 4.2   Sana Musasama in her studio

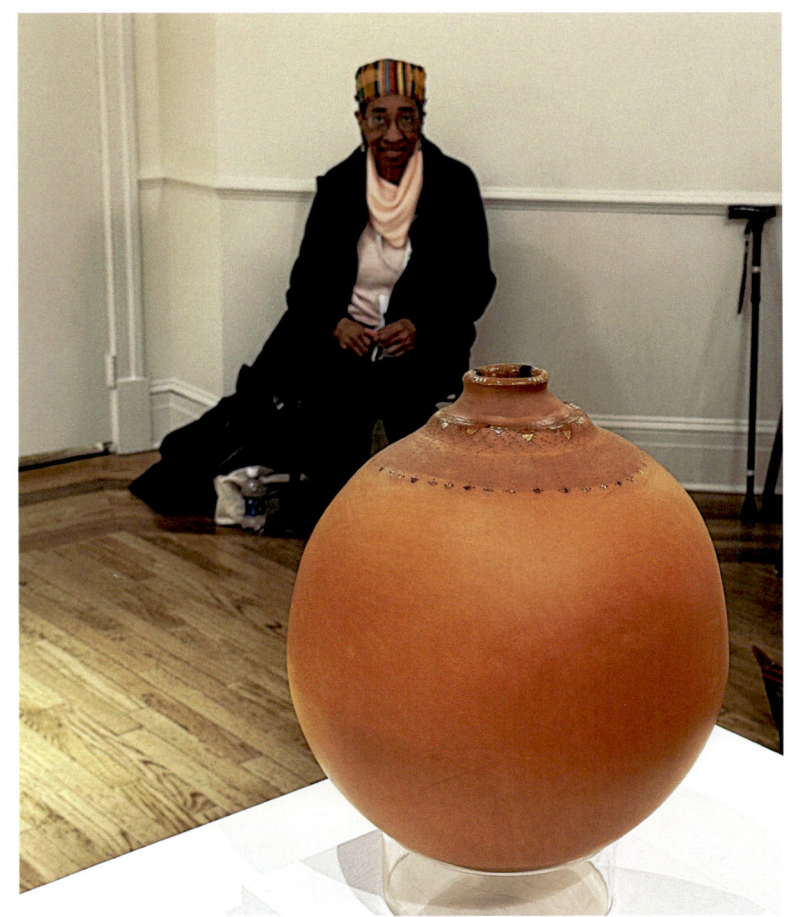

FIG. 4.3   Winnie Owens-Hart. Photo by Syd
Carpenter, 2024

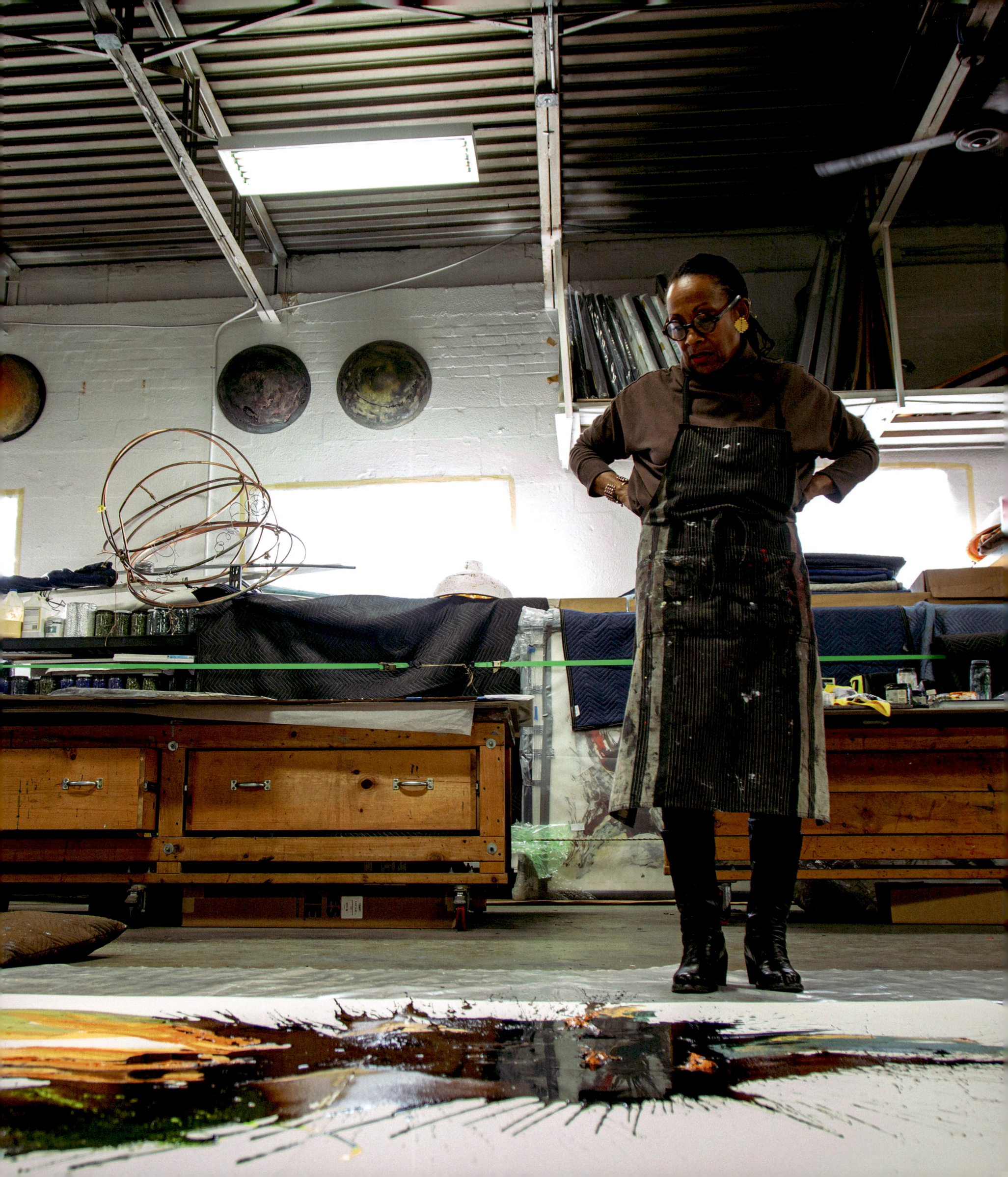

FIG. 4.4   Martha Jackson Jarvis in her studio. Photo by Kelvin Bulluck, 2020

FIG. 4.5   Judy Moonelis in her studio. Photo courtesy of The Lo-Down, 2014

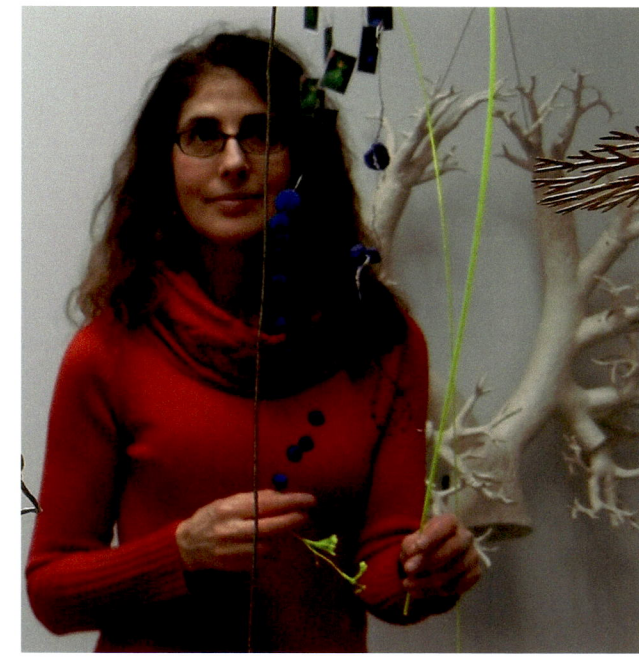

Syd, I feel a very special honor to be here, and very proud to be here as one of the supporters for your beautiful work and show, and connected to you. I don't know all of you well, but I know some of you, and it's just lovely to be part of this. I'm a New York City–based artist, I've made a studio there for—since graduate school, basically.

It's been an interesting challenge, and as a woman, it's a very interesting challenge, just art in general, finding ways to keep going. The support of fellow artists, especially women artists who have helped each other and continue to create communities that support and give mutual support, in particular. I feel like there's a lot of that in this room. Syd, you've been amazing that way. I feel like one couldn't ask for a better friend, colleague, inspiration, and I'm so happy that this is happening to bring us together. You inspire me, and I'm sure everybody, with the quality of your work and your efforts. The content of your work and the way you think about the site in your work, the way you plan exhibitions, the seriousness you bring to all that. I think probably everybody here does that version, but especially right now we're talking about you. I would say it's just lovely to see this kind of attention being brought to your work. Well deserved and long deserved. It's about time. [LAUGHS] So that's what I have to say.

KING-HAMMOND   I feel it is critical to respond to these remarks. When Lowery Sims and I were approached to work on this exhibition for Syd Carpenter, one of the many questions was, what are we going to write? How are we going to approach this project? Lowery is an exalted curator and wanted to address the content context of Syd's work in the contemporary art world. I have spent my professional career in academia educating visual artists. My focus has been increasingly concerned with creating opportunities to hear the voices of underrepresented and women artists. This is an aspect of art history that has been woefully invisible, erased, forgotten, too often hidden in plain view. In the discipline of art history, the voices of white male scholars, critics, poets, intellectuals, or philosophers have been prioritized over the authoritative voices of the creative makers. This has been a significant disadvantage to the remarkable intellects and brilliant artistries of women and artists of color.

I am especially excited to convene this dialogue to address the magnitude of this exceptional exhibition and your careers. It is so rare to see you all together. It's so much more powerful than seeing you all independently, which is always wonderful and exciting, but this is a moment that we need to really talk about how important it has been to your lives at this point in your careers.

Sana, I want to come back to you because you said something very important. Syd wove you into her life and her work. I want to know how—give me some examples of how that happened for you.

MUSASAMA   Oh, in many, many ways. One way that comes to mind right now is a letter that she wrote to me that's probably maybe sixteen or seventeen years old that I held on to because I was suffering from depression. I wrote to her one night, and she responded by listing all the important things that I do for her and the world, and just raised my confidence and my self-esteem.

I was applying for tenure-track jobs and never getting them, and losing them out to someone half my age, and to the point that I just gave up on it. She just injected this kind of fuel into me to keep pushing and keep moving when I didn't have anyone else to do it for me. So that's what was so monumental.

Anytime she's curated a show or anytime she's curated a talk, I'm on the list. During the pandemic, when I lived in a senior community and was incredibly isolated from my four sisters, who I only saw on Zoom because they were trying to be protective of their grands, it's Syd that invited me to come stay in her house to get out of mine. It's her community that she walked me through the cafés, the children's shops, to just bring me back to Sana. So she's been healing, she's been loving, she's been caring, and she's made me feel whole when I didn't.

CARPENTER I should interject here because Sana also said she didn't know how we met. Sana, I met you through your work. I was aware of you. And at an opportunity to speak at a national conference on education in ceramic arts, I had the opportunity to show other artists that I was impressed with and wanted to know you.

MUSASAMA Yes, I remember that.

CARPENTER You were one of them and you were at the conference. That's how we met, because I knew about your work. Now, how I knew, maybe it had shown up in *Ceramics Monthly* or something, but I needed to know you.

OWENS-HART I remember meeting Sana when we were at Baltimore Clayworks, and she was always very caring, sensitive—I mean, I could say that about everybody in the room, but she was taking care of her, I believe it was, nephew at that time. That's how I got to know her as a person, as a mom, and as an artist. She makes such exquisite things that you are attracted to them and vice versa. I've always just loved looking at Sana's work.

MUSASAMA Well, I remember something you did for me. You gave a talk and I was in it, but I wasn't at NCECA. Debbie Bedwell came up to you and said, I'd like to know more about Sana, and you handed the whole package over to her, and she called me maybe six or seven weeks later. I did have my nephew. I was caring for my nephew, my sister was ill, and he was probably maybe eleven months old, pulling on one leg and screaming.

Debbie Bedwell called me about an opportunity, and I said, I can't do anything now. I'm trying to take care of my nephew and get my sister healthy. She said, well, what would you like to do? And I said, I can't talk! She said, no talk! And I talked to her, and Debbie wrote the grant while my nephew was screaming on one knee, and I was sitting on the edge of the tub on the other. So that was you Syd. That was you.

JACKSON JARVIS Yeah. OK. Wow. Syd, weaving into life, I know wherever Syd was, she'd find a way to invite you in. I remember at

Swarthmore, you invited me to come up and have a solo exhibition there in the gallery.

CARPENTER Fabulous. It was just always as someone said early on, the connection has always been through the work. I think I knew. We met when I was in grad school, and you were there, and you were a Black woman at Tyler in the '70s kicking butt. [LAUGHTER]

JACKSON JARVIS I was hanging on by a thread, but I was there.

CARPENTER You were pregnant and had a baby, and you were kicking butt!

JACKSON JARVIS I was being secretive about being pregnant. I had a big fur coat that I wore, and I walked into the studio, and this one student said, you know I had a dream about you and you were pregnant? I opened my coat, and there I was pregnant. So she predicted my first daughter. Niambi is now almost fifty years old.

I have three daughters and a son. Gina, my youngest daughter, we collaborate and we work together every day. So Syd had this, I won't say uncanny ability, but uncanny amazing ability to include you. It was just always extraordinary to keep an eye open for Sana's work. I always think of—what is the tower that gets built up to the sky that never ends?

KING-HAMMOND The Tower of Babel.

JACKSON JARVIS There we are. I always see it as this tower that's never ending. So I keep my eye, my inner eye, on that work, or Syd's work. And for Syd, the connection and again, Judy was there at Tyler also. We met at Tyler, which was an intensive environment, and it was a man's world, let's face it.

The sixties and seventies for clay. The Peter Voulkos, the big dudes from California, the West Coast. I mean, we know that whole scenario. But there we were.

CARPENTER There you were. Then you went to the Clay Studio, and you were a star there, making these amazing pots. Well, we saw one at a show recently.

JACKSON JARVIS Again, making my way as a creative, trying to invent. When Sana talks about life suddenly happening, I wasn't just a single person. I had four other people—six, really, when I count my husband—that you have to work around and with and bring along in the creative process. What these women did in terms of being there at Tyler, you were like food for energy. Once we got in that clay studio, the material itself was so consuming and giving and delicious, right? You could smell it. You could almost taste it. I might have eaten it at some point. [LAUGHTER]

That studio, I have to say, was the energy of these individuals. Tyler, for me, was not welcoming, except for you guys, when I hit that studio. I kept all of the ceramic studios and work. Then I would also make paintings. Those were my two loves that I've always combined. It was just extraordinary, finding the voices. I've kept up with everyone's work as much as I possibly could. Looking and seeing and feeling the energy. I just appreciate the work that everyone's done. It's cumulative. It's magnificent.

CARPENTER Martha, whenever someone would write about who was doing significant work, I remember Greg Tate just zeroed in on you and just thought you were one of the best working, but under the radar a little bit.

JACKSON JARVIS I never knew that.

CARPENTER Yeah, oh he was a big fan. I was watching this in amazement, because Martha was just powering through all of these male spaces and landing these amazing commissions and producing awesome things to look at that were permanent. They weren't going to get rid of this woman's stuff. Still continuing to do it with blinders on. I'm going for this! What I admire so much about you is this propulsion that you demonstrate in the way you exist as an artist, as a female artist. By the way, she drives this big pickup truck! [LAUGHTER] The symbolism of that fact is real and powerful! [LAUGHTER] Her roaming through areas in her truck, with all her stuff and getting it done, and getting it done beautifully—and not having to apologize for it.

JACKSON JARVIS Thank you. I'm going to say, I think it was the final crit of coming out of Tyler, and I'm not going to name the person, one of the professors saw I had my work on the table. I asked, well, what would you suggest in terms of going forward? He said, well, I don't think anyone would ever be interested in buying or purchasing any of this work that you're doing. [LAUGHTER]

That was his final critique. I just remember, OK, well, all righty then! I remember packing up all that stuff, throwing it in my little VW through the sunroof and drove away, with a level of determination. That comment for me was *food* for just, let's just keep going. When those kinds of things happen, and they do, and they still do. They're subtle and some are not, some are unsubtle. It was always the food that kept me going because the work itself demanded it.

CARPENTER The focus that you had was, I have to get this done. Whenever I would speak to Martha on the phone over the years, her voice was in business mode. [CHUCKLING] I knew that. OK, let's get to the point, because Martha does not have time.

JACKSON JARVIS No, I don't have time.

CARPENTER She did not have time. I got that, she conveyed that. That attitude, it just made me love her more, because I knew Martha don't play. [CHUCKLING] I love that about her.

KING-HAMMOND None of these people play. Come on now, this is very serious business. [LAUGHTER] Judy, let's hear your thoughts on this subject.

MOONELIS Oh, wow! I have really amazing memories of our time at Tyler's undergraduate school. I think all of us started off in painting and ended up finding clay. It was an interesting thing that we didn't plan on clay, or at least I know I certainly didn't, but there was that greenhouse. For me, Rudy Staffel was a major

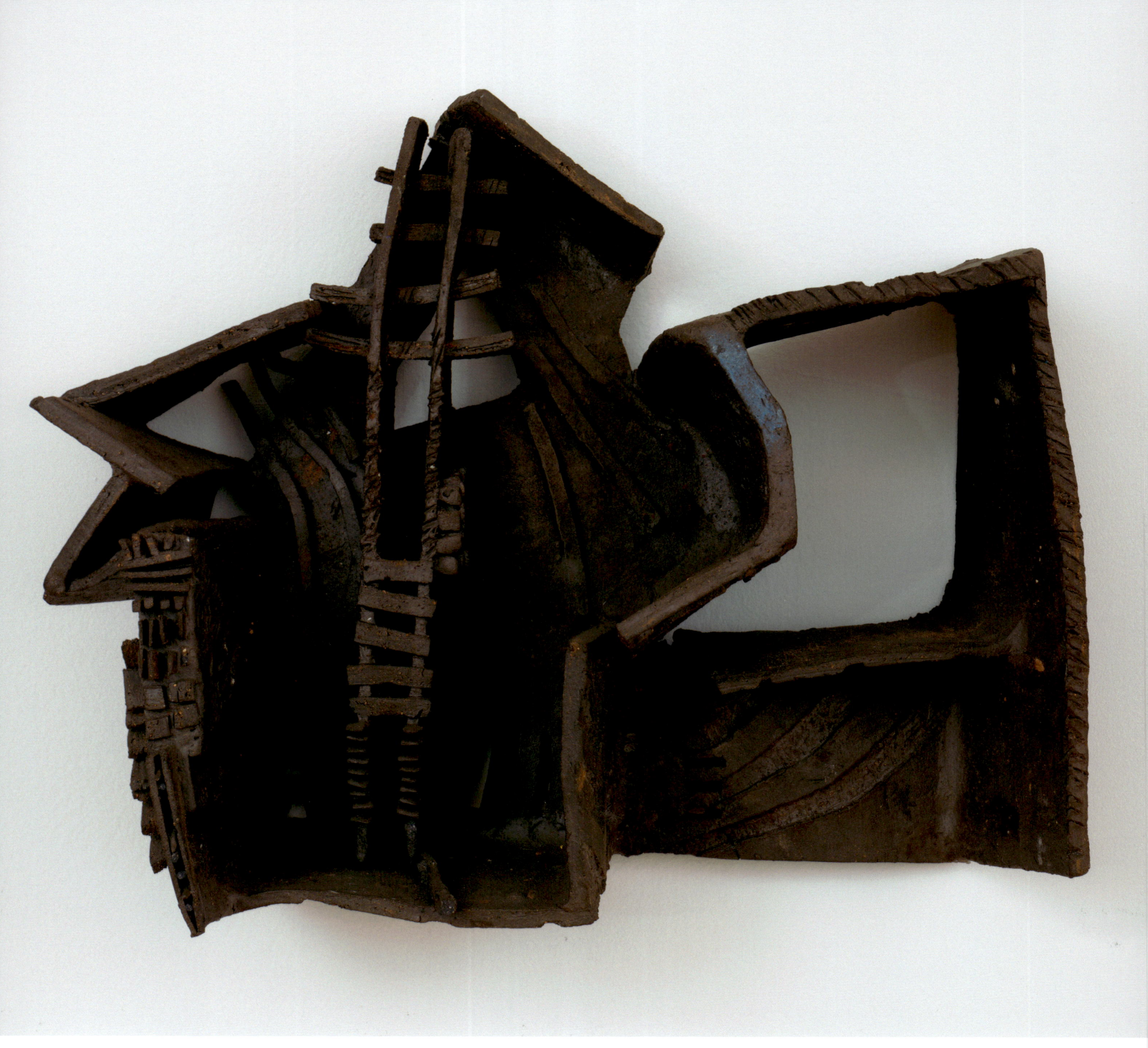

FIG. 4.6   Sana Musasama, *House Series*, 1983,
ceramic, 12 × 14 × 9 in. (Collection of the artist)
Photo by Dawoud Bey

mentor and an incredible teacher, and he just opened this material up. Suddenly, it was the magical thing that I wanted to work with more than anything. We had a community of these great women artists, all inspiring and encouraging each other and to see how much of it has continued since then. I've been lucky enough to have to go to Philadelphia for personal and professional reasons often over the years. Almost every time, I got to see you Syd, and we just kept that going, watching everyone's work.

Sana, the content of your work in Cambodia, the ways that you became an activist through your work, as well as the earlier content in the tree pieces and then moving into the Cambodian situation there. All of that work you did, and do in your projects, the content in your work [POINTS AT JACKSON JARVIS], I'm excited by all of this work. I feel like it moves me that there are people who are out there who really believe in what they do and don't give up. I think that determination, that's the word you used, and I think that's something that any serious artist has, if you just really look at what kept them going. It was just the attitude of don't give up. [LAUGHS] We're just getting up another day and doing it again. It is the thing. It's the thing that we need to do. There will be a lot of challenges, and there certainly have been, lots of different kinds or challenges—just keep going.

KING-HAMMOND I want to move the conversation into the essence of what this is all about—the materiality of clay. You each have had a lot of history and experiences in working with clay. We have here behind us in this space a wonderful collection of clay objects in the Maguire Museum collection. Can you each talk about this phenomenon? What is it about clay that is so impactful? What were your first experiences with clay? It's so fascinating that you each started painting, and then, for some reason, like a magnet, something happened. Clay just sort of sucked you into its vortex. Am I right in these observations? I am sure you each have a different response.

MUSASAMA Well, I guess what I should start off with is that I didn't have the support of my family to be an artist. Both of them were two generations from being sharecroppers' children. They didn't see art as a vision for me. So I was going through

life with their deferred dreams. My father wanted to be a lawyer. My mother wanted to study anthropology. Those dreams weren't there, born in 1916 and 1915. So they became military people because that was the opportunity for Brown people of their generation.

I grew up around a dining room table of people who traveled from many parts of the world, because my dad was very gregarious and a great storyteller. I grew up with people from all parts of the world that came on Sundays, and we listened to stories, me and my four sisters. I heard stories beyond the landscape of how I was growing up, then following my mother and father's dreams, not my own. I happened to bump into a ceramic room by accident my final year of school on my way to the anthropology department, and I stood by the door and peeked in every time I walked by. I was late to my anthropology class. The teacher finally came to the door, Paul Chaleff, and said, why don't you enroll?

I said, I don't have any art background. He said, it doesn't matter, just enroll and go get the paperwork. I got the paperwork and enrolled in the class. When I picked up this material and my thumbprint was there so easily without any prerequisites, I didn't need a piece of paper. All of a sudden, I began to make these forms, and I didn't know where they were coming from. At the time, there was no syllabus, there was no instruction. Our teachers made their own work, and you were involved in their practice. You helped them create their work. You helped them fire the kilns. You helped them go to shows. You sat there when they cried and they didn't get tenure. I lived their lives vicariously. I graduated that semester, and all of the people in the room with me were going to grad schools. I couldn't go to grad school, I'd only taken Ceramics I.

So I love this material. It was obedient to me. It listened to me. I did some research and found out that clay was a material that came from all over the world, and it comes in as many colors and personalities as we do as humans. I thought to myself, why don't I travel and learn about clay, recreate my dining room table like a map and go to every place where every language was spoken at my dining room table. I learned about clay around the world, and then compiled all this information and went to Alfred for grad school. So there was no other material for me other than clay.

There were no other prerequisites for me, and the world was on my agenda and it always has been.

KING-HAMMOND Winnie, tell us about your journey with clay. Why clay? I know you were at FESTAC (Second World Black and African Festival of Arts and Culture, 1977).

OWENS-HART It started before FESTAC. It started with my parents, George and Mildred Owens. I made clay when I was about five years old. When I said that's what I wanted to do, they didn't stop me. They've never stopped me. My first solo show was in Hartford, Connecticut, and my auntie and my mom rode the train, and I went to open it. So it's always been clay, and I can't imagine anything else. I knew that in the 1960s. I went to San Francisco State just to be in California, not really expecting anything. Yeah, absolutely. It just seemed regular. That's what it was supposed to be. My mom died, and a lot of years have passed, but my sister, we were cleaning out the house, and my sister, evidently, was the one who put this thing up under the dining room table. And when I looked at it, I said, that's a piece I made at the community center when I was a little girl.

I don't know who had the foresight to happen, but everybody made clay. In this neighborhood, I found a deed, also in our house, it said that in 1887 we owned all this land in Falls Church, Virginia, in the Black neighborhood. So it was just meant to be.

Those of you who are familiar with my work, all the work that I do, I do it to cleanse myself. I know of the piece that says "never forget," it's a traditional round piece, but there are men being hung all around it that can glow. I'm hearing all of you. There's only one person that I don't know at that table, so hello.

MOONELIS Hello.

OWENS-HART We'll meet when I can open Safari. [CHUCKLES] The piece underneath the table was the first pot that I ever made. It will be in the show. I remember going over to Martha's house with the kids and my best buddy, her husband.

JACKSON JARVIS Jimmy Thunder, you mean? She called him Jimmy Thunder. [LAUGHTER]

OWENS-HART Yeah, now, ladies don't think in that direction. [LAUGHTER]

JACKSON JARVIS It was some song and singer. I never knew who he was, but you would call my husband Jimmy Thunder.

KING-HAMMOND His name was Johnny Thunder (1931–2024), a rhythm, blues, pop singer with a 1963 top hit, *Loop de Loop*. [LAUGHTER]

OWENS-HART I had a lot of meals at Martha's house. I had a lot of fun with the girls. "Johnny" was a little boy then, the only man— only man among females. You all are beautiful, really beautiful in the spirit. Martha, when you come over to the house, you're going to see something, it's going to be interesting for you.

I'm glad this conversation is being done, because I also write a lot of stories. Usually they're about traditional ceramic pieces. For those of you who know, I've been saying for 35,000 years, I'm going to write that book. [CHUCKLING] I acquired a little cousin, and she's helping me dig out from all that work. It's a lot of work, and I need to do it soon because time flies and people fly. So hopefully, I'll have it. I've been saying that, but when it's time, it will happen. Thank you for inviting me to this.

KING-HAMMOND Winnie—You are so crucial to this dialogue. This was the core of individuals that I felt compelled to bring into a conversation to shed light on your stories about your creativity with clay as the medium and the muse. This is not just for Syd Carpenter—but how to explore issues about the genre of clay, women such as yourselves, in an era where women have not been afforded critical recognition and agency in the under-researched discourse on American art history and women who have emphasized in the medium of clay and ceramic arts? In the early phase of our careers as art historians, if Lowery and I had not had each

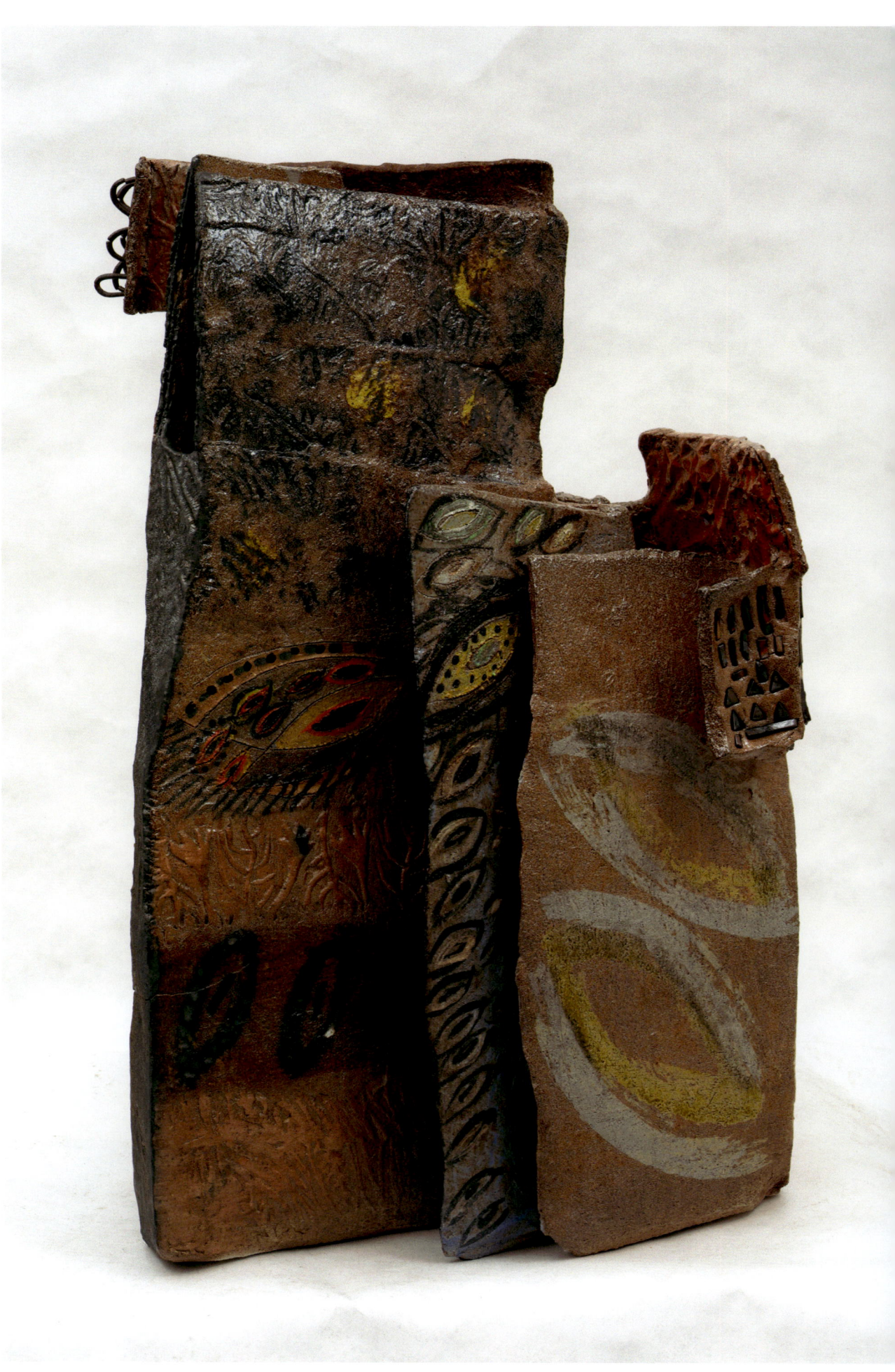

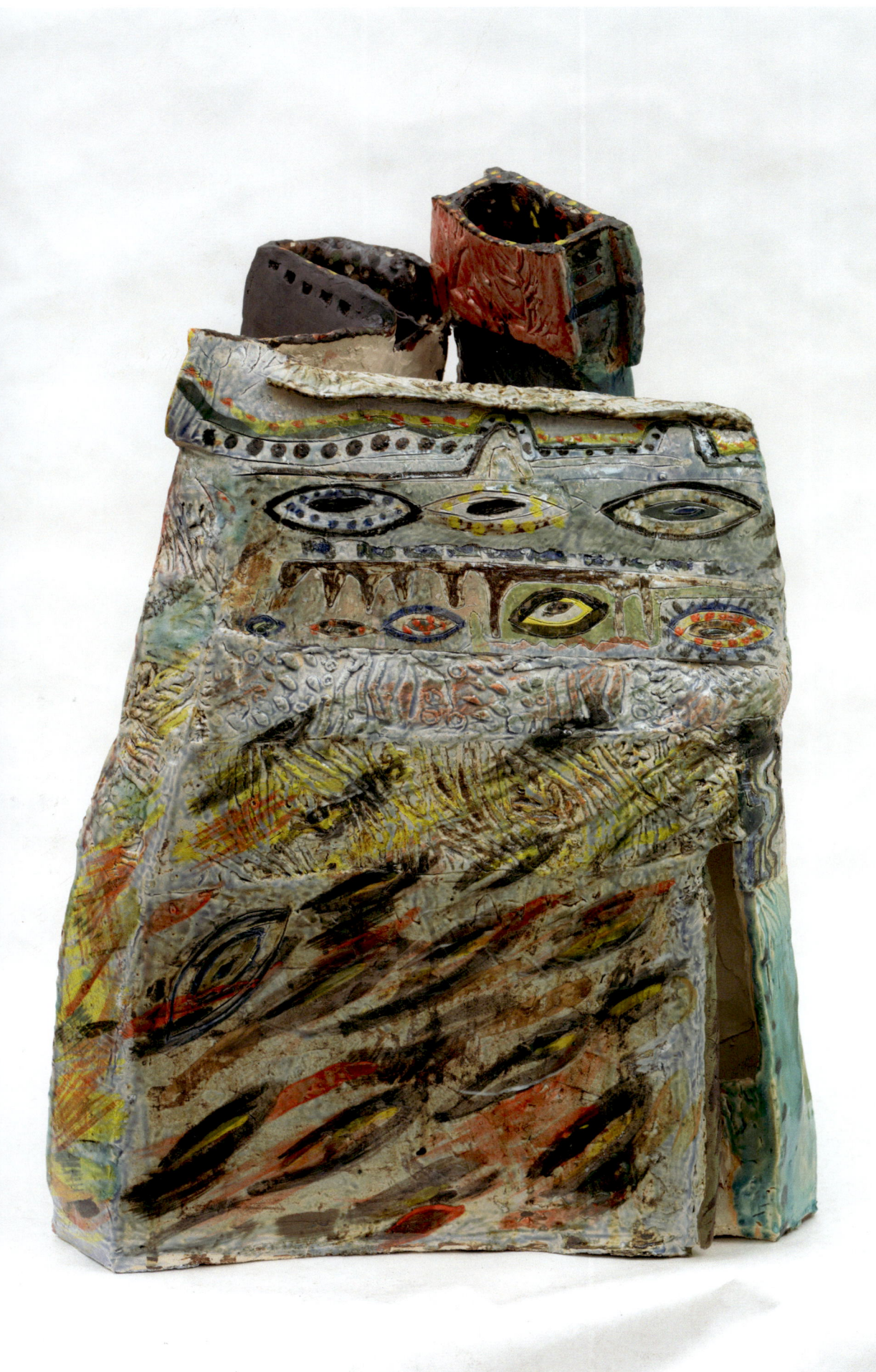

FIG. 4.8   Sana Musasama, *House Series, Returning to Ourselves*, 2024, ceramic, 24 × 16 × 12 in. (Collection of the artist) Photo by Sana Musasama

other's support, we would not have survived the weathering process of working in a nation hostile to the accomplishments of women and people of color.

Judy, as a white woman in this collective of sculptors, what has it been like being a member of this exceptional collective of women? Why was clay so compelling to you?

MOONELIS So back to the clay.

KING-HAMMOND It's always about the clay as a driving force of inspiration. This is the prime mission. It's all about the power and importance of clay in each of the individualized aesthetic realities of your artistry.

MOONELIS Regarding clay, I would say that I personally think that when most people touch that material they notice immediately that it responds to touch. It has this really powerful effect that you push and then there's a record of your touch. It's not just that it moves, but there's also this evidence that your hand just did that. There's something about that connection that we can make to this earth material that is very special and different from how I might feel with paint at the end of a paintbrush. That's a very different connection to a physical material. There have been scientists who talk about the idea that life may have originated in the minerals in clay. I read that some years ago. I thought, uh-huh, I believe that totally. There is something about that substance—it is an *alive* material. It does not feel static or dead. I don't mean the mold that grows in it or anything like that. The fact that Sana was mentioning, this is all over the whole globe, constantly, clay is being formed. We all connect—every culture, every time period is connected to it in some way.

It just has this kind of universal appeal, I think, that most people connect to. As artists, I guess we found our way with this material. I know myself and I think maybe most of us, it's not the only material that we work with, but it's a primary material.

MUSASAMA I think I also love that Mother Nature makes it, and man doesn't have a damn thing to do with it. [LAUGHTER]

CARPENTER My connection with clay, I have to go way back before I actually started using it as a primary material. I was always identified in my family as the artist. Now, that meant to me, or to the other people who identified me as such, that I could draw, that I could make things look nice and look pretty. That was my understanding of what my calling would be. I had to draw well, and I had to make things look nice and pretty.

The actual essence—we're using that word—of what it meant to be an artist was never anything that was in my consciousness. I knew that people identified artists as those people who made things look nice and could draw, and especially draw realistically. Your goal was to draw like Leonardo da Vinci or some other, basically, European-based artists. Those were artists.

There was never any discussion of what was being made in Africa, rarely in India, certainly not in South America. Those were cultures that were considered below the European model. So going to art school, I was going to learn how to paint and draw like European masters, that was the goal, not having any sense of what making art would be. I was wandering through different media, taking printmaking at Tyler, taking painting, certainly, because I was going to learn how to paint and draw, and that was going to be the ideal. But of course, you had to take a 3D elective, which was life-changing for me. I went into the greenhouse, as was mentioned by Judy, that was where ceramics was. It was a remote location in an old greenhouse on campus.

And the teacher there was Rudy Staffel. I should mention that in this very kind of macho environment, Rudy Staffel was an older white male who did not fit the cliché or any of the standardized tropes of the dominant white male. Here was this person who just took you as a person. Said little, but was just this respectful, not condescending—who is this person? And let's see how to draw them out. Draw them out without saying a word, which is what he was able to do. I was there, fortunately, at the time of Rudolf Staffel. Going into graduate school, it was the same thing. No one had still provided me with an understanding of what it was to be an *artist,* what that word meant. So wandering through grad school, the critiques I got were very thin. I was certainly never exposed to African American artists, Africa, at all. I think. Ladi Kwali came to Tyler once. I will confess, I didn't go.

KING-HAMMOND [GASPS] Oh wow! Ladi Kwali (c. 1925–1984) was Nigeria's foremost potter, ceramicist, and educator—a brilliant artist trained by her family in traditional Indigenous Nigerian pottery and revered globally in cultures and communities of ceramic artistry. She came to Morgan State University at the invitation of Professor James Lewis, chairman of the Art department for a demonstration workshop on pottery using large, thick coiled slabs of clay. It was the 1970s while I was a doctoral student in art history at Johns Hopkins University. It was an awe-inspiring experience for me to see a *woman*, a master Nigerian potter, of stunning aesthetic brilliance, power, authority, and elegance. Seeing and being in her presence, watching her process had a powerful impact on my education. This was a crucial example of how a master sculptor bridged and navigated the boundaries between the traditional Indigenous and expressive contemporary ceramic art forms.

OWENS-HART Can I put in for a minute? It's about Rudy Staffel. His wife, Doris Staffel, was my paint teacher, and she was the only one among that whole group, and the craftsmen, who was very sensitive to me and what I was doing. I followed Ladi Kwali around the United States. Not really, not literally, but I think, in this day, it would have been called—what do you call it when you follow—a groupie? When they came to Baltimore. That's how things manifested themselves.

CARPENTER No! You're quite welcome. I mean, I wanted to just get to that point where, when did I find out what artists do? What is an artist? I mean, because the word was flung around as this kind of person who did that kind of work that everyone liked. And for the most part, your goal was to create beauty in a standardized way.

OWENS-HART Well, I have three Ladi Kwali pots.

CARPENTER Oh, go ahead and brag! [LAUGHTER]

OWENS-HART That's not the point.

CARPENTER Sure it is. [LAUGHTER] So, I went through many years of working with clay once I was introduced to it. In this welcoming environment that Rudy was able to create, I was making pots. I was also simultaneously painting. I was a double major at Tyler. In terms of being exposed to other Black artists and being mentored, that was not happening. I was kind of clueless because I was immersed in learning my craft, which at the time I identified as clay, once I discovered it. Clay as others have mentioned and said, is that it takes the mark. It's a reflection of you. So immediately, there was content for me in the fact that the possibilities of this material were endless.

I was doing a lot of high fire reduction pottery. I was doing salt glazing, I was doing raku, just going through all of these different ways to work with clay. The clay studio had opened up. Martha was there already. I could go down and see all of these things. But basically, as I think about it, it was just a holding pattern for me, technically. It was just there learning this craft. What was going on around me, there were the Black Arts Movement, and there was so much going on with different artists, like Howardena Pindell and a number of other folks who were speaking out and making their presence known and challenging the status quo around the presence of African American and folks of color as part of the conversation that was going on in contemporary art.

So I'm hearing all of this stuff. Not being an activist person, but being aware that there was something happening here. So I'm continuing to make work, and getting into shows with the work that didn't identify myself in any kind of political way or any kind of personal way. I was making nice pots and they were selling. But there I was. There was a presence there because people were starting to invite me to do things around these nice pots. And I was also showing at the Sande Webster Gallery. Still, the clay was my medium, the clay and I were able to take these kinds of processes that I had learned and begin to think about what they were as a voice.

What happens when you allow something to crack? What happens when you allow yourself to put some kind of dreadful glaze on something, but it speaks? So those things start to awaken me, I become aware, and begin to look for those things that could be translated through this medium, which is touched by earth.

FIG. 4.9 Syd Carpenter, *Adjust Pressure to Normal*, 2005, clay, graphite, and acrylic, 78 × 10 × 8 in. (Collection of the artist)

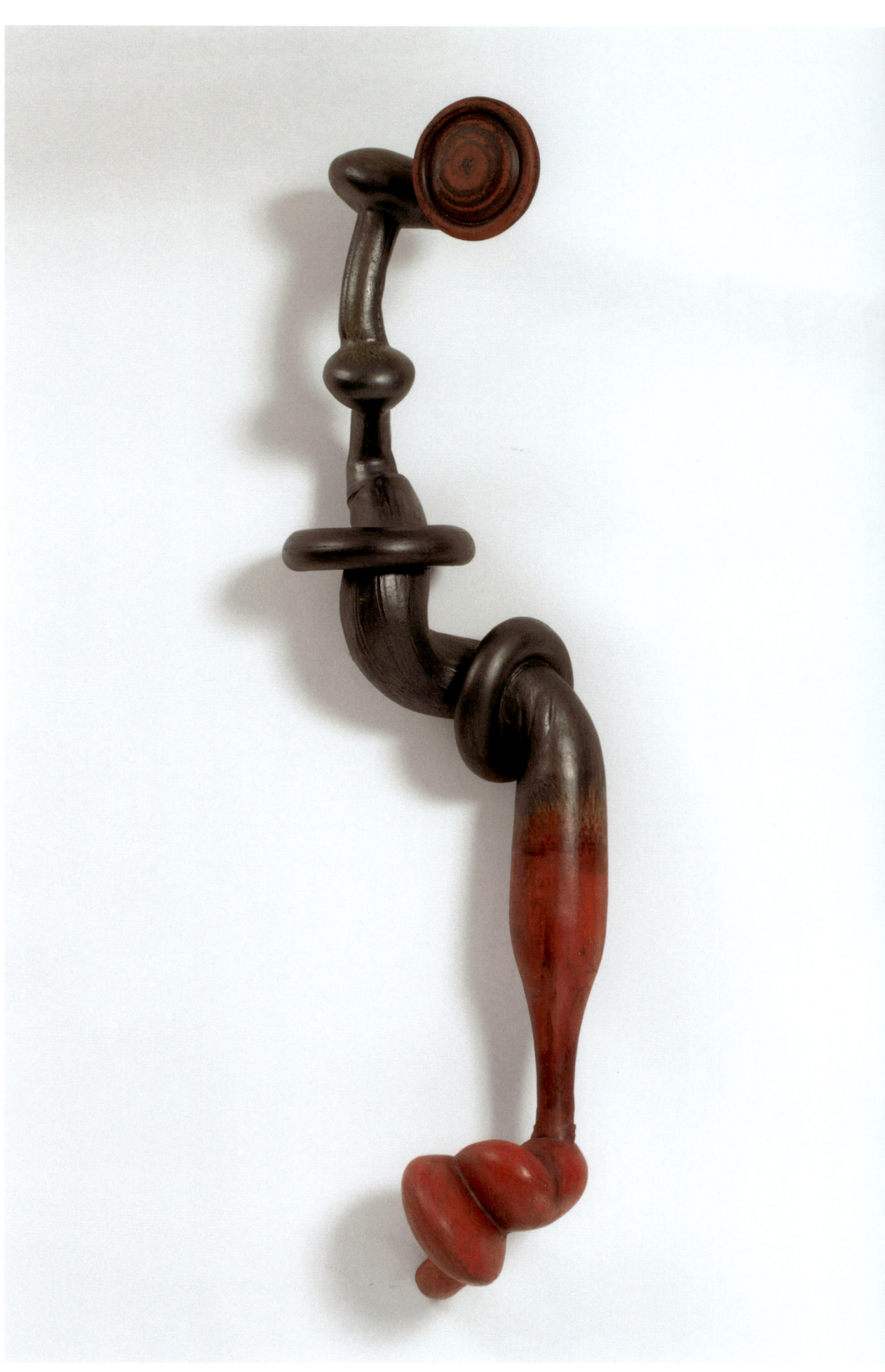

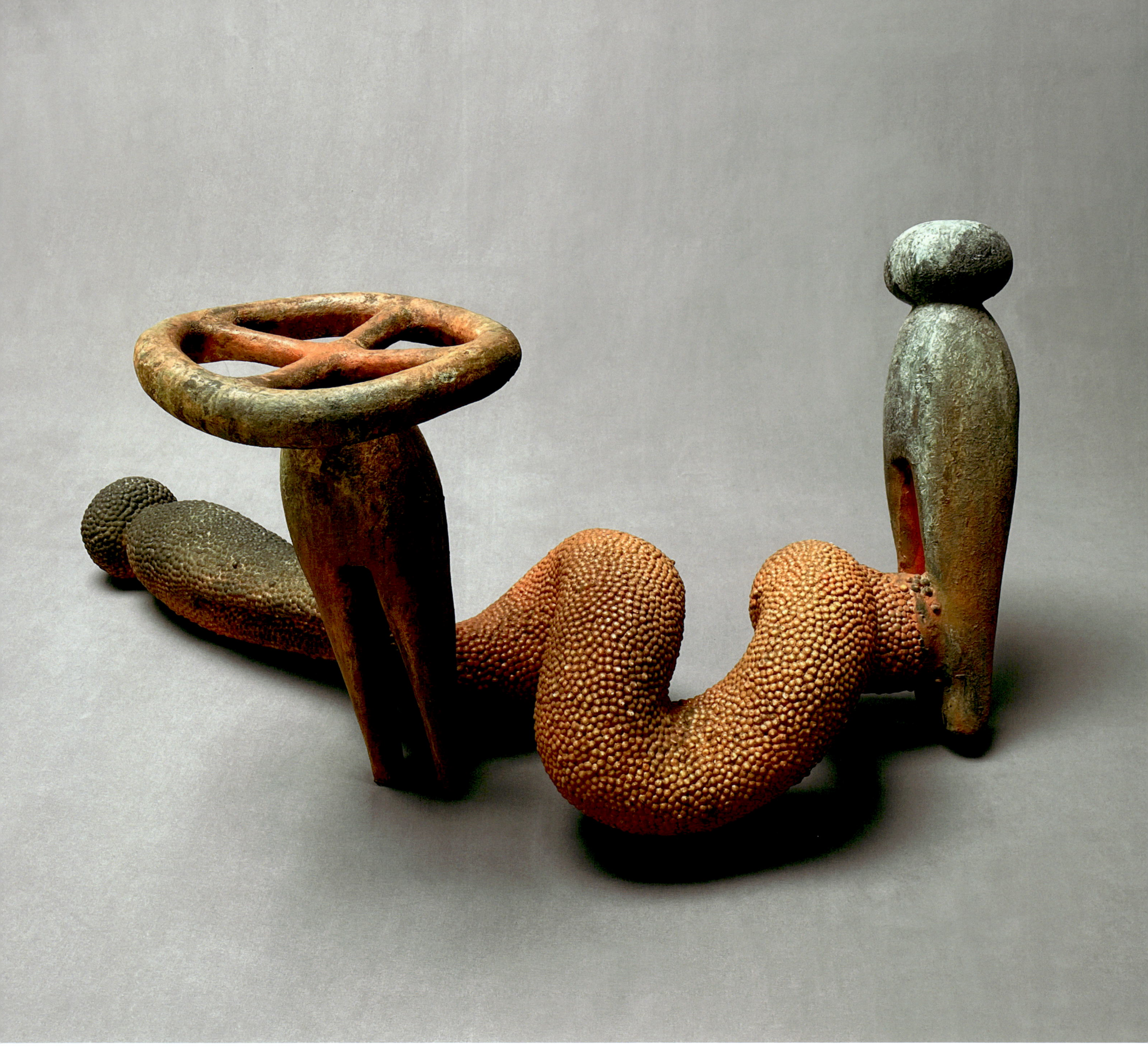

FIG. 4.10   Syd Carpenter, *Three Mother Pins on a Vine*, 2021, clay and mixed media, 18 × 37 × 26 in. (Collection of the artist)

I remember I was in Brazil, and one of the people that we visited in Brazil talked to me. She was some kind of a visionary, and she zeroed in right away. She looked at my hands and she said, earth. [CHUCKLING]

It was true. So that alone, someone halfway around the globe or down the globe, who could recognize something essential in me that was about this material. So that was one of those intangibles that became very, very tangible. It was a primary material that I started to learn its language and use that language to develop content around things that became important to me. It had to do with not only making pots that had narrative to them, but then sculptures that were clearly making use of clay's ability to absorb your identity and reflect it back to you. So that is why I still need to start with clay. I've wandered around it and through it, through doing mixed media pieces, working in glass, steel, wood, all kinds of things. Right now, there's always a clay component in there. I'm rooted there, and I'm still in the earth because I garden.

OWENS-HART My experience at PCA (University of the Arts, Philadelphia) was rough. When I was in my last year of study, I was frustrated because the teachers there were combative. We had weekly critiques, and usually I was the only student who brought in all the work completed during that week. There was a teacher who had a beard—I don't remember his name—but I decided that he wasn't going to just walk away from me without saying something anymore.

I had been experimenting with glazes, and I had done a lot of pots with colors on the surface. The teacher had said to me in past critiques, "You don't have anywhere to go with what you've been doing." It was like my work and I were invisible. That day when he came to the studio, I yelled at him, "We're going to have a crit because my mother and father pay a lot of money to send me to this school!" He looked at my work and said, "Well, this is inadequate." It was totally insignificant to him that I had about fifty-two works on the table in front of him. I decided that I really didn't want to be at school anymore. It didn't matter to me because I was going to continue to do my own work. This is an example of the type of teachers I had to deal with at PCA. If I had been a sweet, compliant female, I might have gone crazy. It

was very difficult to learn in an environment where people don't see you and make you feel invisible. This was probably going on in every school as African American students began to enter colleges in this nation.

After PCA I began working and studying at Ile Ife Humanitarian Center in Nigeria. The teacher brought a visiting artist to the studio to critique the work of the students. At that time I was transitioning from Euro pot forms to more Indigenous styles. The guy came up to my pots and slammed my work. He then began to take clay and demonstrate how a pot should be made. The Nigerian students burst into laughter—they ousted him because his ideas were so negative and revealed how little he knew about Indigenous traditions. That has been very much my experience with these issues in my career.

KING-HAMMOND These are powerful and telling narratives on the challenges you each have had to navigate to find the path of your personal vision and relationship to clay. Martha, please share some of your insights and experiences with clay?

JACKSON JARVIS OK. I'm going to roll it back to the beginning of clay. I have to say, painting was never first in my life. It was clay. I discovered clay when I was three years old, my sister was five, and we moved to the country with my grandparents. In the country, like Southern Virginia, in the foothills of the Blue Ridge Mountains and growing up there, the red clay of Virginia, it's beautiful. Within that environment, that small rural Black community, I witnessed from my grandfather, grandmother, and aunts, and 30,000 cousins down the lane and up the road, that sort of community, the work ethic. My grandfather had a tool shed, or I call it a studio now, but we call it a shed and he had his tools there. And he would go into that. I followed him around, and he let me, a little girl with one hundred boy cousins, he let me follow him. Whenever he would go in that shed and take out a tool, I had to follow, because I wanted to see everything. He could go into that shed and come out with whatever was necessary. He was always building something, brainstorming, creating. And I loved that.

Growing up in the country as a kid, with lots of cousins, every five minutes of a child's life was not curated. You could get up early in the morning and go into the woods and forage for blue-berries, huckleberries, blackberries with your cousins, digging, going to the spring. I remember there was a natural spring not far from our house. Because there was no running water, we got water from the spring, that sort of close living to the earth. I just remember one day they had all gone to work and come back home. If you've been in Virginia for a spring rain, the red clay and the earth, and then it would rain, and then the sun would come out again, and you'd have this magnificent wet clay. I just remember working out and building the whole driveway, and I just got consumed with this material. It was all over me, covered in clay.

I had built these mounds and shapes and dug holes and all this stuff. I just lost myself. I lost sense of time. It was time for all the adults to come back home. They drove into the driveway, and there I was, covered in mud and clay and all this stuff. They all got out of the car and said, who did this? I'm standing there covered, thinking that I am going to get the whipping of my life. But they were like, I can't believe you moved all this stuff by yourself. The earth and all of this material. I had this innate connection with the material. Then I rediscovered clay when I was a teen-ager. I moved to Philadelphia with my mother, and I rediscov-ered clay again. I accidentally walked into the art room, and in the back of the room were these bags of material. I opened that plas-tic bag, and I said, oh, that's my material. I know this material. That's clay.

I just started working with it, playing around with it. I went to Howard University and they had clay there. Jim Kane was teaching in Philly while Winnie was there. I had met Winnie at Ile Ife (University of Ife, now Obafemi Awolowo University, Nige-ria), where she taught ceramics as an artist in residence. I think when you left, I started teaching ceramics there. So there was this whole network that happened. Clay, for me, was always the magical receptacle. When I touch it, it plugs me into such an immediate force, and I can create anything. It can deliver any-thing, and it's a receptacle, and at the same time, it doesn't play. It demands certain things of you, and you must give it or else. I love that about the material.

KING-HAMMOND I have an interesting question that has come from our primo curator Lowery Sims, who asks, how do you con-sider the descriptors of art, i.e. sculpture versus craft, where do you see clay? Is this a dichotomy, a tension between high and low, fine art or craft? Part of the reason might be about why peo-ple don't know how to treat this material, in terms of the hier-archies of art. There is the formality of architecture, painting, and sculpture, then there is the question of the role clay plays in that conversation.

JACKSON JARVIS Syd talks about finding your way in your own consciousness about what art is and that sort of thing. When I applied for a National Endowment for the Arts grant, they used to fund individual artists. Remember those days before they wiped that out? I applied as a sculptor in with the pool of painters and artists. I didn't apply as a ceramic artist. For the first time in their history, they gave me, a clay artist, a grant as an individual artist. It was really interesting when they made a list of the artists, and they were all painters and sculptors, there was another artist who won, and it was for clay. It was for my work.

So for me, it was transformative that, for the first time, the NEA had acknowledged clay was not a stepchild, but it was in the pool. So from there, it was like, oh, it's on now. It was fantastic, for me, in my thinking. You always have to live in relationship to what happens for you. In the studio, that was transformative in terms of, the boundaries don't matter. In painting the hierarchy of the art didn't matter. It still doesn't matter. But as creative peo-ple, you have a handle on all of these materials, all of these disci-plines that you can wield. You pull it out of you—you don't pull everything out of the magic bag at the same moment, but it's all there. When you talk about preparation and learning and hon-ing our crafts of what we do. The crafting of whether it's painting or sculpture or steel or glass or clay, all these materials. Syd, I'm going to let you do it.

CARPENTER During the Renaissance and before, everyone was a craftsman. Then somehow or other, a hierarchy appeared. I think you have to follow the money to find out when that happened.

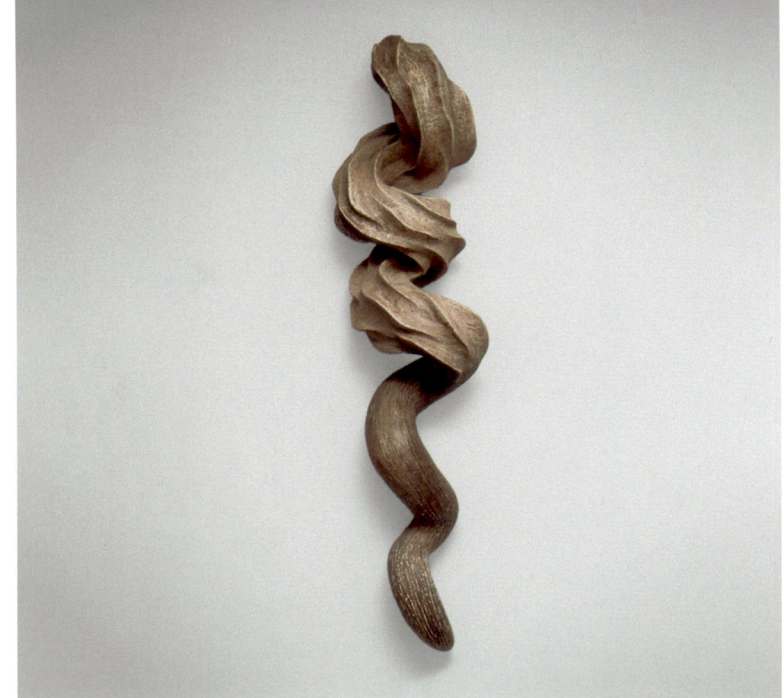

[LAUGHTER] My sense of this art versus craft dichotomy is false. It's a completely false idea. Primary to that thinking is the fact that each object has merit one way or the other. So to make the assumption that someone is doing bad paintings and that makes it better and more important than good pots, I find that contradiction just ironic, useless, and, once again, it's, follow the money. What's the difference between a pot and a vessel? $5,000?

I think you're looking at an object, and if it possesses these intangibles that associate it with, at least, resonate with us as a work of art, that's what art is to me. So I have a problem with the word craft. It has to do with being as good and as inventive and as resonant as anything that we would consider high art. It has to. I can look at a gorgeous mug and see amazing sculptural qualities in it, and then look at a bad piece of sculpture, but one's art and one's craft. I find that tedious. I find that annoying. I can't teach that. I will not teach that. So it depends on the person who's doing it. It also has to do with the intellect and what you bring to it. I mean, if you're going to bring to it only technique and there isn't that intangible, and its accessibility makes it repetitive or somehow lacking in imagination, I think, well, there's a problem there. I'm not going to think about that as good art. But I'm trying to think of the artist who is making art with bottle caps from Africa—El Anatsui. Nobody has assigned him this lower status as an artist.

To me, it's about who comes to it, what they bring to it. So if you're going to use bottle caps or you're going to use clay, it has to be seen with this sense of vision about the possibility of the imagination. That's what art is. So the word *craft,* you craft something, we learn our craft. There are works that the artist does not want to be—the maker does not want to be identified as an artist. They've perfected a technique and they want to do that. They acknowledge that. In terms of having a discussion around art versus craft, that is so tired. So very tired!

KING-HAMMOND Yes—it's because craft really talks about the process, skills of the maker, and imagination.

CARPENTER It's process! To me, it's about what you do with the process. When does it become more than the sum of its parts? I look at objects, I'll look at a basket, there's a woman down in South Carolina doing these baskets and I think, wow.

KING-HAMMOND Mary Jackson is an African American fiber artist known for her sweetgrass basket weavings that combine contemporary designs using traditional West African methods brought by enslaved Africans to coastal South Carolina in the 1700s. She is a member of the Gullah community and was awarded the MacArthur "Genius" award in 2008 for advancing fiber design traditions in America.

CARPENTER Thank you for those words.

KING-HAMMOND This is what we're here for.

CARPENTER We feed each other. It's that notion of taking every object on its own and not walking it. I was making pots, and I knew curators were not coming to those shows, because they decided there was no art there. So they would miss all these amazing people making fantastic things. That's my take on the art and craft idea, that you have to take it one artist, one maker at a time, one object at a time, and not be willing to just blithely categorize something because it's made out of clay, it must be less. It gets different consideration. I'm not going to consider it. I'm not going to look for the subtleties in it. I'm not going to look for the imagination of it. I'm not going to look for the expansiveness of this bowl.

On the subject of feeding each other, Winnie and Martha, you mentioned Ile Ife, and I want to acknowledge Barbara Bullock, an amazing Philadelphia artist who takes painted, curled, and sculpted paper to an entirely new place of meaning. She created the art program at Ile Ife back in the 1960s and 1970s.

KING-HAMMOND I want to take the conversation now to another level, connecting it to a more global, regional, national, local level, and it moves into the realm of social justice, the work that

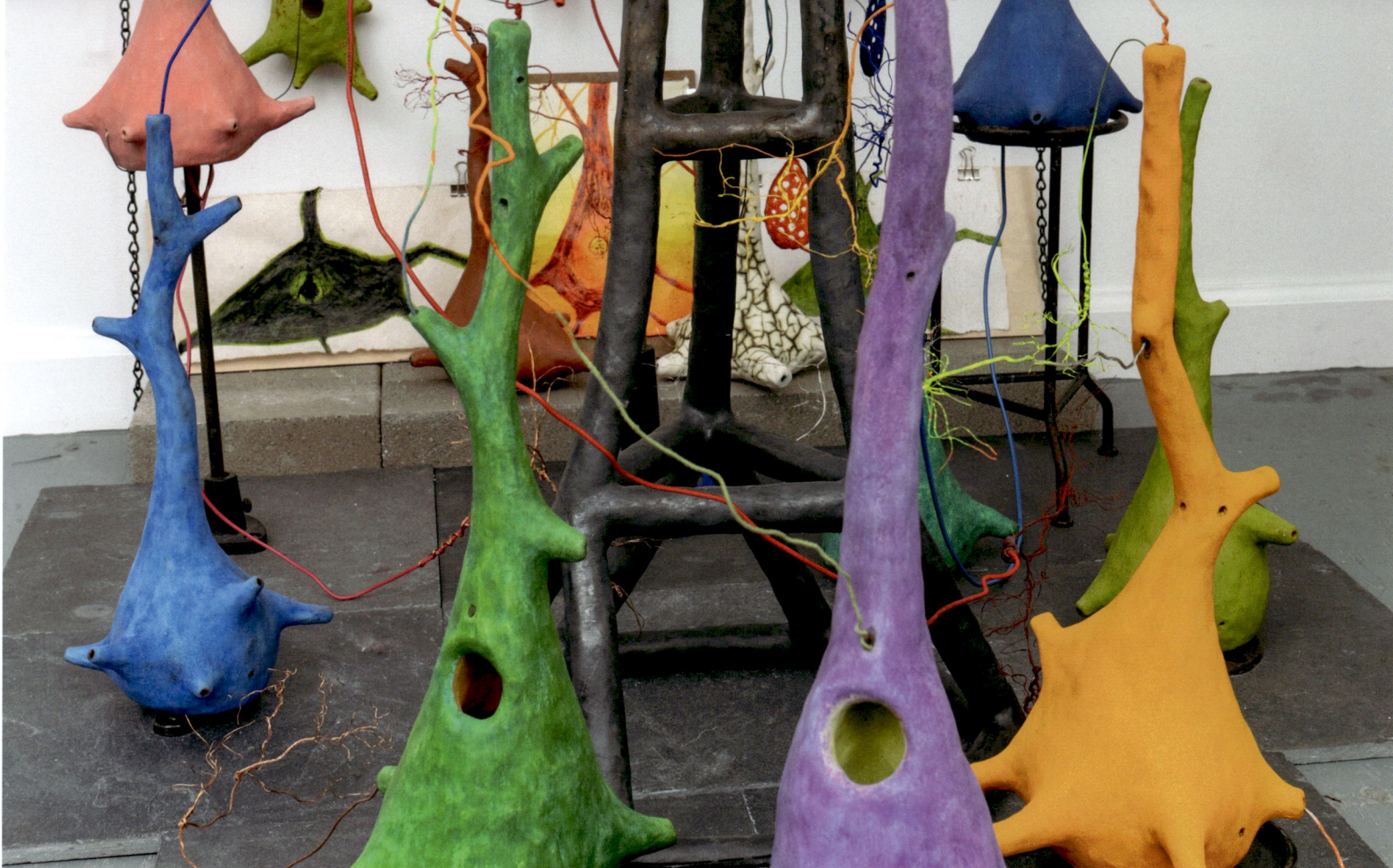

FIG. 4.12   Judy Moonelis, *Neural Home* (detail), 2023, clay and mixed media (clay, wire, chain, paper, ink, gouache, root, repurposed materials, and slate), 102 × 36 × 67 in. (Collection of the artist)

you all do as an extension or connection to the work that you do within your studio practice. Sana, I want you to talk about your work in Cambodia, how you work with your clay and working with the young women that you have been committed to caring for, for so many years, in so many ways.

MUSASAMA   Yes. The work that I'm doing in Cambodia is not with the material clay. Not yet. It may possibly be down the road, but when I came here seventeen years ago to work with girls that I know were rescued from the sex brothels, and I came from working with alternative incarcerated women, and watching the projects that I did with them, and telling them the stories about victimization of women all over the world, regardless of color, even though I knew that the population that I was working with was there because of color.

When I went to Cambodia, I went with dolls, dolls that my inmates had made. It was a wonderful project that an art therapist did with them where she would bring a blank doll into the room, and one side of the doll was their past, and the other side of the doll was their future. When they began to work on these dolls, I observed, they all were dealing with the present and why they were in incarceration centers. So these dolls had cut marks on them and weapons on them and scars on them, and they were terrible to look at. But soon after a few weeks of working on it, they reversed the doll and talked about where they were in their lives now. That side of the doll became so beautiful, and they spent three and four months just working on that part of the doll.

When I read about the foundation in Cambodia with Somaly Mam, I took a globe into the classroom to show them where Cambodia was, and I wanted them to look at other girls in the world that were victims, that didn't look like them, so that they wouldn't, at fourteen, fifteen, sixteen, only grow up saying, it's only going to happen to me because I'm Brown.

I wanted to demystify that, even though a lot of it was the truth. I took these dolls to Cambodia, and that's what we worked with. One of the things that the girls in the incarceration center said to me after they read the story, they said they were never little girls. I said, yes. They never had the chance to be little girls. They were sold at seven, eight, ten. They said, we had a chance to be girls and we redirected it. I said, yes, and we're going to redirect your lives and I'm going to go to Cambodia. When I went to Cambodia, we did the doll project, and then I looked out into the environment and saw all these materials that were rich right there, like grass and straw and thatch and clay tiles and mosaics, and I thought, if I could do something there, why don't I do it with what's available there instead of me interjecting something from where I come from?

Teach them how to work with what's existing so that when I'm not there anymore, they can continue. I have so many students that have joined the Peace Corps, and I would visit them, and as soon as they would leave the Peace Corps, the project they had been working on stopped. It didn't come from the source of the land where these people lived. So I didn't want that to happen with the girls in Cambodia.

We started weaving baskets and making shoes and making hats, and then we started thinking about what do you need in your own safe house? They began making rugs, and it just developed from there and from there and from everywhere. Now I think about doing ceramics with them, but I developed the apron project with them about nine years ago, and it was with the older girls that get rescued at 15, 16, 17, and they have no formal education and there is no remedial program.

These girls will stay in the safe house for five years and learn self-defense, fish farming, English, math, dance and recreate family. But when they leave the safe house, they don't have enough skills to really survive in the communities. Unfortunately, sometimes walking themselves back into a brothel is really the only way that they can support their families. They're born into two and three generations of poverty. A girl that I'm working with now is not only taking care of her mother, she's taking care of her mother's mother. I developed the apron project with them. Clay happened more for me in Africa, where they make their deities out of clay, where they make their kiln gods out of clay, where they make their calcium pills out of clay. Their manganese, where they put clay on their face to cool them off when it's very, very hot, or when they put clay on a wound to tighten it or—to an astringent on their skin.

So there, it was so easy to work with clay because it was just already being used naturally in the environment. In terms of the thing that sits out so brilliantly about craft and art, I never paid attention to it because I didn't come from any art school training to hear that double lie. In Mendeland, when I worked with potters and we worked in an assembly line, and I saw the love, the passion, the history, the carving, the firing, the burnishing, the handling of the piece, to me, it was so artful. There was no other word to use but that. There was no distinction between a deity and a pot that was going to be for indigo, or a pot that was going to be made to bury a baby. And there were no division lines. So for me, coming back to the United States and going to school, I just thought that it was a form of racism within the arts, and I just was not going to participate in it whatsoever.

So whenever the conversation came up, I said, this is incredibly boring and I'm not going to engage in this conversation. I left it at that. There were always debates going on. It just wasn't interesting to me, having had the world behind me, supporting me with the different ways that people related to what you made with your hand.

KING-HAMMOND Winnie, what were your experiences in Africa?

OWENS-HART Well, I've been to two villages, one in Nigeria where I went back and lived. My desire to work in an African village started when I was a teenager. I was really, really determined that I was going to end up that way. I finally got a free ride and went with the first group, and when we all got off the plane and kissed the earth and all that stuff, we got to stay an extra week.

What Ladi Kwali did at Howard and when she came and worked around the places here in the US, that's what helped me concretize what I want to do, how I want to do it. Basically, what I do is work with traditional shapes, and find out the truth about what was the purpose of the pot. The first year I was there, after FESTAC, I ended up staying there for another year with some money that was given to me. I came back to America and met Gilbert "Bobbo" Ahiagble, and he was a famous Ghanaian Kente weaver. Again, I was able to go back for another year. It was a beautiful experience. I tried to immerse myself in the culture and everything, it was really nice.

I learned how to speak Yoruba because I took a course at Howard University, I was working with the women, you find more—you pick up the language that all of these women were speaking to me. I found myself going back to the weaver's place, because that's where my dad and the weaver became friends. I went there in my early twenties, and I'm still going. So it's just like you have a family and you didn't even know you had a family because it was just so smooth.

KING-HAMMOND Judy, you've chosen a very interesting path in your work with neuroscience. Tell us a little bit about that, and how it intersects with your life in clay, your realities. What's the energy?

MOONELIS Well, it's interesting when you think about what we are as humans and other living creatures, right? And when you start looking at our insides and get smaller and smaller into that kind of world, you start to realize that we're very complex creatures. I had an interest in human imagery and anatomy, and I started getting more and more involved in the neuroscience aspect. At the same time, I was very interested in memory and the important role memory plays in who we are, how we define ourselves, and art and science together start to become this really interesting way of describing something about who we are and how we can define ourselves.

In my own case, I have done quite a few pieces based in some way on that. I started getting really interested in site-specific work, where responding to a particular place and then doing some research, finding out something about the history, et cetera, and then bringing some of this information into that site. So one of my more, I guess I could say one of my favorite experiences was actually here in Philadelphia, the Eastern State Penitentiary historic site. I was invited to create work there. They practiced solitary confinement there, when it was considered this wonderful, revolutionary new technique at that time. Now we know how damaging it is to people's brains, let alone their whole being. I did one of my pieces there. I did it in one of the former cells called *Brain Cell*. I used a lot of references to the inner workings of our bodies, the organs as well as neural connections, et cetera.

I did another piece in the women's former laundry based on circulatory systems within our bodies and representations of human beings hovering above the floor there and suspended from the broken skylights. That kind of idea of layering the history of a place and humans' interaction with it, our individual selves with that, I find really interesting. It gives us a real opportunity to speak about many things and bring it into our present. Interacting with a place that had all these stories and histories, I connect strongly with Syd's pieces in this way. They're not site-specific, most of them, but that you do bring place as a very important element in the work. For me, that is a very strong connection that we all have in some way to our past, to where we are now, where we have been or where we might go. So it's part of—that's maybe a short answer to what could be. I don't want to go on.

No, no, what it does is I'm trying to create opportunities so that when the public, and when this becomes a published document, they can see all of the ways you can cross-pollinate, fertilize your intellects and your energies and your aesthetic sensibilities. The anatomical studies that Santiago Ramón y Cajal did at the turn of last century, 1905/1906 when he won a Nobel Prize for his discovery that neurons are separate individual units. They don't actually have a physical connection, they speak across synapses, that there's this little gap. This was a revolutionary idea at the time, and we've since proven his theories, so many theories, to be correct. His drawings are exquisite, he did hundreds of them. I got to actually go to Madrid and see little scraps of paper, backs of envelopes, and handle them. They're just amazing. I've done a lot of work inspired by his studies. It led me to really explore and understand neuroscience more, and then bring it back to contemporary interpretations and scans and all of that. So it's just part of the journey there, I guess you could say. He's a particularly important element in that neuroscience discussion for me.

KING-HAMMOND Syd, you have been focused on the legacy of the Black farmer. We are dealing with numerous aspects of clay, which is earth, the essence of all that we are indebted to, in your work. It is very provocative in the way we rethink our relationship to the land and to those individuals who are the stewards who produce the foods that we eat, that we take for granted. Too many people have no understanding about the processes on how this happens, because they have the supermarket to supply the need for food. Farmers markets are a more contemporary phenomenon, but basically, it's the supermarket where everything has already been processed, packaged, and shelved together. What has been the intent and mission of your concerns in the way you address this distressing conundrum?

CARPENTER The perception of African Americans, people of color, on the land in this country is that we don't belong there. To me, the irony of that is, I'll use the word appalling, given, initially, the reason why we as a people were brought here by force is because of our knowledge of and connection to earth. We were brought here to teach Euro-Americans how to grow indigo,

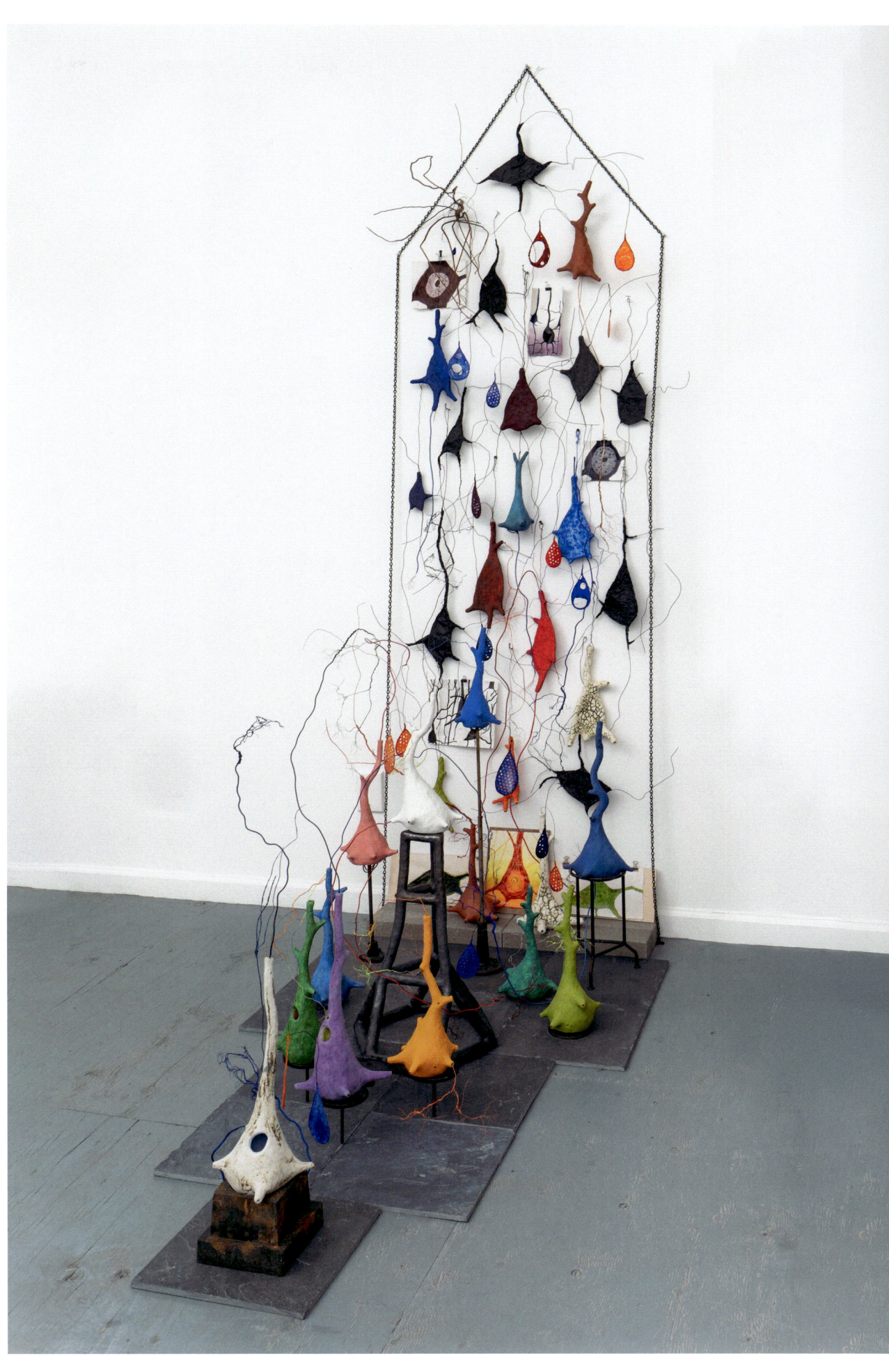

FIG. 4.13 Judy Moonelis, *Neural Home*, 2023,
clay and mixed media (clay, wire, chain, paper, ink,
gouache, root, repurposed materials, and slate),
102 × 36 × 67 in. (Collection of the artist)

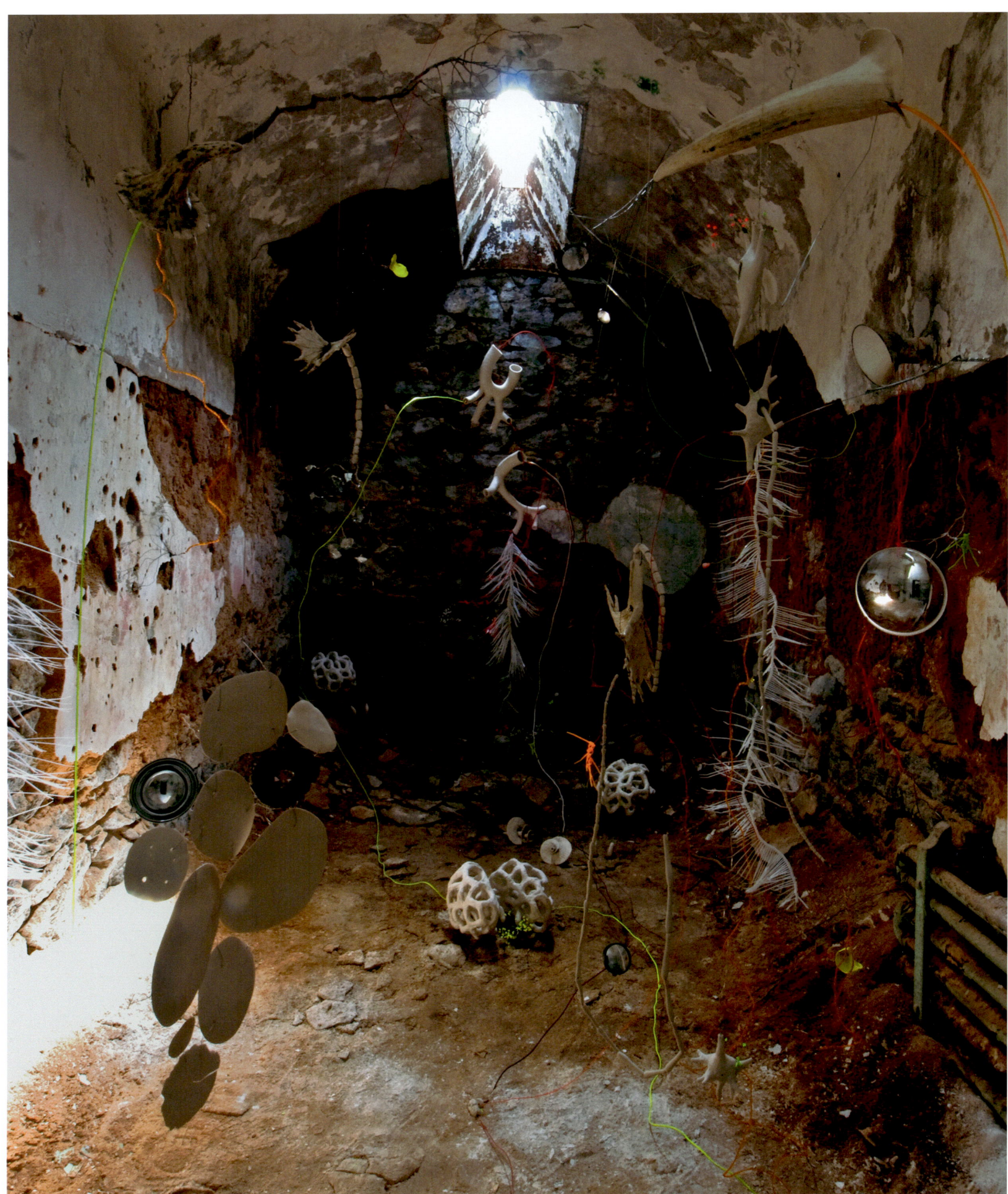

how to grow cotton, to teach them how to grow all these different things from which they then profited. We're at a place where we need to be reintroduced, at least that is the perception, that is a way of thinking about it, that African Americans need to be reintroduced to the earth. Black people have never actually been disconnected from the land and the earth. There has been an aversion to it, but in terms of looking at who was on the earth, stayed on the farms that had been acquired, we have been quite consistent. The burgeoning interest in recycling and creating urban farms, we are at the vanguard of that. Early on, during the Great Migration, when we got here and could, the first thing we did was plant gardens.

We would bring that knowledge and that practice, that desire, that connection to the earth, to every little scrappy piece of ground we could. We did that and it's been consistent. This idea of us being disconnected, where African Americans do not want to be associated with the land because it recalls a memory of being subordinate, to being downtrodden, and it's associated with poverty, it certainly has nothing to do with modernity. All of these issues during the Harlem Renaissance, we were trying to overcome and to disassociate ourselves. There was always that farm that they left. I started doing a series of pieces that I thought of as legacy farms, looking for farmers and farms that had been retained. Because even though a lot of us, millions of us, left during the Great Migration to go north and west, there were those courageous, steadfast stewards who stayed on the land despite the abuse, the intimidation, the attempts to take the land, and it often was, most of it was.

Those folks, when I could find them, hear their stories, that these were multiple-generational farms, they had stayed on their land. That, to me, represented a certain kind of courage and belief in the self. A lot of those farms and the people who owned them became the creators of the churches and the schools. These farmers were supporting the growth and the sustenance that allowed us to continue to survive. To me, obscuring and skewering our role on the land, as stewards, as rejecters of the land because of its history, that has to be re-examined very carefully, because it's a complex relationship that we have over time, over the last century with the land. But it has never been a disconnect.

It's just, to me, telling that story to our children, reminding our grandparents and our mothers and fathers of that wealth. I think that's wealth. It is a major imperative to keep land, to get land, whether it's just a row house with a backyard, own it.

When you start these gardens in your city or town, don't just land on it and ask permission to do it. Buy it. And so there are different ways of establishing yourself and being present on the land. And so I'm a big advocate of that. I also want to recall those folks who stayed on the land. So often, the titles of my work are a roll call of these anonymous people who would never, ever gain any kind of remembrance or—or just to have this place in history. I like the fact that my titles lived with these pieces who are going to be in these museums, and they're going to be in these shows. I think I get to say their names. That is really important to me, is to be able to say their names. I often begin my lectures or end my lectures with a roll call of anonymous Black farmers from the South.

KING-HAMMOND This conversation is moving in the direction that needs greater input to address some of the greater fault lines in American art history. In the course of your lives what has motherhood, marriage, parenting, mentorship, and "woman as artist" meant in your life?

MOONELIS I have never been a parent. My mother, Goldie, was a creative person who encouraged an appreciation of art in the family. I always felt she could have been an artist herself, given different life circumstances. My parents never attended college. They were both smart, creative people who often took us to art and science museums, where my love of research in support of art making was born. My father taught me to use tools as a young girl, very uncommon at that time. I appreciate the opportunity to mentor students and interns in my own studio practice. As an art professor I created a residency program which engages alumni with current students. My longtime partner, Jeffrey Mongrain, is also a working visual artist; we have mutually and strongly supported each other over decades as artists. In my art practice I have always felt an important approach is to make the best possible work I can make.

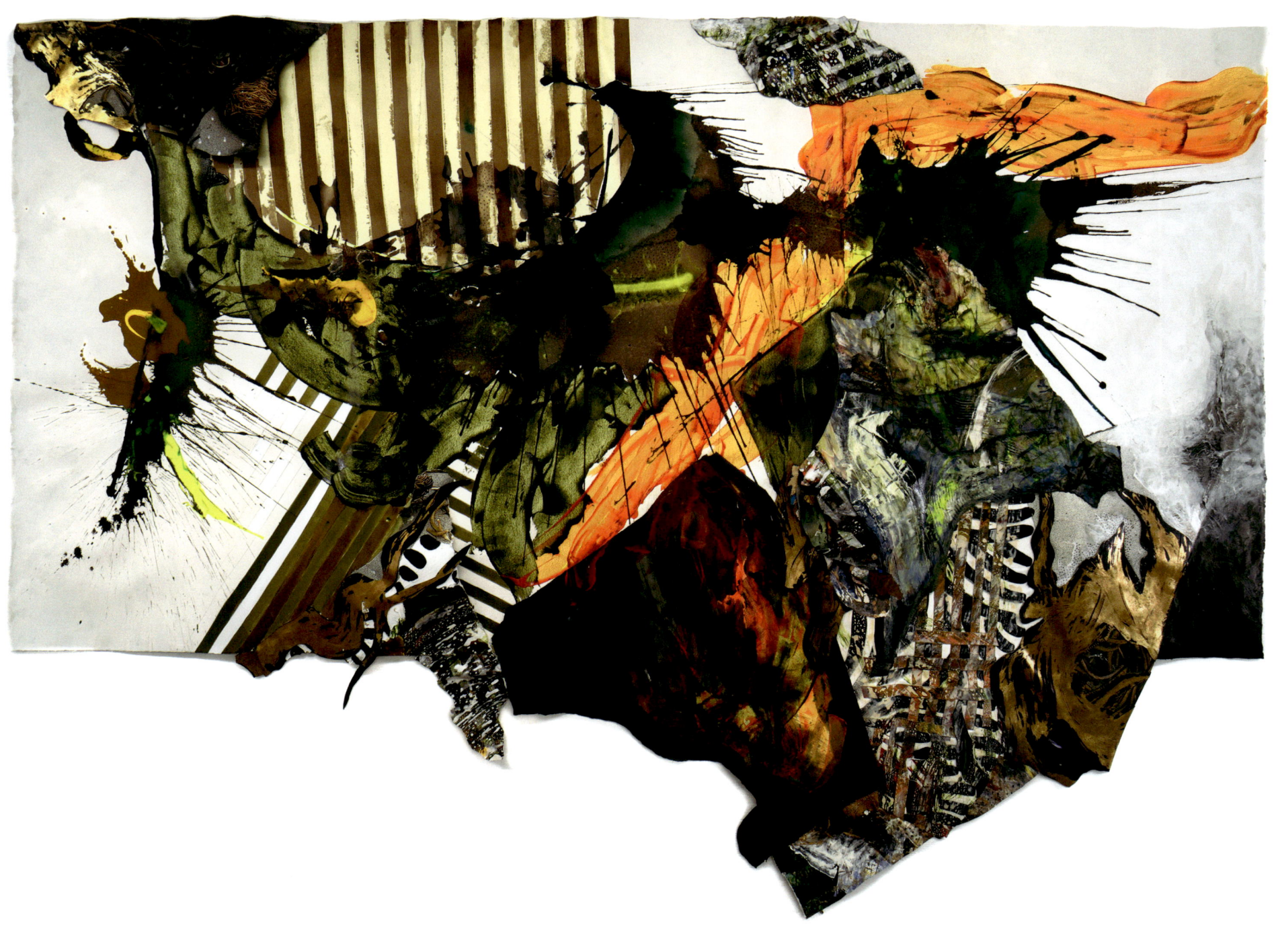

FIG. 4.15 Martha Jackson Jarvis, *Crossing Land*,
2020, oil, acrylic, watercolor, black walnut ink, and
canvas, 84 × 120 × 2 in. (Collection of the artist)

JACKSON JARVIS Through assemblage, sculptures, and site-specific work, I reference traditions like African American quilt-making, translating them into contemporary forms that layer personal, cultural, and historical narratives. Woven into this is lived experience of family life as a creative sustaining force that I very carefully wove around my creative life as an artist. "Family Life" is a force that has required tremendous discipline, organization, courage, and compassion. I married a wonderful man who understood my passion and unwavering commitment to my art practice. My four children, whether blessed or cursed, were born to an artist. They never knew anything but a mother who worked in her studio as an artist making things . . . for a while they all thought all mothers were artists. I never told them differently. I have been the recipient of love and support from my dear husband, Bernard Jarvis, for forty-six years, who passed away in 2022. My family life has expanded to four children and four grandchildren. Competing as a female artist I have simply stood my ground, and let the work speak.

CARPENTER Because I have no children of my own, I can describe my relationship to motherhood in two aspects. First, I view motherhood through my experience as a child of Ernestine and understood motherhood through her. Second, I taught for more than thirty years, and a few of those students have come to be known affectionately as "my children." My connection to them includes feeling a responsibility to them as support and friendship rather than the conventional role of parent. My over forty-year marriage to the same individual has been a gift, a successful partnership through mutual respect, friendship, and uninterrupted connection. Our union has provided me with support of every aspect of my work. I respond in kind. We are both "all in" to maintain momentum in whichever direction the work takes us.

I am dedicated to supporting younger artists. Being an artist and a woman is both challenging and to my advantage . . . being marginalized, ironically, can be a liberating position in which to make art. You can do and say whatever you want because no one is paying attention until the noise from the margins becomes too loud to be ignored. I am not compelled to overtly represent feminist tropes in my art. I do not make work that can be described in masculine terms to avoid being categorized as "too feminine." The strength in the work comes from the extent to which I maximize what I put into it at the moment of making.

MUSASAMA Mother has always meant a broad term for me. I grew up in an extended family system. Of course I had a biological mom and dad but many, many extended moms as well as aunts who were also classified as moms. I was considered a mom to younger cousins, relatives. As a woman traveler, little girls caught my eyes first and have remained the topic of my work for over two decades. The inequalities, gender biases, lack of education, health care, child labor, wars, poverty, droughts, incarcerations, and life-threatening ritual practices—little girls suffer these atrocities the worst. I was very aware of these crises.

Gender makes me a mom in most cultures I have lived in. Little girls in villages became my mentors. They taught me their mother tongue, how to eat and sit like a Mende woman. They taught me morning and evening greetings, the tune of the death chant. They kept me safe. Our roles switched like the seasons, sometimes they were actually my mommy, other times I was theirs. All the time we were girls in our ritual of sisterhood. I have shared with others, never wanted fame alone. I wanted my buddies alongside me. I taught from a place of offering. I never saw myself as a mentor. In Cambodia, I saw evil and I *stepped up!* I was being *human*—simple as that. My mom taught my four sisters on what humanity feels like. She was a good person and often said, "Be a good citizen."

KING-HAMMOND At this juncture, is there anything else you all would like to talk about, or perhaps what you envision in your futures?

CARPENTER Well, I'll say that mentoring is becoming very important to me. There are plenty of big-name artists out there who are just making magnificent, awesome work. But I think that maybe younger artists, artists like myself who were not that visible or not attempting to be visible, can find some support, find some encouragement through me reaching out to them. I like to go find them.

OWENS-HART   I've been going around for the last year or so since orange man and Muskrat are throwing their dirt all over the world. I really have asked people, everybody that I know, and it's not about a clay request, but I think that's really important that we write our own self stories, and keep it, because we're going to be looking for a book soon, the ones they burn. I just ask everybody to tell you their own story.

CARPENTER   One of the things that I started to initiate on social media is this declaration that they're coming for the books, the libraries, and they're coming for the museums. I would like to have meetings at libraries and museums to talk about how to protect and defend these institutions, because it's easily the case where federal funding will be cut off and these libraries will have to close because their salaries can't be paid, the heat can't be—they will cut these resources and just fire people and there will be no access. Of course, there will be the censoring of books. We all know from history that they come for the artists. The playbook is so obvious. I'm thinking, we can't sit here, the museums, the colleges holding meetings to brainstorm about in the event that they cut off all this funding and they start demonizing curators and writers and censoring and all of that. How do you fight back? Because it is inevitable. It's not a "if," it's a "when." All has to be organized. I read all of these people who have been saying, yes, do this. Really? You have a meeting and figure out how to save your space, how to save your town library, how to meet with people who are in museums, curators. How do we save this? Because they're coming for it.

And so that's one thing, as an artist, I feel like I can call attention to. So we're hoping to have some meetings in Philadelphia. I need to get in contact with the people at the Free Library. I don't know about the people at the museums, I'll talk to Bill [Valerio] maybe, he'll have a meeting, at some point. But we have to be seen to be fighting back. Can you imagine that the federal IMLS "terminated" a grant to Woodmere for $750,000 that was intended for care of the museum's collection? And worse things are happening.

We have to actually do something. We have to have an idea. What if they decide to censor all of these books? And what if they close your local library? Don't forget that local library is also where a lot of people get access to the internet. When they start to wipe out funding for these institutions, it's a domino effect. You're talking about the dark ages. So we can't be passive as museum administrators and librarians. You have to actually get organized. Don't think they're not coming, because we didn't think he was coming. [CHUCKLES]

KING-HAMMOND   His intention is to completely disrupt, dismantle, and leave us in a state of chaos. Now, we have to remember, as Toni Morrison has often said, in times of trouble and strife, that the arts are the place where we have to be far more diligent and double down on what we do. This is a time where what we do—and I think you're absolutely right about mentoring, reaching out.

Lowery and I just had an incredible experience this past weekend, working with the American Craft Council at their winter market. And we did little what we thought were just casual workshops. We were inundated; we were overwhelmed with the number of people who came in. We did a little project, just patchworking, showing them how to take scraps and to repurpose them. It was the whole conceptual idea that people who had never put their hands on anything creative or artistic had the capability "to make something from nothing" as people are witnessing the world unraveling increasingly.

JACKSON JARVIS   Oh, visions of the future. The future belongs to us. We have to claim it. It's time for all of the beings and all of your talents, gifts, things that have been gracefully fully bestowed upon each of us, right? The future is open, but we must command our space. Stand your ground. It's time to stand the ground. So what does that mean? It means look around you. There's plenty to be done. Claim something. If it's a small patch—or learn how to thread a needle. Most young people don't know how to do it. Plant a garden. Do something. Say hello to somebody passing in the street. Don't be a zombie. "Good morning" won't kill you, but it could save somebody's life.

So we have to claim the power that we have. Orange, blue, pink, man. None of it. He's not going to win. What we have is long of the earth. Long of the universe. And we will be sustained if we

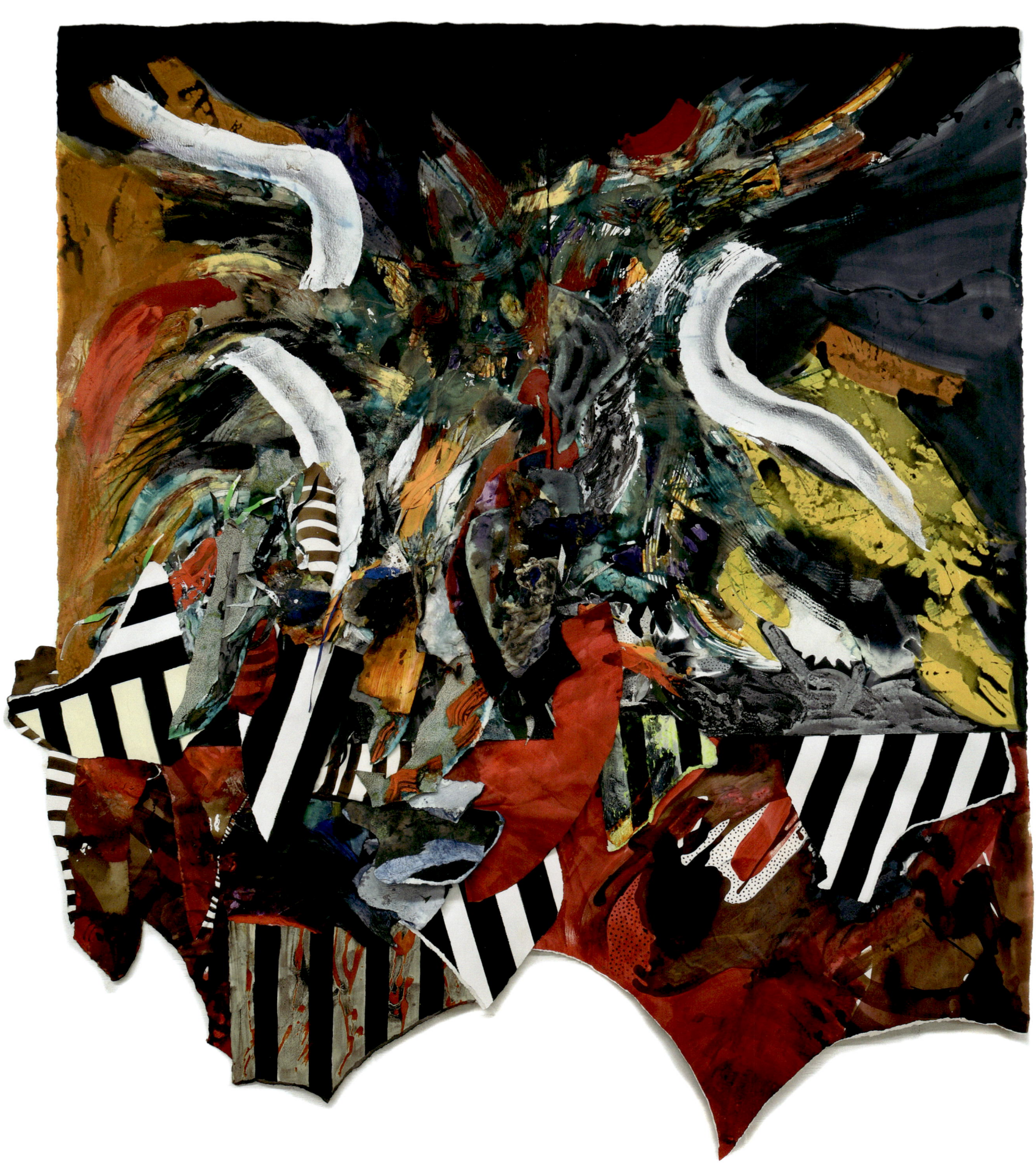

do our work. And if we don't, you will perish. You will perish, and the earth will keep right on breathing. The animals will do better without you.

We have to make a stand. We have to make a stand as humans. Are we going to be here? Are we going to claim the waters and the air and acknowledge the power of the trees and the things that we grow and eat, that we're all connected? That your destiny is intertwined with mine? And they will never be separated. The sisters in Cambodia, working seventeen years or more. The threads, these universal threads, shall not be broken. There's no amount of greed, lying, stealing, corruption, and just plain old-fashioned evil will disintegrate this. But we have to stand our ground.

CARPENTER Passivity caused it. We need to be vigilant because half of folks didn't think it was important, and here we are discussing how to save it. So the idea of passivity is an issue, and I don't know if this crisis that we're in as artists is how we contribute to the wakeup call. And not its—

OWENS-HART Did y'all see the movies that I made for NCECA for this—not the one that's coming up, but the one in Richmond?

KING-HAMMOND You made a movie? You didn't tell us. You have to get the word out, Winnie. That's all right, that's all right. Tell you what, I'm going to find the movie. I'm going to find the movie, and I want to wrap this up—

OWENS-HART It's not out when we show—we showed the movie. It's Joseph Jr., I don't know if you know him, but he's a genius and he teaches at Hampton. And so we shot a lot of stuff that he said, don't say that. Don't say that. But we gave him the movie, and it was a presentation. It was one of the categories. And it wouldn't play. And I'm going like, damn. And then everybody stayed. Nobody got up. They wanted to hear what we had to say, it was a very powerful movie.

KING-HAMMOND I can tell you that this has been a dream of mine come true. I don't know about the rest of you. I hope you all realize that this is an unprecedented moment in history, where we

have a major retrospective being installed on Syd Carpenter and complemented with each of your visionary creations. Syd is in the company of her cohorts, her posse, her sisterhood, is so incredibly significant and such a monumental achievement of kinship and collaboration between artists and institutions.

JACKSON JARVIS Can I say one more thing? I want to thank Leslie King-Hammond and this beautiful lady sitting over here. You all have made—you talk about connections that we have? You all have threaded the needle, and you have woven the garment. When I think of *Art as a Verb*, and not just us, you could fill this room with all the artists and the women and men from that one exhibition, one exhibition that you two, Leslie and Lowery Sims, in 1988. You can go through the list. Adrian Piper, Faith Ringgold, Betye Saar, Joyce J. Scott—the list is just endless. And the vision. I can't even count how many times I wrote to this poor woman and said, could you please write me a recommendation? [LAUGHS] I know I wasn't the only one doing it. And she would do it. You would do it.

KING-HAMMOND That's correct and that's what we do. We are continuing to do it. We are not stopping. We dovetail, we counter and complement each other in our work. We talk about, all the time, what are the issues? What do we hope to achieve? This is a collaboration, to be aligned, with intentional commitment, grounded in community engagement.

CARPENTER I think it also has to do with momentum. Because we're not really aware of the level of momentum that can build. It's like that butterfly flaps its wings and something happens on the other side of the earth. What can an individual do? Flap their wings. [CHUCKLING] So my sense of this is doing what you can, staying connected. The idea of identifying a project. Thinking about libraries and museums, and what can I do? I'm going to be making work. I mean, that is, that's unquestionable that is going to happen. In the face of what's coming, we do have to react with the powers that we have. Each person does have a power. It's those individual actions that build momentum, not to feel powerless in the face of all of what's happening. As an artist, my sense of it is that we are being called upon even more now, because we represent thinking, we represent creativity, we represent imagination. Those in power do not appreciate or welcome any of that. We are in those positions to promote and to create these kernels of energy that need to be spread. Plant those seeds.

JACKSON JARVIS I must say one last thing, may I? Talking about the small things that we can do that can save someone, Leslie, I will never forget you. When my husband passed, and the next week, I had to go in to mount my solo exhibition at the Baltimore Museum of Art. I had to pull myself up from losing my mate of forty-seven years. I walked into that museum numb. I could just get out of bed and get up, stand up straight and get there.

You walked into that museum. I'll never forget it. You walked up and you hugged me, and you whispered in my ear, with a hug, welcome to the widow's club. It let me know I was not alone. I will never forget you for that moment. Because it gave me strength. We mounted that show.

CARPENTER So what I see here, I have a show that's about reuniting. It's not just the five of us that are doing it. I am really very grateful to be at the kernel of this, but knowing that it's beyond me. That this was just my turn to do something, and the Woodmere and the Berman and the Maguire give me a foothold. Give me a platform to do it. I love this union of folks from the museums, from the curatorial and scholarly level, to the artists, and how that reunites and ignites.

KING-HAMMOND I would like to thank each of you for this critically essential conversation that will bring significant light to the presentations of your works at three sites. I am so humbled, honored to know and work with such powerful women of fierce determination, innovative vision, and artistic integrity.

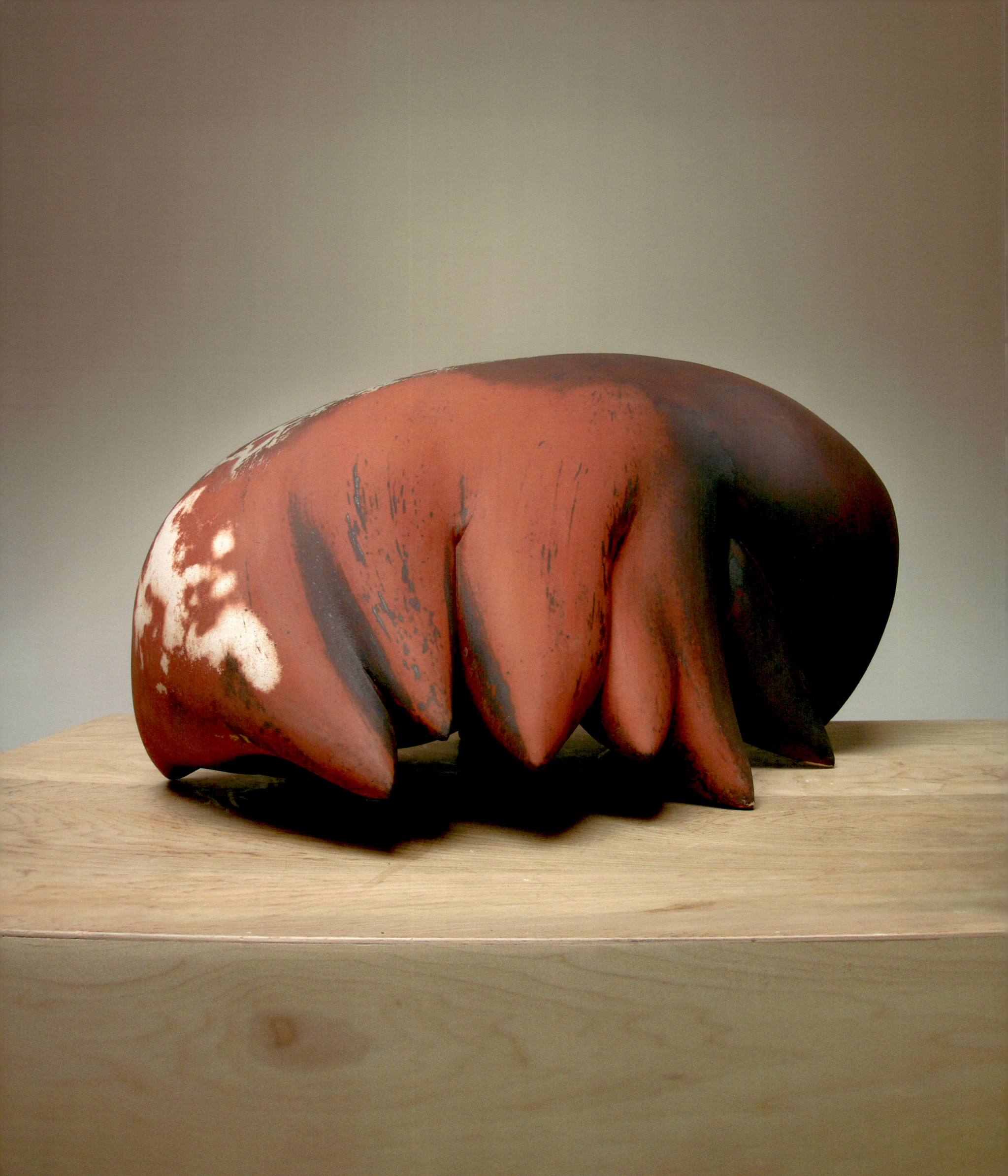

Echoes and Evolutions
Transformations in Syd Carpenter's Creative Practice

LAUREN MCCARDEL

WHAT MAKES AN EVOLUTION in artistic practice truly transformational? Not all evolutionary steps can be described as revolutionary, surely—markers of growth or segues into new experimental processes are often just that, evidence of some type of momentum or perhaps simply the absence of stagnation.

Transformational evolution, I think, takes time. It may occur quickly, seemingly at once even, but it is the result of a durational process of absorption, digestion, reflection, experimentation, and finally, maturation.

In considering Syd Carpenter's recent sculptural practice, particularly the work following her 2022 retirement from a thirty-year teaching career at Swarthmore College, this word *transformation* keeps recurring in my thoughts. I first encountered Carpenter's work in 2018 at a solo exhibition at the Center for Emerging Visual Artists in Philadelphia and later heard her speak about her most important influences: the familial and educational relationships that shaped her early practice, and how the discovery of Richard Noble Westmacott's 1992 survey, *African-American Gardens and Yards in the Rural South*, opened new pathways for exploration into the legacies of African American farmers and gardeners. Having been raised by a mother and grandmother who kept gardens, for nourishment and for pleasure, Carpenter understood from an early age the importance

and implications of owning and cultivating land for African Americans. For more than a decade, her practice has been shaped by extensive research and travel to meet Black farmers across the southern United States, embedding and amplifying their stories in her multidisciplinary work.

Carpenter's convictions about the primal importance of land ownership, her practice of naming the individuals whose farms and legacies she documents, and her experimental approach to collecting materials and forms have, in many ways, stayed consistent over the course of her career. Crucially, though, her recent practice has expanded to incorporate new materials and vastly differing scales, far beyond those she typically employed in earlier work (which have necessarily led to creative partnerships with other artists). The resulting work is a triumphant culmination arrived at via the passing of time: of decades spent scanning, noticing, documenting—collecting information for future use; of a mastery of materials achieved through constant practice; of a confidence in her ideas, and, perhaps, an absence of the fear of failure at this stage of her life; and of the enduring support of the communities and individuals at the center of her storytelling. What follows is a much-too-brief reflection on the recent works included in *Syd Carpenter: Planting in Place, Time, and Memory*. These newer works, on view at the Berman Museum

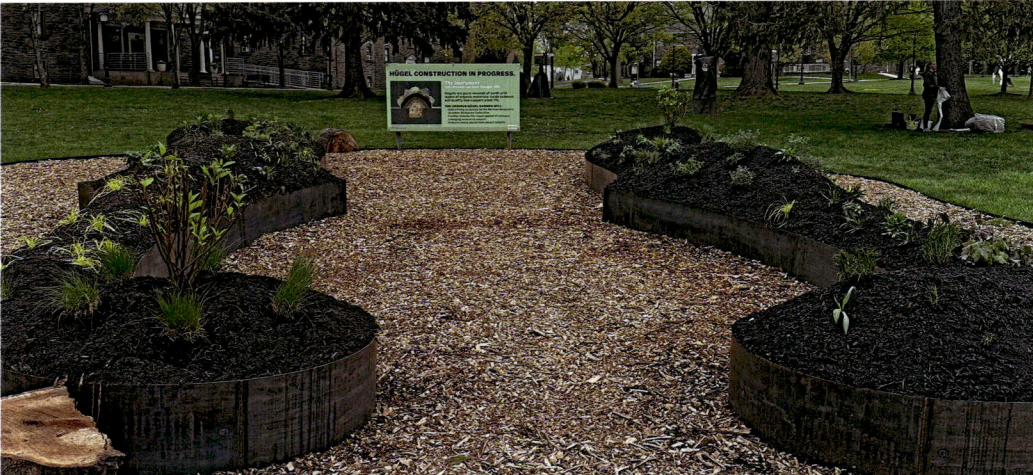

FIG. 5.1   Syd Carpenter and Steve Donegan, *The Instrument*, 2024, hügel garden (The Philip and Muriel Berman Museum of Art, Ursinus College)

of Art at Ursinus College in the satellite installation entitled *Syd Carpenter: Home Bound in Wood, Steel, and Clay*, speak to the transformational nature of the artist's practice.

Carpenter's work can be productively situated within a broader lineage of African American artists who have utilized form and material to challenge dominant narratives and reclaim agency. Like Simone Leigh, who merges ceramic traditions with monumental sculpture in works such as *Brick House* (2019), Carpenter employs scale to assert Black female presence in space. Betye Saar's assemblage works, particularly *The Liberation of Aunt Jemima* (1972), provide a crucial historical parallel in reclaiming domestic and labor imagery, while her daughter Alison Saar's *Sweeping Beauty* (1997) explores similar intersections of Black femininity and physical labor. Theaster Gates's immersive exhibitions, such as *How to Build a House Museum* (2016), resonate with Carpenter's recent works, including *Home Places* (2025, described in the following pages), transforming familiar structures into multilayered installations rooted in cultural memory that honor the Black experience. Likewise, Magdalene Odundo's hand-coiled ceramic vessels and Joyce J. Scott's beaded sculptures interrogate form, history, and identity through tactile materials, much like Carpenter's multi-material explorations.

From a theoretical perspective, bell hooks's *Art on My Mind* (1995) provides an essential framework for understanding the liberatory aspects of Carpenter's sculptural practice. hooks writes, "For Black bodies, the fear has not been losing touch with our physicality but how to be in touch with our bodies in a way that is liberatory, that does not confine us to racist/sexist paradigms of subjugated embodiment."[1] Carpenter's sculptures, particularly the *Mother Pin* series, reflect this ethos, transforming domestic and agricultural symbols into forms that assert female presence and resilience while resisting imposed narratives of limitation. Her commitment to decolonizing material practice aligns with hooks's assertion that "decolonization of our minds and imaginations" is central to artistic liberation.

Richard J. Powell's *Black Art: A Cultural History* (2002, 2021) further situates Carpenter's work within a broader trajectory of African American artistic innovation. Powell examines how Black artists have continually redefined artistic traditions to assert cultural identity, writing that "Black artists have long used art as a means of self-definition and cultural affirmation, challenging the limitations imposed by mainstream institutions."[2] Carpenter's sculptural practice, with its emphasis on history and embodiment, aligns with this tradition, asserting Black presence within contemporary art discourse. By engaging with symbols of labor and land management, she recontextualizes these forms as sites of strength and continuity through engagement with visibility, material transformation, and historical reclamation.

• •

In March 2022, I had recently joined the Berman Museum as director when I reconnected with Syd Carpenter at an artist talk by Shirin Neshat at the University of Pennsylvania's Perry World House. We began to discuss the possibility of an exhibition. During a visit to the wonderfully sprawling studio Carpenter shares with her husband, artist Steve Donegan, the two told me about the hügel garden they had recently completed at Woodmere, featuring sculptural raised beds designed to beautify the museum's grounds and create a place of respite, with plant species carefully selected by the artists for year-round visual interest. Together we made the short trip to Woodmere to see *La Cresta* (2021), composed of two raised beds shaped into abstract forms and bursting into spring blooms. Struck by how such a garden could create and foster cross-disciplinary learning experiences for students, I asked Carpenter and Donegan if they would consider partnering on a commissioned project for the Berman Museum, and in 2024, we broke ground on *The Instrument* (figs. 5.1 and 5.2), a site-specific hügel garden designed and planted with the participation of Ursinus faculty and students and members of the local Collegeville community.

Our work together on the Berman hügel garden brought Carpenter's deep knowledge of gardening and the aesthetically transformative power of plants into new perspective for me. While hügels are a new form of creative expression for Carpenter, embodying the interest in a more expansive scale referenced above, gardens, including her own at her home in Philadelphia,

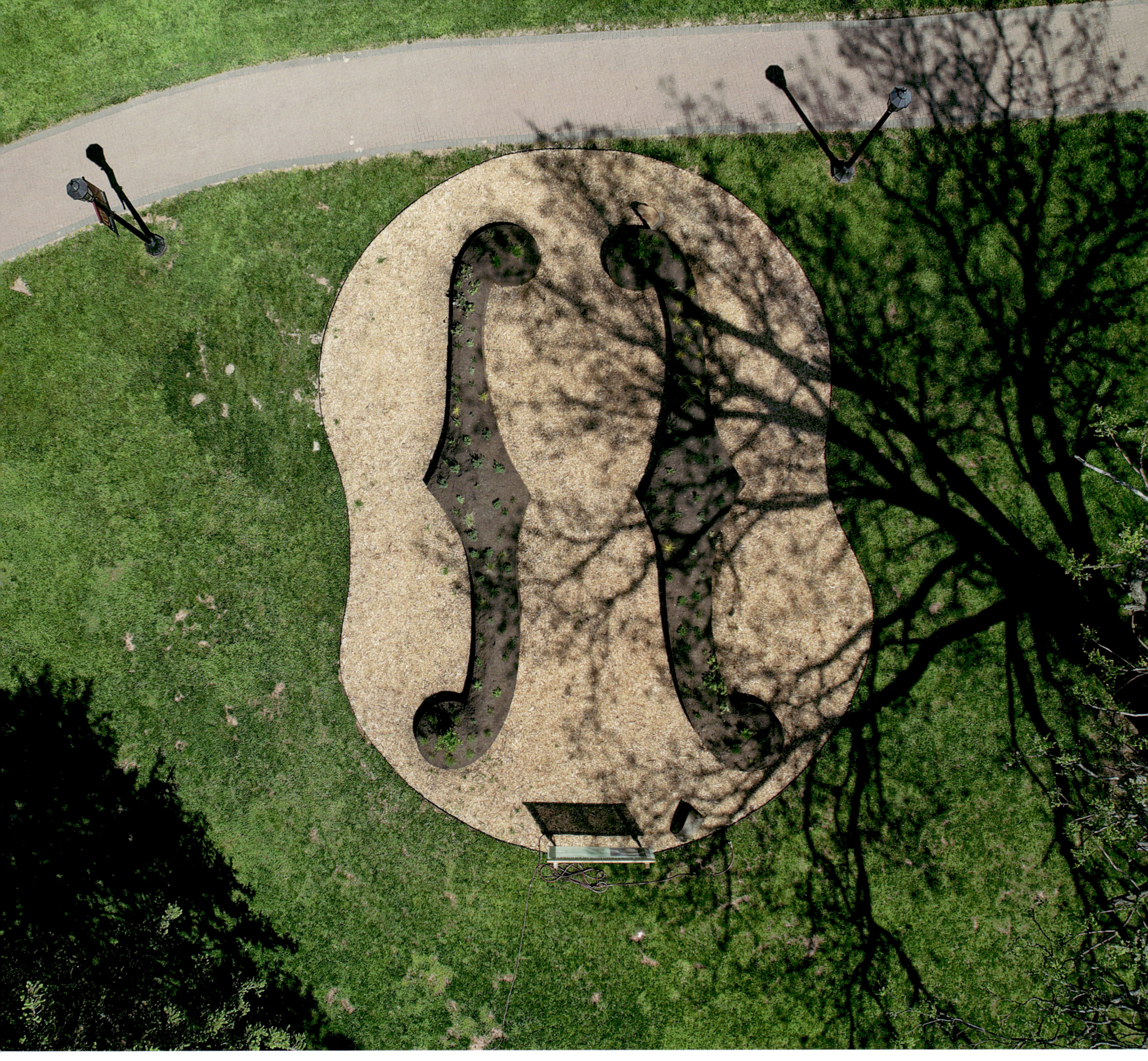

FIG. 5.2   Syd Carpenter and Steve Donegan,
The Instrument (aerial view), 2024, hügel garden
(The Philip and Muriel Berman Museum of Art,
Ursinus College)

107   ECHOES AND EVOLUTIONS

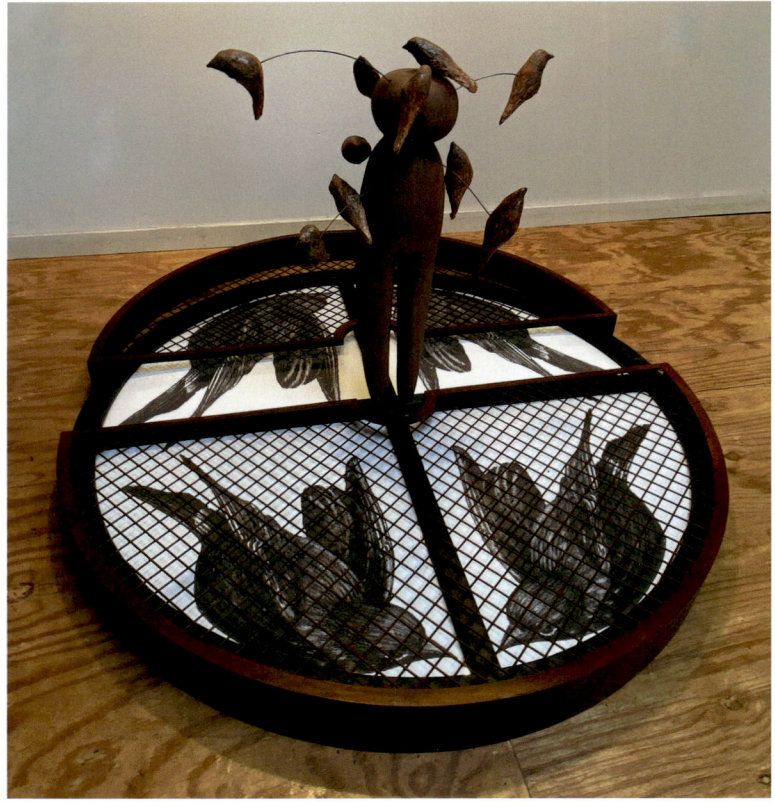

FIG. 5.3 *Release*, 2021, steel, clay, and papier-mâché, 28 × 64 × 64 in. (Collection of the artist)

have always served a crucial role in Carpenter's artistic process. The rhythm of the seasons and resultant changes to the landscape provide her with a never-ending source of ideas and inspiration. "I look at the garden as another medium. I see it as material. I see plant forms, textures, colors, as something to be manipulated and changed."[3] As an artist concerned with the histories, personal legacies, and social dynamics of place, she thinks deeply about land stewardship and her own agency in both owning and tending to places of meaning. "It was the purchase of my own land that set me on the path of unearthing more complex and nuanced understandings of African Americans on the land," Carpenter has said, "not as enslaved victims but as creators of beauty, community and providers of home places remaining in families for multiple generations."[4] Her work has consistently reflected this sense of purpose—in the mother pins honoring her mother, Ernestine Carpenter, and grandmother, Indiana Hutson, both master gardeners; in the farm bowls created as personal responses to the people, farms, and gardens she visited in her travels through South Carolina and Georgia, featuring farm crops and vernacular buildings, and honoring the histories of African American farmers who have stewarded the land for generations; and in her use of organic and sustainable materials, from clay and wood to plants and site-specific land art.

As the essays herein examine, Carpenter's extensive research into African American farming communities deeply informs her work. Sculptures like the farm bowls are not merely representations of agricultural structures, or even portraits of individual

sites—rather, they are vessels of memory, embodying the stories of resilience, labor, and innovation that Carpenter pays tribute to. She has a keen understanding of the precarity felt by Black American farmers, who over the last century have lost more than twelve million acres of farmland due to inequitable access to markets and biased government policy, and her response is a celebration of the individual and collective beauty of these legacies. "The history of decline in numbers on rural farms can be attributed to systemic discrimination, mechanization, and the Great Migration north that occurred between 1910 and the early 1970s. But the story doesn't end there. There were many, many farms and gardens that remained in families sustained by those who did not migrate north and who were able to withstand the pressures of a dominant discriminatory culture. . . . People are going back to the land."[5] Carpenter is too, in her own way—revisiting, reconsidering, and rearticulating ideas and questions that have been central to her practice for decades, that have never lost their saliency, but that she is finding new ways to examine.

• •

Since her retirement from Swarthmore, Carpenter has had a creative renaissance, embarking on more ambitious projects and expanding upon her earlier series. "It's been an open door for me," she says, "in terms of developing more ambitious projects and working off earlier works. The *Mother Pin* series, the standing farm pieces, the wall pieces. All of these have generated a lot of new ideas. There's a good flow towards the new work that I'm doing."

That new work, including the pieces on view in *Home Bound in Wood, Steel, and Clay* at the Berman Museum in 2026, represents a continued exploration of themes deeply rooted in memory, heritage, and the land, embodying her evolution as an artist while maintaining a profound connection to her foundational inspirations. This period has seen her experimenting with scale and materials, resulting in works that are both monumental and intimate, personal—evidence of a dialogue with representation, a complex process of reasoning with the form, site, and purpose

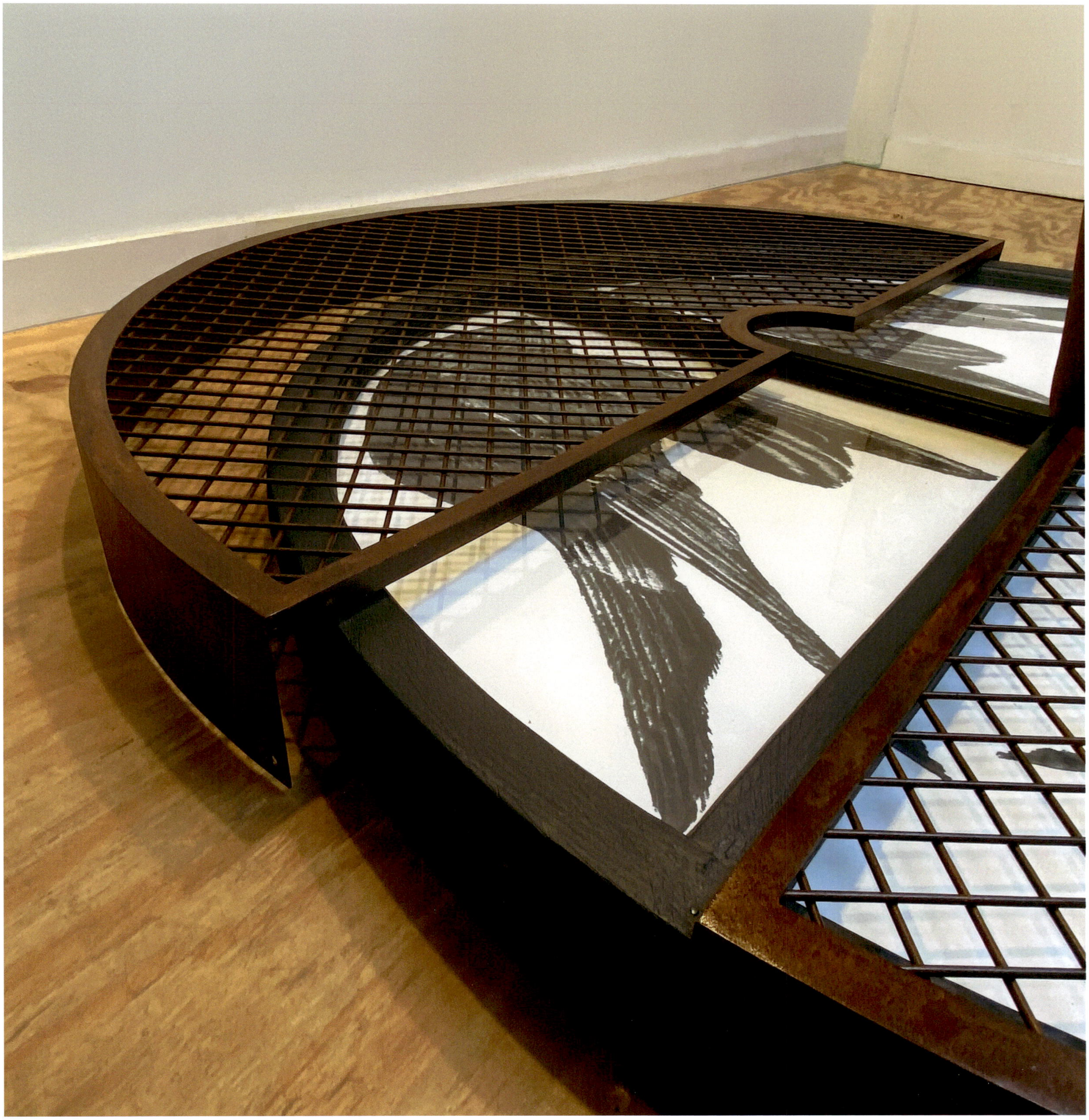

FIG. 5.4 *Release* (detail)

of her designs. How do elements combine to evoke the experience of a place, real or imagined? The narrative potency of Carpenter's sculptures is in their visual complexity, a unique logic belied by her frequent use of simple geometric or vernacular forms. The manipulation of those forms is clearly a source of joy and constant discovery for Carpenter, resulting in a diverse body of sculptural work that is cerebral, sensuous, and often celebratory. Light—a critical through line between her sculptural and agricultural works, the element that enables photosynthetic processes and teases perceptions of form and depth—dynamically affects how these works are experienced in space, yet another connecting link to the legacies of Black agricultural practice, land stewardship, and sustainability Carpenter engages in so much of her work.

Carpenter's ongoing dialogue with her own ancestry manifests physically and symbolically in works like *Mother Pin Ascending* (fig. 5.5), a triumphant addition to a series she has engaged with for decades, exploring notions of protection, community, and familial bonds. The new work makes a stark break from earlier mother pins, typically scaled in the twenty-inch range. This life-sized clothespin, an abstracted but clearly recognizable female form, stands approximately six feet tall, with a commanding physical presence. Here the form and symbolism of the mother pin is transformed into a much different kind of entity. More than an object one might view on a plinth or mounted on a wall, *Mother Pin Ascending* is totemic—a monument to a feminine lineage Carpenter has spent a lifetime seeking to represent.

The figure, Paulownia wood turned by sculptor Jack Larimore, is consistent with the form of the antique clothespin Carpenter has requisitioned for so much of her oeuvre. At this scale, the woodgrain is a key feature of the work, organically undulating around and through the figure like a garment. This effect is heightened by the light blue stain Carpenter chose as a surface treatment, drawing the wood grain into sharp contrast, which fades into a slight rust around the edges, nodding gently to the ruddy coloring of the sculpture's base. Standing atop a sculptural six-foot disc of steel—an exquisite material itself, splashed with subtle gold speckles, fabricated in partnership with Carriage Creative—the mother pin is self-aware in the space it occupies, a

phenomenon that feels somewhat new to Carpenter herself. She connects her interest in working at this scale to the monumental hügel gardens she designed for the Woodmere and Berman museums, which opened the possibility to think more expansively about space and her agency in inhabiting it. "I want these newer objects to feel as if they are full-fledged occupants of a space, rather than being adornments," she says, a sentiment that recalls hooks's reflections on liberation. "These pieces become substantial occupants of the spaces they're in." The collective components of the sculpture are simple, spare, yet its quietly imposing presence conveys a power that might be felt as almost shamanistic—a matriarchal force connecting the present to the past and refusing to let us forget.

Another significant expansion of Carpenter's practice is her foray into printmaking, which she incorporates into her new body of work in ways that speak to her experimental and curious approach to materials. *Home Bound in Wood, Steel, and Clay* includes three multimedia prints that integrate ceramic and aluminum elements. Small mother pins, bisected and affixed to handmade paper, are collaged over by deconstructed prints Carpenter created during her 2023 artist residency at the Brandywine Workshop and Archives in Philadelphia. "The print pieces came out of being frustrated with what the prints looked like originally," she told me. "I thought, I have to fix this. I have all this beautiful paper, and this print is just not working. So I kept working on it—I connected half mother pins to it, and suddenly I had a new series." She finds working with paper to be somewhat similar to working in clay. "I think about all of the different possibilities of combining materials and forms—that is something that I am absorbed with right now. That's where ideas are coming from, the combination of materials and how they function as a language of visual connection." As those connections are made across mediums, forms are transformed, and different points of entry are made accessible. Sentences, then stories, emerge from the unique vocabulary of shapes, forms, and materials Carpenter uses to convey a narrative.

Home Places (2025) is an ambitious evolution in Carpenter's exploration of these themes. Here, she engages the architectural form of a barn, or shed, as a site for both memory and

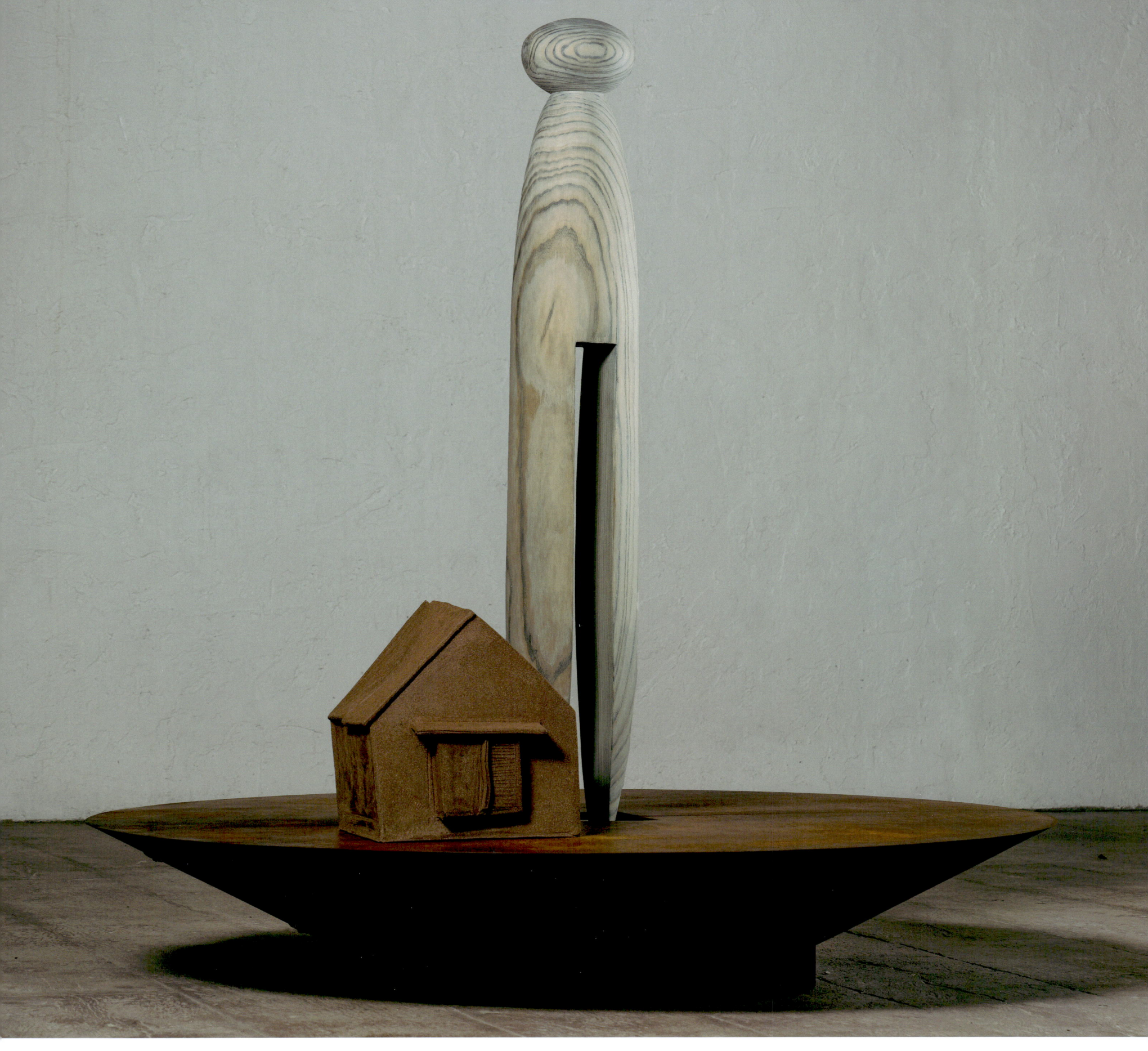

FIG. 5.5 *Mother Pin Ascending*, 2025, wood,
clay, and steel, 65 × 60 × 60 in. (Courtesy of the
Petrucci Family Foundation Collection of African
American Art)

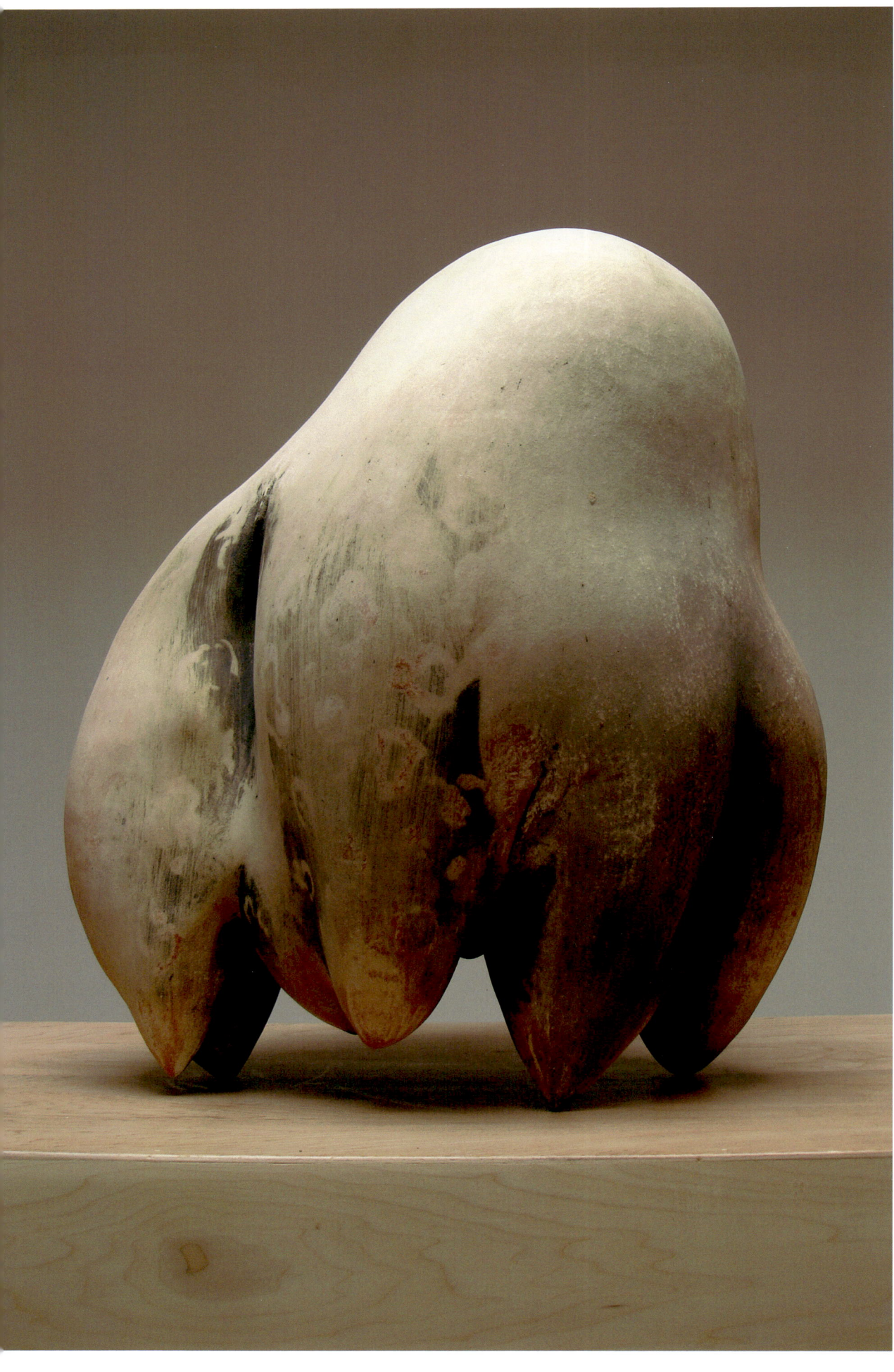

FIG. 5.6 *Bite Down*, 2006, clay, underglaze, and oxide, 26 × 22 × 12 in. (Collection of the artist)

memorialization, incorporating light, sound, moving image, and sculpture to create an immersive environment that honors the agricultural histories of Black farmers in the American South. Use of the ready-made, in this case a standard steel utility shed, is not typical for Carpenter. *Home Places* marks a point of clear departure from the organic, handmade forms and unobtrusive scale of her earlier work. Like the monumental *Mother Pin Ascending*, its intention is to take up and hold space. Constructed from sheet metal with one side left open, *Home Places* invites viewers to enter and engage with images and recordings collected during Carpenter's travels through the South. There is a light, joyful spirit reflected here, as Carpenter experiments with architecture within architecture—a space within a space, again engaging ideas of place-making and agency. The installation marks a culmination of Carpenter's longstanding interest in the intersection of sculpture, land cultivation, and cultural memory. Rather than simply recreating scenes of rural life, *Home Places* acts as a living archive, embedded with personal and collective histories—a testament to the endurance of Black agricultural traditions and to Carpenter's ability to translate personal narratives into forms that resonate with universal metaphors of nature and the body.

In *Shine: The Visual Economy of Light in African Diasporic Aesthetic Practice* (2015), author Krista Thompson notes that "Black subjects have historically been denied access to the mechanisms of visual representation and thus have developed alternative ways of producing and controlling their image."[6] Carpenter's integration of ceramics, found materials, and large-scale installations exemplifies this intervention, challenging traditional sculptural norms and embedding Black histories into tangible forms. Incorporating sound, light, and moving images, *Home Places* can be understood in this context as an act of reclaiming historical presence.

Among them, *Home Places, Mother Pin Ascending*, and Carpenter's prints show clear signs of the connective tissue that brings cohesion to this new body of work. But there is also evidence of shared ideas with the *Animated Leaf* sculptures installed in the adjacent gallery at the Berman Museum, a series Carpenter began in the early 2000s when a walk through her garden sparked a question about what a leaf might look like if it were animated in three dimensions—"what would happen if the thing inhaled." The resulting ceramic sculpture, *Of and About the Skin* (2006) (see p. 47), was the first in what would become a series of leaves, typically standing over two feet tall, that are bulbous, fleshy, almost animal in their presence and form. Improbable in the balance with which they stand, the works reflect a sense of movement, growth, evolution, change. Sensual and at times almost grotesque, the leaf sculptures document Carpenter's process of working through conceptions of space and volume—how to manipulate and stretch them in ways that subvert the familiar. She finds endless inspiration in the sublimity and fractals of nature, where self-similar patterns—not identical, but loose, soft—offer a sort of comfort in their irregularity, speaking to our human instincts about space and place.

This experimental approach to imagining two-dimensional forms in the round also informed Carpenter's earlier *Farm Portraits*, where, using Westmacott's maps of African American farms in Georgia, South Carolina, and Alabama as a guide, she created sculptural documentations of the farms in clay, each named for the farmer who owned and cultivated the land. It was this process of visual translation and naming that led Carpenter to embark on her own project to document the stories of Black farmers in Georgia and South Carolina in the early 2010s. "It wasn't a subject that artists wanted to take on. It was something people wanted to leave behind. But I saw it and continue to see it as this incredibly resonant experience of Black people on the land here in America. Not just as enforced laborers, but as creative stewards of the land, making their mark and doing it in a way that other people didn't. [Farming] was a source of survival. Owning land is critical in this country, because if you don't own land, you are a displaced person. Even if your land is just your twenty-five-square-foot backyard—own it. Don't give it up, try not to sell it. If you can, keep it in the family. So that whole idea of land and Black people on the land—that narrative is underlying everything."

Carpenter's work is deeply informed by her relationship with materials, which is often circumstantial: highly specific, localized, informed by and responding to immediate environment. Clay, her primary medium, is a tactile link to the earth, a foundational substance she builds on with organic material and found objects to create sculptural vessels and shapes metaphorically representing land cultivated by African Americans, and her belief in the importance of creating "one's own foundation"—a conviction steeped in a deep understanding of the historical inequities and sustained, systemic discrimination that have been devastating for rural communities of color. Beyond clay, Carpenter's material choices reflect and deepen her conceptual investigations of Earth through several other literal associations, whether intentionally or subliminally. Ceramics, hügels, gardens, and farms are, of course, iterations of earth itself. Plant life is central to her agricultural practice, but also to her recent experiments with handmade paper, and the turned wood of *Mother Pin Ascending*. Carpenter marshals materials that are reciprocally responsive to and dependent on the subjects—human, vegetal, place-based— she engages, mirroring ways in which communities have historically shaped their environments, using available resources to build, sustain, and protect their livelihoods. Exploring the physicality of creation and the stories embedded in the land, the textures, forms, and finishes of her pieces often mimic natural patterns, a signal of her reverence for the people, processes, and productivity that have kept those histories vital. The rich dimensionality of this layering of mediums, and the earthen sensuality with which many of Carpenter's forms are imbued, invite us to come to the work with our own associations and memories, and to find something new among the familiar.

Carpenter's engagement with community extends beyond the themes and processes she explores in her work. "My greatest strengths tend to be from the observations of other strong people," she has reflected.[7] She frequently works with collaborators, finding inspiration and mutual support from former students, other artists, and institutional partners. A recent example is a partnership with Philadelphia's Colored Girls Museum: Carpenter curated a garden and walkway when the museum was granted zoning approval as a library and cultural institution in 2024. For Carpenter, to be a steward of place means more than caring for the land, though that is always a central concern. It means being a neighbor, a mentor, a partner—being in community with those who share the spaces we inhabit. The present multi-venue

exhibition examining Carpenter's work across her career is a fitting way to acknowledge and celebrate the commitment to collective care the artist has embodied to such noteworthy effect.

When I ask her to reflect on where she is now—what forces or personal qualities have gotten her here, and what she's looking forward to—Carpenter talks about how much of her process has had to do with consistency of practice. "Even if you don't have anything, show up because something is going to happen. That's been true for me." She ruminates on the importance of learning how to "notice what you notice," of documenting the things that catch your attention. The objects and elements she has noticed over her life have come back to feed into her creative practice over and over again, often in unexpected ways. Creative collaboration has opened new doors for an expanded practice, too. "Some of the things I'm doing now, I get fabricators to help me. I get an idea, and I think, I don't know the first thing about welding. But there are people who can do it, and if I provide them with a good enough drawing, and I'm there when they're doing it, then that collaboration is how you get it done. . . . So that's where I am right now, and it's so much fun. You get to work with these brilliant people you might never otherwise cross paths with. And you learn the process."

And it is finding joy in process, ultimately, that best characterizes Carpenter's practice, one of constant growth, adaptation, and regeneration—of transformation. Ideas follow each other in what appears to be a constant flow, one series leading naturally into another. Reuse and reconstitution have been integral to this consistency and the development of her work over time. "Until [an object] is out of my studio and in somebody's collection, it's fair game. It's part of my resources. I can go back into pieces and start again. . . . It's all there. There's an advantage to accumulation," she says. She frequently returns to earlier work to harvest elements she sees new uses for, implementing them in ways that are at times continuous, at others completely new. There is no preciousness about how she views her earlier works—they, like many of the objects that catch Carpenter's attention, are subject to the tireless curiosity that keeps her experimenting with new and found materials, and with expanded dimensionality and scale. This dual focus on past and future is particularly evident in her recent projects, which use her established visual lexicon and mastery of materials to speak to a forward-looking vision.

"You know, the idea of success is that you can make your art and you have an audience. And I did. I didn't feel any pressure. I had a good teaching job at Swarthmore College, which allowed me to meet a lot of people and interact with all these other academic disciplines that were very stimulating. I've always been nourished by my life as an artist."

Carpenter's recent work represents a profound exploration of identity, collective memory, and community. While many of her sculptures are documents of specific places and people, they yet transcend their contexts to speak to universal themes: resilience, familial legacy, and the human connection to the land. As she continues to push the boundaries of her practice, the work serves as a powerful testament to the enduring significance of story-telling and the transformative potential of creative expression, reminding us of the deep, often unseen labor that shapes the spaces we inhabit and the stories we carry forward.

NOTES

1. bell hooks, *Art on My Mind* (New Press, 1995).

2. Richard J. Powell, *Black Art: A Cultural History*, 3rd edition (Thames and Hudson, 2021).

3. Ceramic Artist Syd Carpenter on "Discovering a History: The Farm Portraits" (audio transcript), Swarthmore College, 2015.

4. Syd Carpenter: Farm Bowls & Mother Pins, 2020–2022. *Ceramics Now*, August 11, 2022.

5. Discovering a History.

6. Krista Thompson, *Shine: The Visual Economy of Light in African Diasporic Aesthetic Practice* (Duke University Press, 2015).

7. "Syd Carpenter: Places of Our Own," Woodmere, 2022.

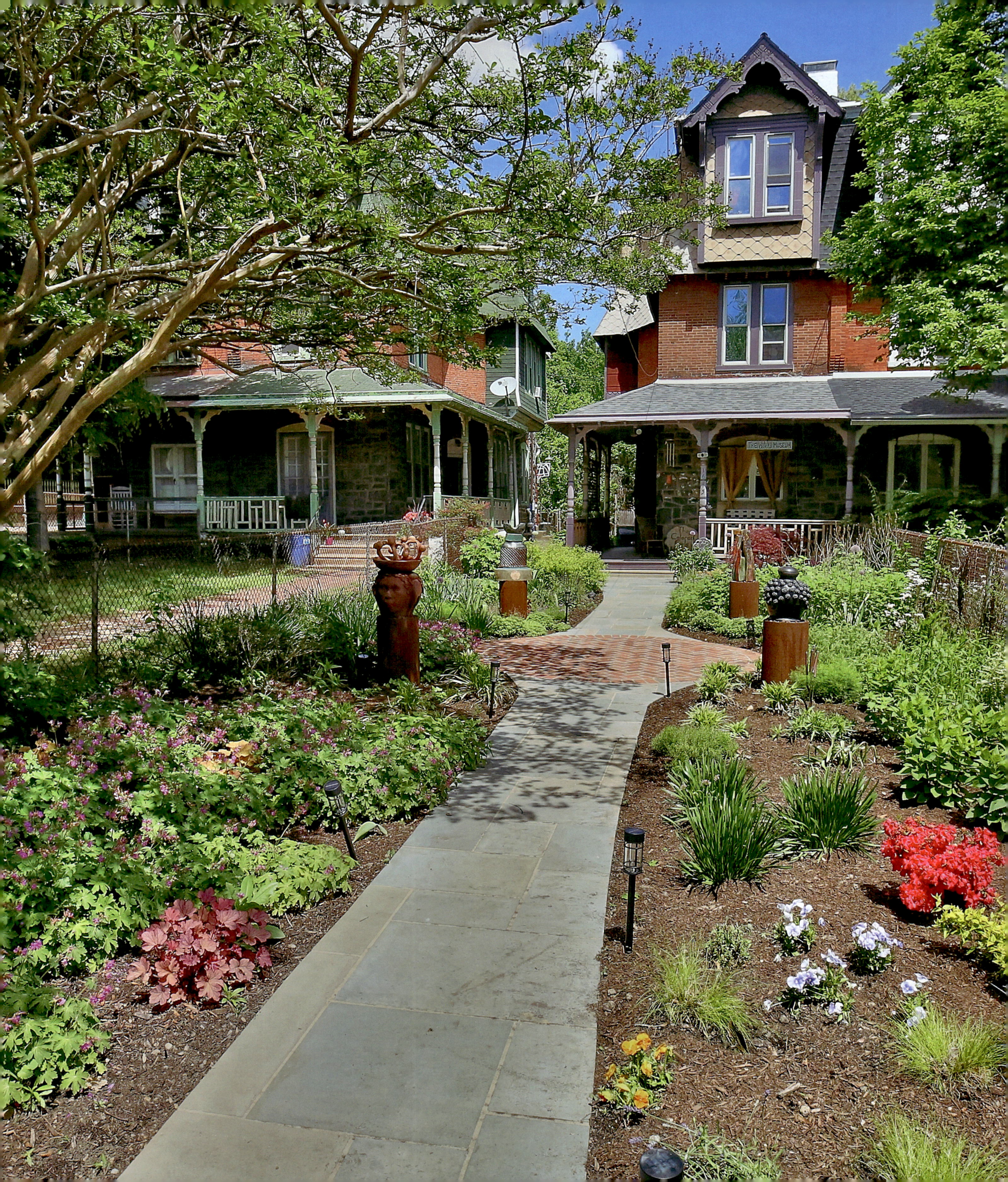

A Conversation at the Colored Girls Museum with
Syd Carpenter, Linda Goode Bryant, and Vashti DuBois

MODERATED BY WILLIAM R. VALERIO

VASHTI DUBOIS Thank you for being here, everyone, and especially Linda, for making the journey to Philadelphia today, specially to visit the Colored Girls Museum. We are a unique museum, dedicated to the experiences of Black women and girls. It is a truly an honor.

WILLIAM R. VALERIO Thank you, Vashti, and the honor is ours. Linda, when I think about your accomplishments, both at Just Above Midtown and Project Eats, your history and interests seem to rhyme with those of the Colored Girls Museum and Woodmere in the context of the partnership we both share with Syd and the part of her practice dedicated to outdoor spaces and gardens. Just Above Midtown Gallery, the alternative space (1974–1986), was dedicated to providing a platform for Black artists back when there were none, and it launched many important careers. I should say for readers that my internships there—in my college years—formed my beliefs about what arts organizations should be, and I mean this in a spiritual, creative, welcoming, inclusive sense. Boy, did I have a lot to learn! Now your journey with Project Eats brings together creativity and greenspaces. Both of them seem mission-connected to Vashti's project here in the amazing front garden at the Colored Girls Museum.

DUBOIS We should say that garden project is fully Syd's.

SYD CARPENTER Before I arrived on the scene here, this garden was well tended by Vashti. It was well designed, perennials undulating in a kind of peak order manner through the seasons. The first thing I wanted to change was the path from the street to the house itself. It was a flat, uneventful passage with no texture or sense of pattern, nothing going on with it. And there certainly wasn't an entrance experience to announce the special aspects of the place or catch your attention if driving in a car. There was a sign that said Colored Girls Museum, but basically there was an anonymity about it. Unless you knew about it and knew to come, there was nothing to announce it as a museum, certainly not a Colored Girls museum, certainly not evocative of a culture and a history. And so my thought, when Vashti approached me to do something, was to emphasize the identity of the place as a protected sanctuary. An inviting experience is the key, countering the idea of museums as exclusive. Exclusivity is something I'm against. Vashti doesn't want this to be a clubhouse. This is a place where everyone is welcome. I remember when I was a teenager in Philadelphia knowing that my calling was to be an artist, but I was somewhat intimidated by the museums of our city, with

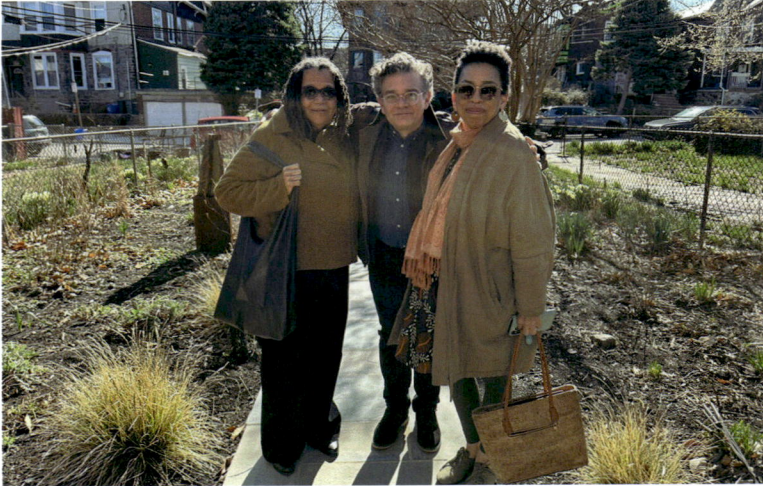

their grand stairs and towers. The icebreakers were the teachers who took us on field trips to the museums. So anyway, I want this museum, The Colored Girls Museum, to be the opposite, 180 degrees away from that kind of interface with its community.

GOODE BRYANT It also seems like a place for a visitor to activate, to ignite with, to connect to your own story.

DUBOIS That's what this place is about.

GOODE BRYANT Before we talk about the design, the sculptures, and the plants, I'm curious about what you imagined when you first envisioned this garden and imagined what it would be when you walked in?

CARPENTER Luxuriant growth! Looking at what was here, there was already good things in the garden, some of which we retained. Other things we have completely dug up. One of the big desires of Vashti was to have a Japanese maple here, and that was one of the first plantings. Also, we envisioned a place that visitors could recognize from the gardens and plantings of childhood, together with new things that were unusual and of course herbs because of the importance of herbs and health. And being able to see the garden as a source of rejuvenation, as a source of something that you could grab onto, you could go up and grab a piece of lavender or pick some of the herbs.

GOODE BRYANT Can we talk about the special sculpture sitting on this stone slab at the entrance to the porch?

CARPENTER That's a work by the artist MaPó Kinnord-Payton (fig. 6.2). See, it's actually a lantern. She's an artist of New Orleans, and we have it because when Katrina destroyed so much of the city, including the artist's studio, I invited her to come to Swarthmore (where I was teaching) as a visiting artist. She needed escape from the horror of what was happening in New Orleans. She built that piece while she was here. She's a phenomenal sculptor, a wonderful artist. When she was ready to return to New Orleans, she couldn't take it home with her. I got it fired for her,

and it sat it my office at Swarthmore until I retired. I wanted the school to keep it for its art collection, so I left it there, but that didn't work out. A couple of students recognized its beauty and took it to their dorm room. I asked for it back. They gave it to me, and it belongs here now.

VALERIO It looks like a seated figure, a welcoming figure perhaps?

CARPENTER Yes, a welcoming figure. When the spiraea are blooming and the azalea is leafed out, she becomes the star of the garden.

VALERIO As your eye revolves around the figure, you find the heart shape toward the back, which is again, a welcoming, warm discovery.

CARPENTER Right, because it does make you want to come around it. And when you find the heart, it is nice.

GOODE BRYANT Opposite the sculpture is another greeting. Right?

CARPENTER In terms of symbolism, I don't know what the maples represent in traditional art, but it's a reference to a kind of garden: the serenity of a Japanese garden, and it lends that kind of elegance. And because Vashti loved it!

DUBOIS I did!

CARPENTER She wanted the beauty of a Japanese maple in this yard, and we found one.

VALERIO And the empty chair?

CARPENTER The Japanese maple and the chair go together, in conversation with each other. The seatless, old wooden frame of the chair is a sculpture itself, it lends a sense of the presence of somebody having been here before, maybe the person who lived

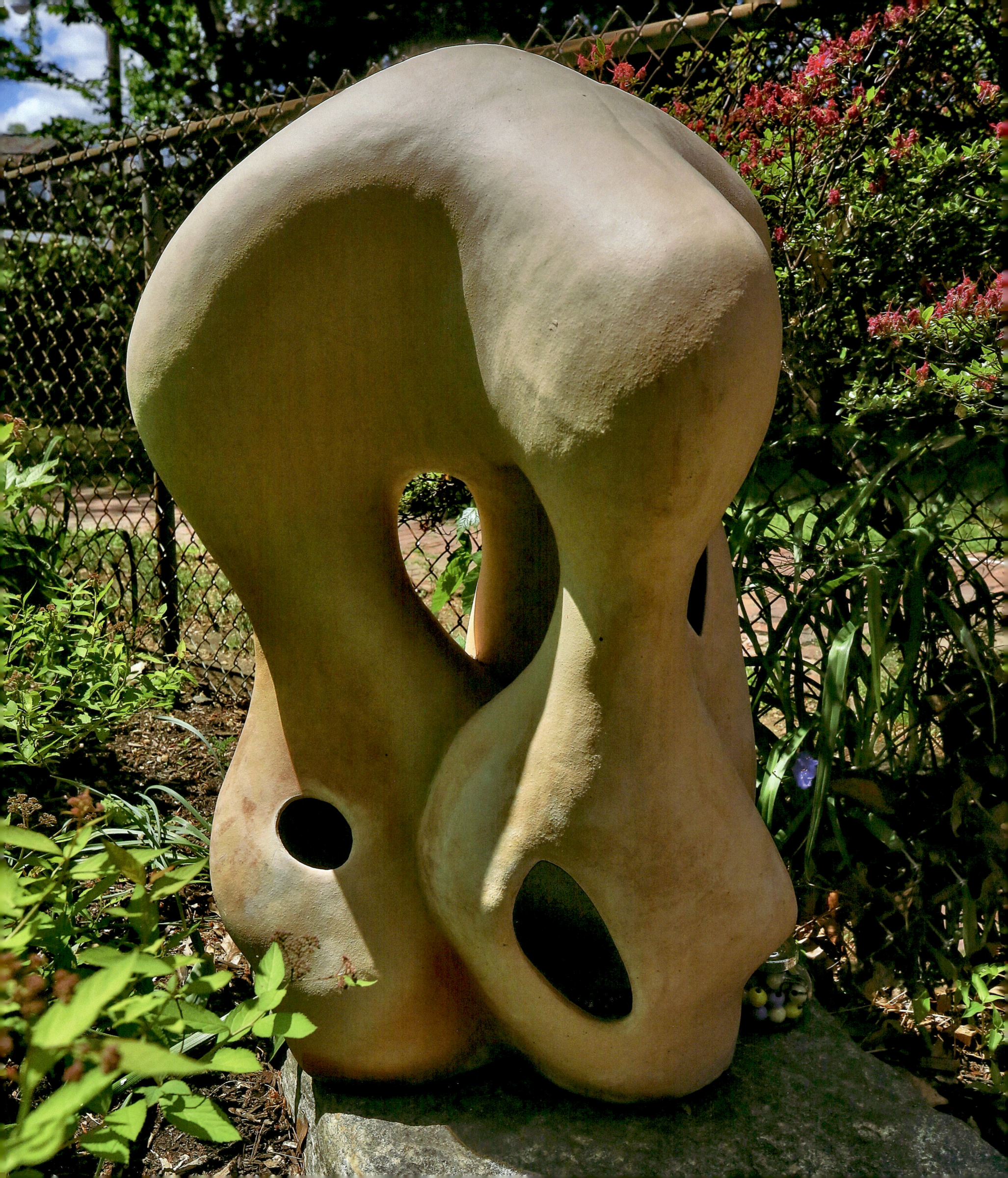

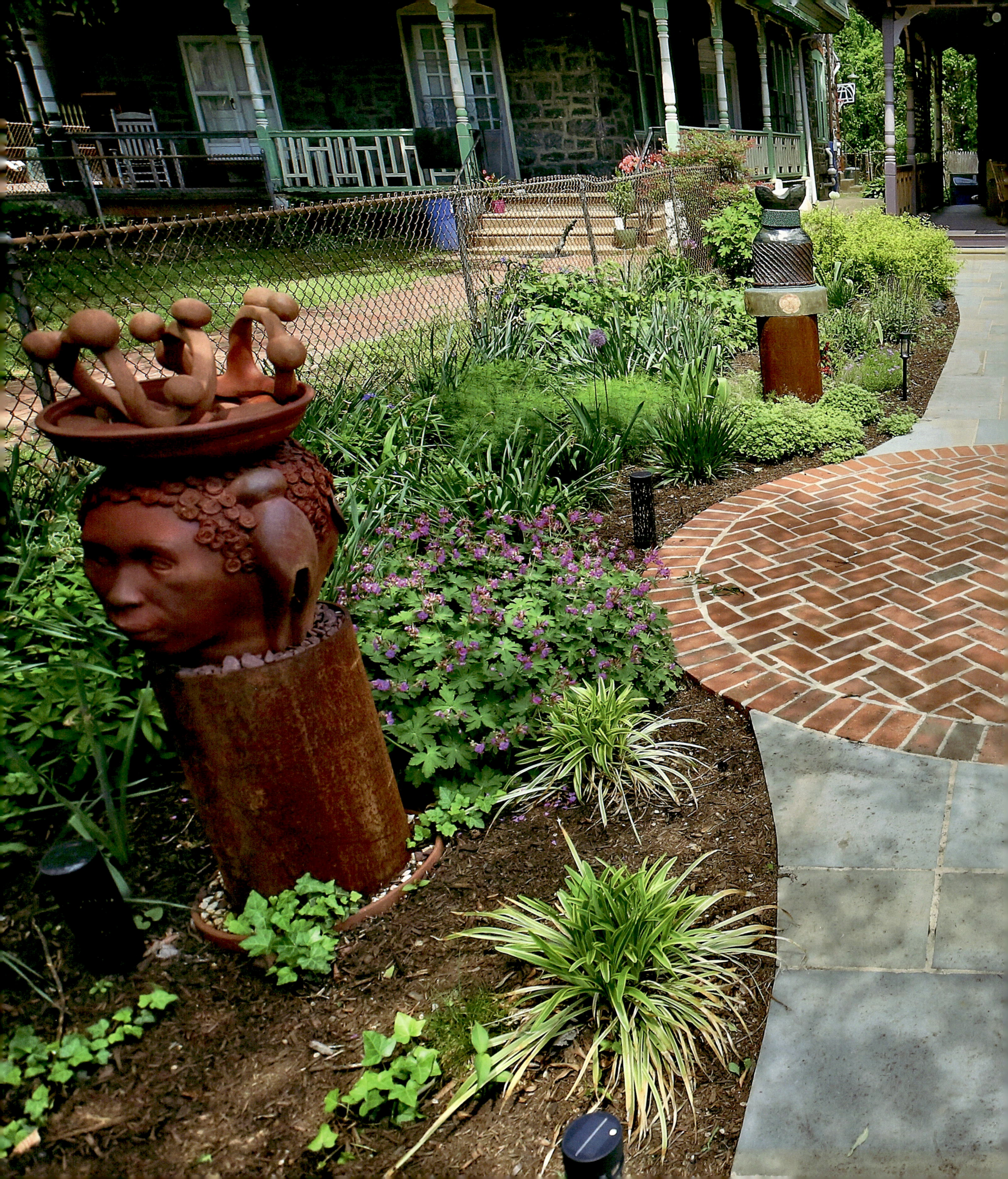

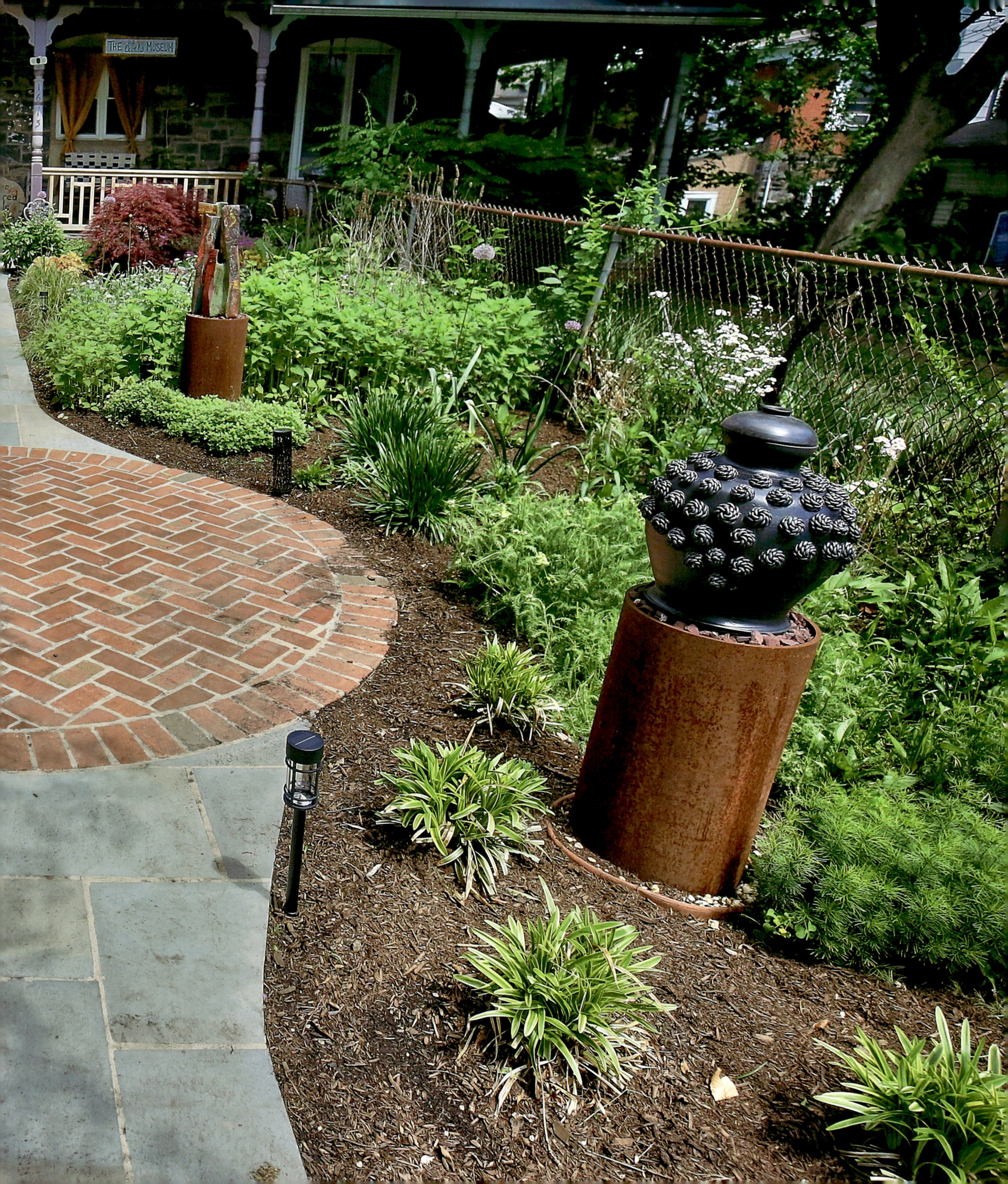

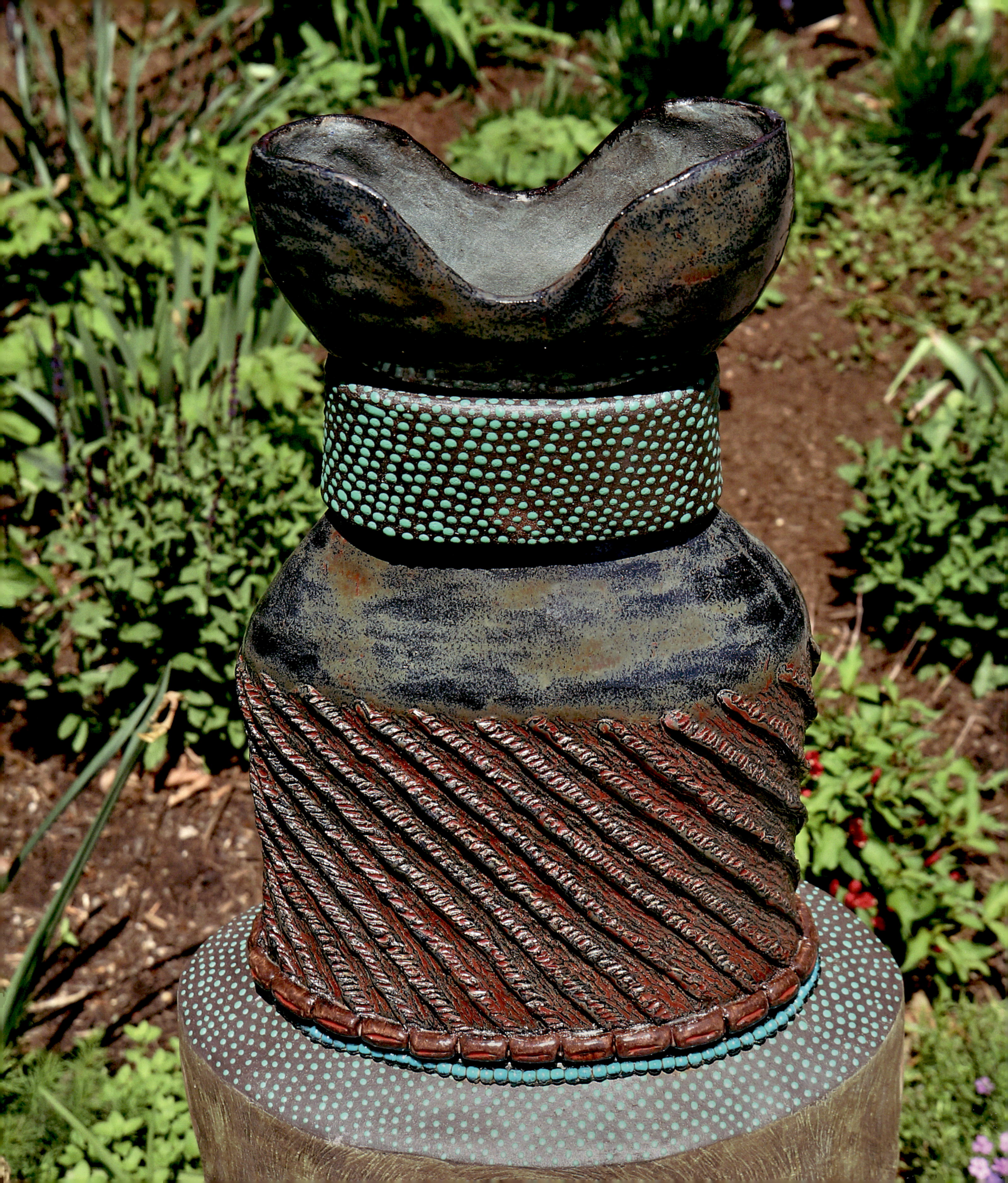

FIG. 6.3 (PREVIOUS SPREAD)   Garden Plaza, The
Colored Girls Museum

FIG. 6.4   Angelica Pozo, *Pot* (The Colored Girls
Museum)

in the house a while ago. The wood is also in a state of decline,
while the tree is growing, a kind of resonance about process,
change, aging, and hopefully also making visitors think about
the amazing woodwork on the house itself and the museum. To
me, the maple, which is about Vashti, with the chair are about
the house and the place.

VALERIO   What's also so interesting in the relationship between
that tree and that chair is the play of scale. If you look at that tree,
which I realize, it's a young specimen, but it has the form of an
adult treat in miniature. And so, if you allow your mind to take
that as an adult tree in miniature like the gorgeous magnolia next
door, it makes the empty chair seem monumental and important.

CARPENTER   That's about this place, and it makes for a meaningful, symbolic entrance moment I think and I totally agree with
your perception of this.

GOODE BRYANT   I feel that presence of a human being in the
stripped-down worn chair, it's what I love about all this. There's
a history of whoever that chair held and supported. It also speaks
of future because you were talking about this being a space where
you're invited in. What better than a chair?

VALERIO   I've been too much trained in art history not to mention the relationship it conjures to the chair that Van Gogh
painted in his bedroom at Arles, which, as we've been discussing,
represents the idea of a chair that is symbolic of people: people
who had been, people who perhaps are being felt in their absence
or loss.

GOODE BRYANT   Let's move back away from the house one more
step and talk about this circle-shaped space you created.

CARPENTER   We refer to this as "the Plaza," a circle of brick pav-
ing in a beautiful pattern that we dance on, where we stop, slow
down (fig. 6.3). A place to sit ourselves so the approach to the
house becomes slow. You have to stop and then take notice of
the four sculpture pots, works of art that are the guardians of

the space. The space is for gathering. It's circular. It breaks
up the linear. And allows us to be collective and experience
something together.

DUBOIS   One of the things that Syd said when she designed the
path is: This is the Colored Girls Museum. It has to be warm
space. Straight-line entrances can be phallic. We needed to break
that up. And when you look downs at this space from the third
floor, it has the curves of a woman's body.

CARPENTER   To me, that was one of the most exciting parts of
this. It took a long time to actually get the artists to make these
pots and get them to me. They are guardians on one level, but
also welcoming figures. There's a certain kind of obviously organic
quality that speaks across the space of the circle. The works are
by Angelica Pozo, Sana Musasama, Yinka Orafidiya, and myself.
Each one is an ornament, a plant-like ornament that speaks
to stability, but also to the female figure, reflective of a kind of
strong femininity, especially Angelica's work. Let's start talking
about Angelica.

She lives and works in Cleveland, and there's a majesty to all
that she does. First, I love the colors that are showing up in that,
nuanced and beautiful. Her mother was dressmaker, and that's
the form, the body and the dress.

GOODE BRYANT   It's very evocative. Folks can stay with it a while.
It's not an idealistic or conventional looking pot, none of these
are. And there's a lot of information in each one, and here especially, pattern and color. So once again, a time to pause.

CARPENTER   It's early in the season now, but there will be herbs
and all kinds of wonderful things growing up, a lot of movement,
shifting, and blowing around. There are some tall grasses and low
grasses that will be in a kind of dance, some of them more blue,
some more green. And here's some artemisia coming up, that's
gray. One of the things we're trying to do is to make the fence participate as opposed to looking so hard, like a barrier. We're going
to be putting some clematis in there and honeysuckle to soften it
and create fragrance. The pleasure of being a gardener is to stand

FIG. 6.5   Sana Musasama, *House Series, Returning to Ourselves*, 2024, ceramic, 24 × 16 × 11 in. (The Colored Girls Museum)

there and notice things happening and seeing combinations happen. The garden invites you, compels you to stop and say, oh, look at that combination! What's happening with those two together?

GOODE BRYANT   How would you describe what it feels like to put your hand in soil?

CARPENTER   Putting my hand in soil is like going home.

GOODE BRYANT   But what does that feel like?

CARPENTER   It makes me feel like this is what I should be doing right now. Because that's always an issue when you're a person who's become accustomed to seeing yourself as being productive. Productivity comes out of well, what should I be doing to produce? And so when I am working in the soil, I immediately get the sense of this is exactly what I'm supposed to be doing. This is not in any way a distraction. I'm not doing this to distract me or divert from something else that's supposedly more useful. I'm doing this with intent that is OK. When my hands are in the soil, I know this is the right thing to do. Whatever I do here is going to be good for the planet. I can't do anything wrong by doing this, OK? And so in terms of the sense of producing effectively, the soil gets me to reach back into myself to some kind of core or root because I think that that is who I really am. My grandmother, Indiana Hutson, and my mother, Ernestine Carpenter—who all my mother pins are about—were major gardeners. My grandmother Indiana had a garden in Pittsburgh that was pretty well known. It was very beautiful with sunflowers and vegetables, and she was able to share all of the produce she grew with her neighbors, friends, and family. And my mother was more ornamental in her garden, which is what my own garden is. The whole idea of putting my hands in the soil, knowing that that was at the root of so much of what sustains me spiritually and allows me to make art.

GOODE BRYANT   I'm from Ohio, same generation. And one of the things that developed within the Black community were these flower shows where women in the neighborhoods would grow their flowers, display them in arrangements, and compete in the shows.

CARPENTER   I knew that kind of stuff was happening, but in my family, especially for my grandmother, it was mostly about growing food. Then a generation later, my mother worked for Doctor Salk. She was in his lab. A lab worker doing the test and studying science through the microscope. They also did tests with chickens and rabbits. Sometimes, the ones that survived the tests would be brought home and they would run around in the back garden, so although her gardening sensibility was ornamental, it was kind of like a farm.

GOODE BRYANT   One of my grandmothers had chickens, and I remember as a little girl, her stooping over and pulling up her skirt and ringing its neck. And the eggs!

CARPENTER   Yeah, I also remember some dispatching of chicken. Dispatching. It was practical, and we learned that they weren't pets. No, no, no.

VALERIO   Your grandmother's farm was what period of the twentieth century?

CARPENTER   World War II and the 1940s were a pressing context always, so there was an urgency. And on top of that, she had seven kids. Four of her own, and three others she took in and raised. There was a strong sense of "reality" to it all.

GOODE BRYANT   Can I ask what part of Pittsburgh?

CARPENTER   The garden looked out on the Monongahela River across at the mills. This was the steel capital of America. The steel mills are still there, and some parts of it are touristy now because those buildings are beautiful industrial architecture, visually powerful. However, my grandfather, my father, and other family members worked in those steel mills and that . . . it was hell. They didn't consider it to be beautiful in those days.

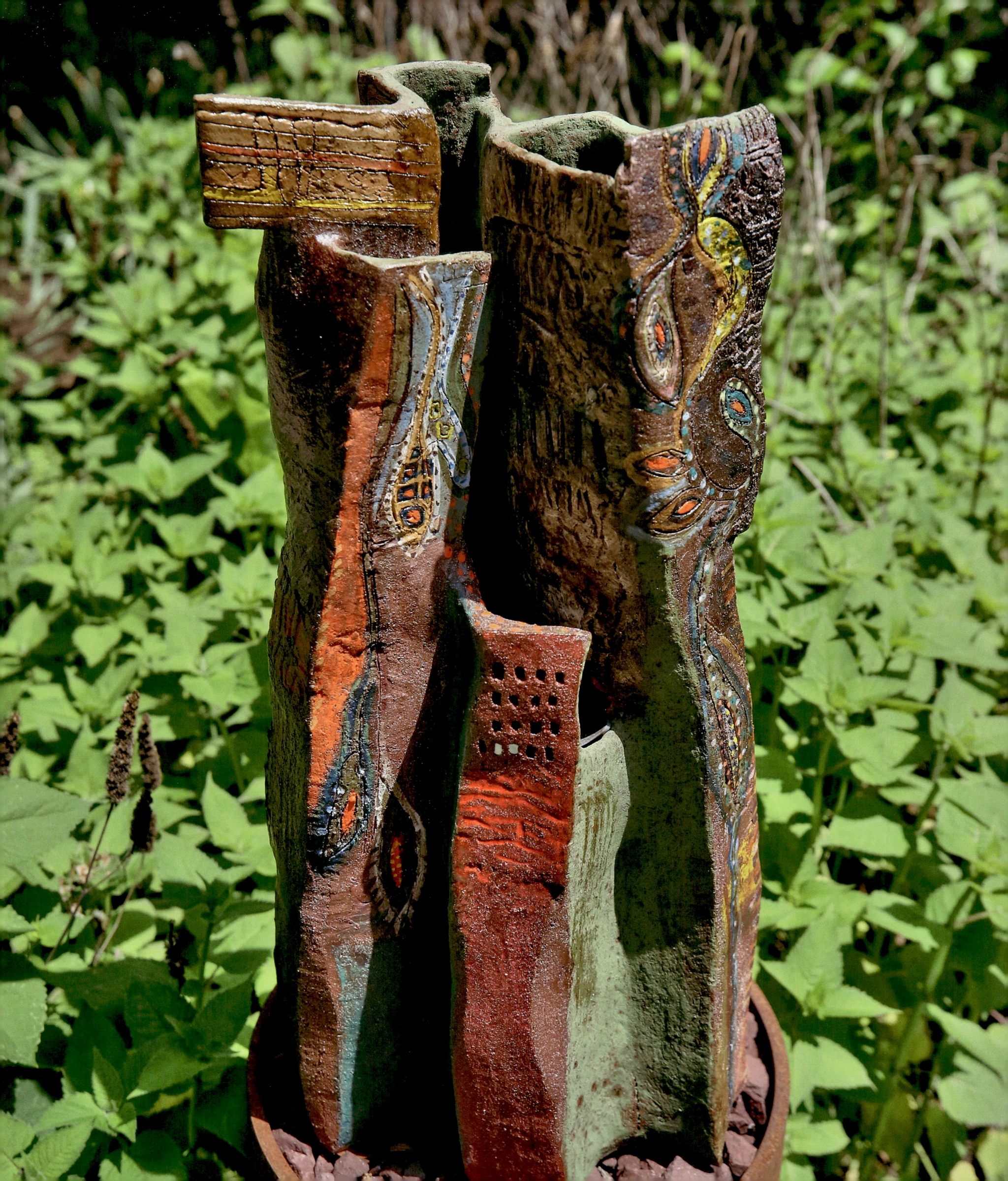

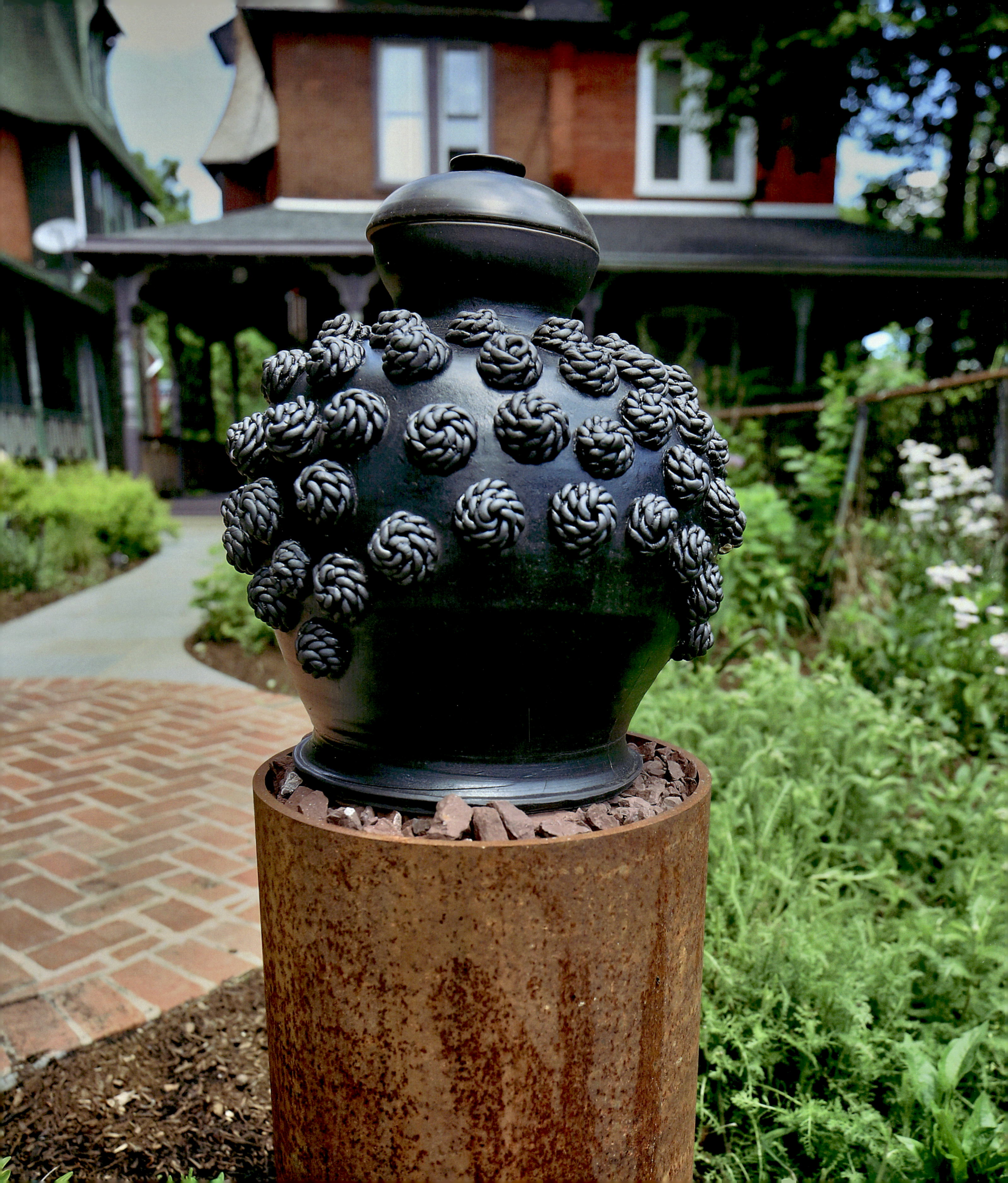

FIG. 6.6 Yinka Orafidiya, *Pot* (The Colored Girls Museum)

FIG. 6.7 Syd Carpenter, *She Still Hears Me*, 2023, ceramic, 28 × 15 × 15 in. (The Colored Girls Museum)

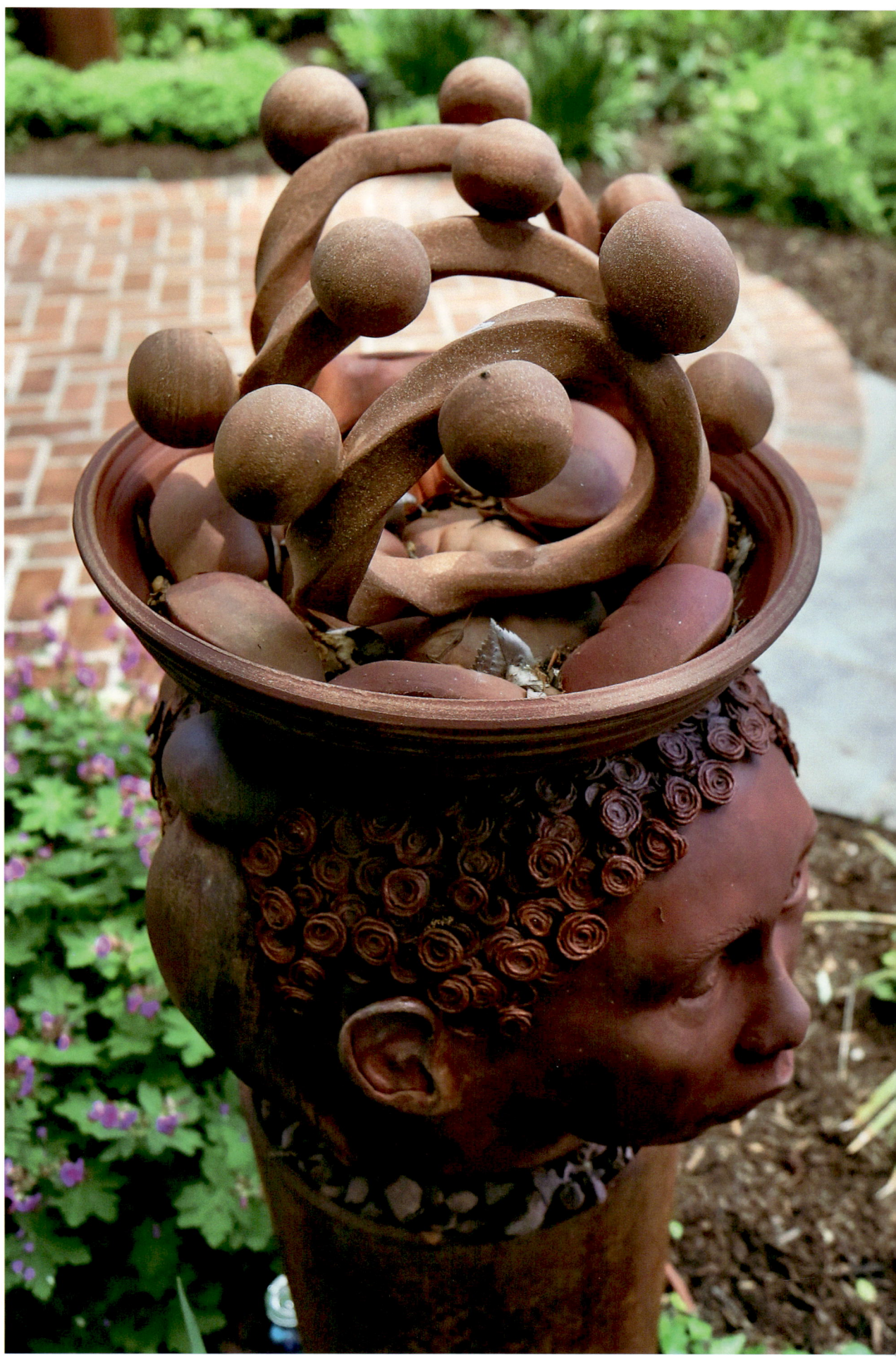

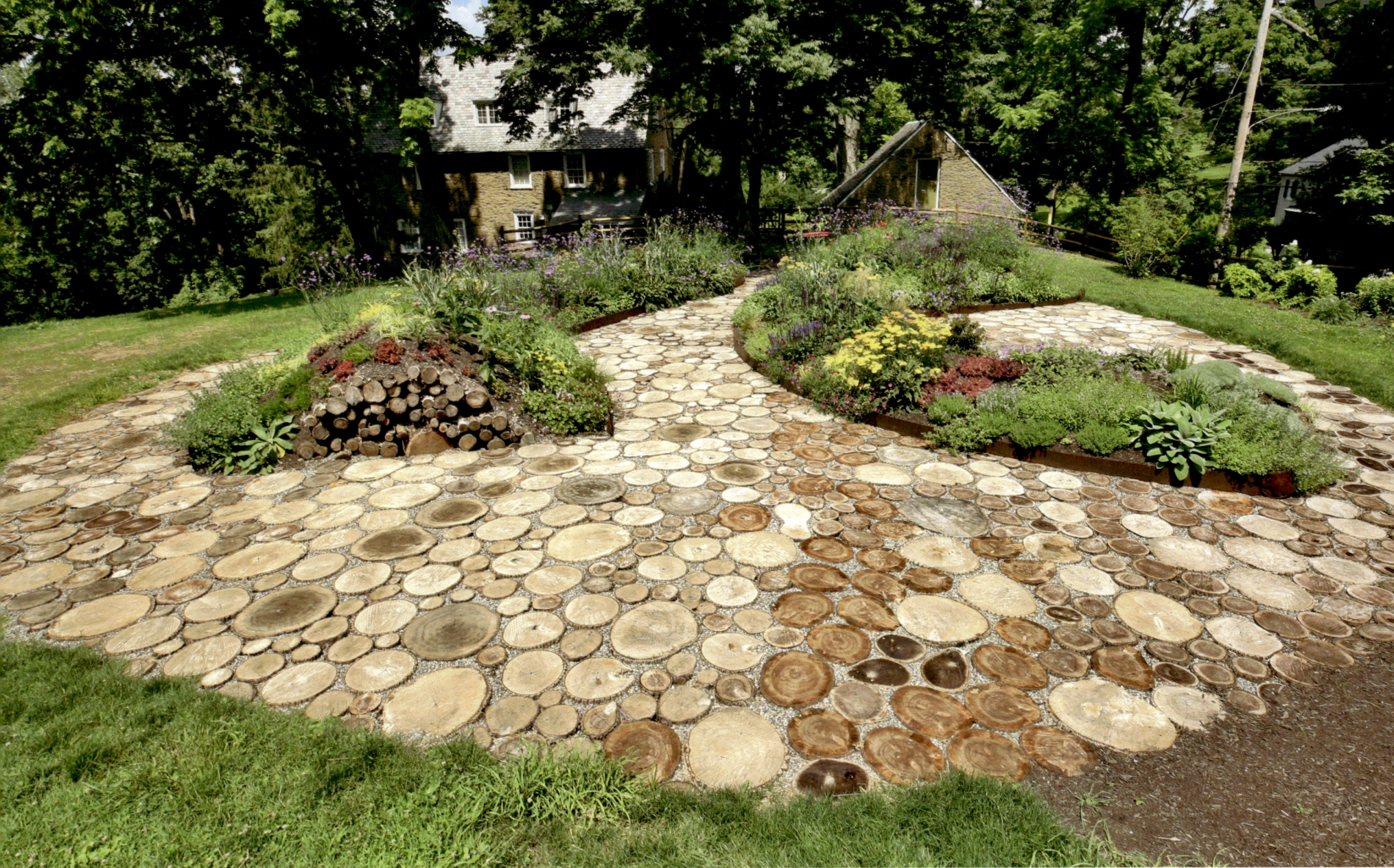

FIG. 6.8   Syd Carpenter and Steve Donegan,
La Cresta, 2021, hügel garden (Woodmere)

VALERIO I have to ask you about the pedestals for these four sculptures. The industrial steel tubes might resonate with that modernist industrial aesthetic.

CARPENTER Initially, I thought that the four sculptures would stand directly on the ground on shallow slabs, and they just weren't presenting well. So I went to good old Fazzio's, the metals supplier just over the bridge from Philly in New Jersey, and they had endless miles of this rusted, steel tubing in different diameters. You could do a whole garden with it and it would be a stunner. But these four pedestals, tubes filled with gravel, are the perfect resolution in height, color, texture. They're just right and not going anywhere.

GOODE BRYANT Can I ask you about native plants?

CARPENTER They're mostly native plants here: monarda (bee balm), Agastache (anise), achillea (yarrow), grasses, and artemisia. Native plants are adapted to the place, and they nurture the insects and microorganisms that are also adapted to the place evolutionarily. And we did get rid of some not natives that were invasives. But that said, I'm not a purist, and there's also a function to a plant that's non-native, if it's just the right color, texture, or accent, or brings a special kind of beauty (if it becomes invasive, it's no longer beautiful). But in thinking about the environment, I want to attract insects, I want to attract wildlife. Well, Bill, but then there are the voles in our hügels!

GOODE BRYANT Voles in the hügels?

CARPENTER The hügels are an amazing kind of planting system that originated in Northern European countries. The Vikings used them in their frigid climates. The word "hügel" or hill in German is the recent name of the horticultural practice, and it was revived in the 1960s. It's actually a type of raised bed: You start with a trench in the ground, and you load it up and create a hill with logs, then branches, and then other compostable materials. Finally your last layer is about eight to ten inches of soil, and so what you've made is this mound. What's beautiful about them is you can see the ends of the logs on both ends, and as the logs and

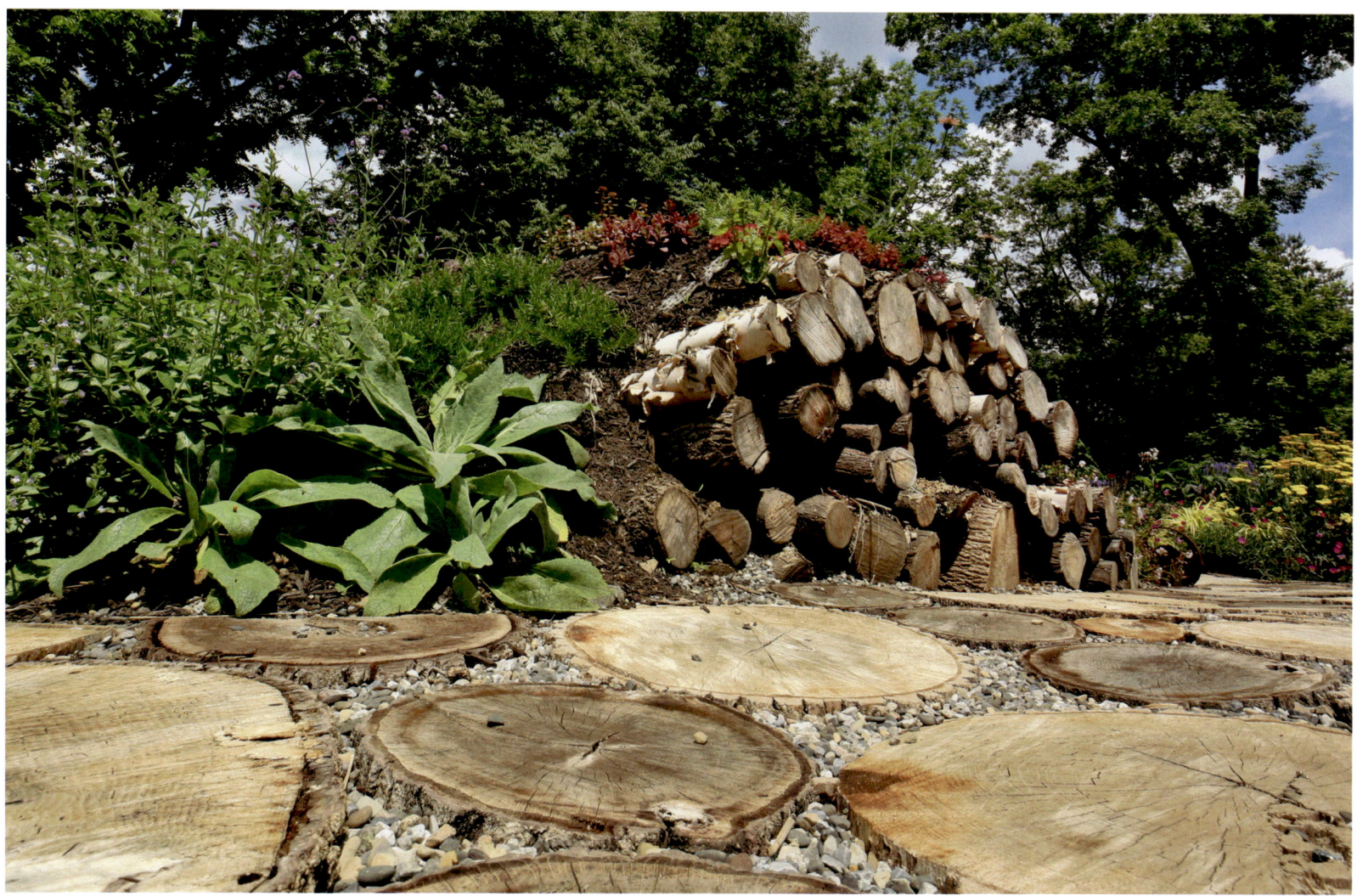

FIG. 6.9   Syd Carpenter and Steve Donegan,
La Cresta, 2021, hügel garden (Woodmere)

other materials start to break down, they give off heat so you can plant into the later season. And so that was great in Scandinavia where the summers are short. You also get a sunny and a shady side of the hügels because they are a hill, and that works for different plants.

VALERIO When I learned about hügels from the landscape architect Darren Damone, who was then part of the team at the firm Andropogon (with whom we are still working), I reached out to Syd, knowing her passion for gardening, and asked if she and Steve (Syd's husband, the artist Steve Donegan) would be interested in designing and building a hügel with us at Woodmere. We were thinking about it as a kind of earthwork garden sculpture. Syd and Steve's hügels, titled *La Cresta*, are actually two curving mound shapes that speak to each other like large, fish-shaped, yin-yang forms. And they are in a defined circular paved space.

CARPENTER And yes, we wanted to attract creatures like birds and insects, but then came the voles. We didn't realize that the structure of the hügel is the perfectly warm, luxury hotel for

voles, and they were eating our plants from below, root first. It has been a battle. And the deer!

VALERIO The voles are worse than the deer, who graze occasionally and do some damage, but our plant choices—lots of alliums and grasses, feverfew, sages, are mostly deer resistant. But the voles eating the allium bulbs from below I wasn't prepared for.

CARPENTER We now have that hawk perch, and my sense is that it's working. Made from a giant branch, it's a sculptural presence. It's our new way to "dispatch" the voles.

GOODE BRYANT As you're talking about voles and deer, I'm thinking about the entirely different issues we have making gardens in New York City. Think about it. There's no ground. There's no ground level, right? New York City is vertical, so Project Eats is focused on rooftops. But then, you're challenged with growing on rooftops. And this is good in New York, because the street level is all about certain difficult creatures: the rats and the groundhogs. And just regardless of whether you're growing food

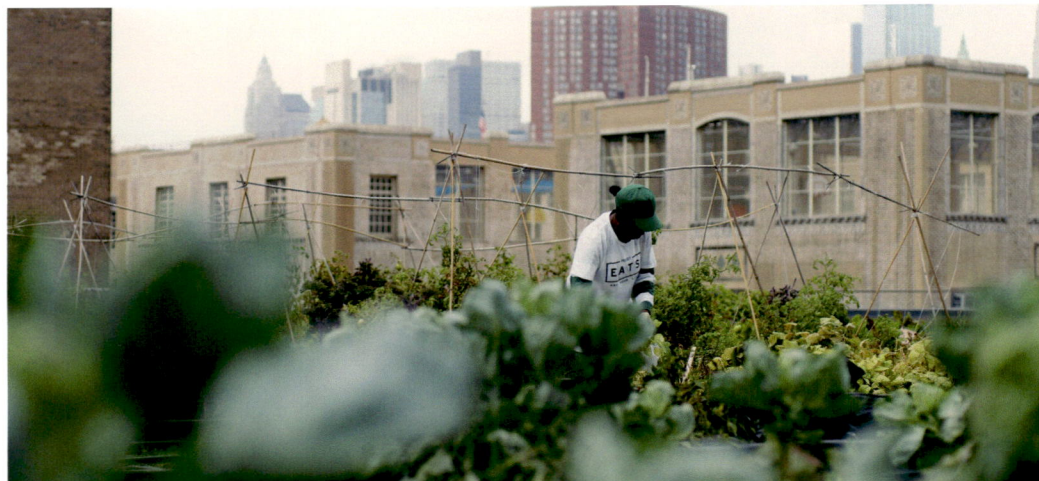

in New York, you have a rat issue. And the thing is they don't eat the food we grow, because they eat our food leftovers in our mountains of daily trash. But they play with the food as it's growing. The same issue is that we have to outsmart the place. So here in Philadelphia, you have a hawk perch for the voles, in New York we grow food on rooftops. And thinking about the idea of a hügel, you're creating other ways of doing exactly that, but in different ways.

CARPENTER   You could grow food on hügels, though, because if you can contain the actual logs with steel or some other kind of support, you could build hügels right on top of concrete and get the prolonged growing season. They're pretty beautiful. And over time they break down. Ours, which was quite a high mound when we first built it in 2021, is almost down to the ground. It started out the highest point was six feet really tall, and now it has settled down to ground level. We're going with that because that is the evolution of a hügel.

GOODE BRYANT   At Project Eats most of our farms right now are on rooftops, and among our biggest challenges is to get the soil up, bringing it up to the rooftop is a strenuous process by hand, but then machinery—like for example a crane—is prohibitively expensive. The point of the conversation at this point right now is just that we find ways, and have been figuring it out for twenty-five years. There are also ways to pump it up. Another challenge is that up on a roof the soil and everything else can blow out and off. Therefore, we find ways to cover our beds.

   What I love about this conversation is that you, Syd, have taken these projects and their challenges as part of your art. It's an art, you know? Please talk about that, because what's so compelling is that you understand these projects—which are so connected to people—as art. And this is an aspect of art that has to be a sustaining component if we are going to survive on this earth.

CARPENTER   What's happening now? If civilization is going to survive the current assault from every direction, there is a critical role that artists and people who act and think with creativity like

artists will do for the survivability of cultures. Culture, intellect, history, knowledge itself is under attack, civilization needs all that in order to change, in order to rebuild. Art is a contribution to change. Artists are in the forefront of change, and that's being said more frequently now than ever.

GOODE BRYANT   When I started Project Eats and said it was an art, people thought I'd lost my mind. Do you see?

CARPENTER   I see.

GOODE BRYANT   To me it made all the sense in the world. Of course a garden is an artwork, and so is all the process we've been talking about. Anything an artist makes is art. Right? That's a principle I believe in.

VALERIO   It's a matter of expanding the definitions of art and artist.

CARPENTER   These days there has to be more interest in different sectors of artists being in the forefront of change because we're constantly observing. We're constantly growing and learning from what we observe.

GOODE BRYANT   Artists see a rectangle and realize, know, understand it's a rectangle. In the context of Project Eats and our roof gardens, green roofs, I've done programs with groups of architects, and I'll sometimes start with the question: What is the most dominant shape in this room? It generally takes a few minutes, and then someone will meekly say, "a rectangle or a square." It's all I can do not to yell! Isn't that what you draw every day, I say? To the extent we don't see what's in front of our face, or what we are doing every day, makes it very difficult for us to imagine something beyond that and then transform that into something that actually creates change. That makes us aware of the fact that there's a dominant shape. But if we can't question that, well, how does that shape our relationships? That we live in rectangles which tend to be hierarchical. What happens if there was a diversity of shapes? You have to see that we live in a world that is dominated by rectangles which do not come from nature. That's part of what makes your circle so special. It's really nice that this circle is here.

CARPENTER Oh, it had to be. The circle is very powerful because it also it turns you around so that you can focus on each of the sculptures. And it, it allows you to not have one of them be the focus, but all four. And you can pivot around, and it's a pretty powerful configuration that again, should it take choices, it allows choice. Somebody can come in and look at them all around. It gives you that opportunity to do that and engage with this or with that. It's not, it's not a uniform experience; we don't all react in the same way to the same things. One of the things the circle gives is the variability to engage. One of the things I think is that it's in relationship. Linda, as you were speaking I was reminded about the experience as a teacher. I always ran into students coming into class and not trusting their own perceptions because it was necessary for them to be given an ordering of what's most important, what's the secondary importance. They wanted to make art that looked like art, and that's a tricky place to be.

GOODE BRYANT How did you tackle that?

CARPENTER So I would introduce the notion of a person as an individual. You have to notice what you yourself are noticing. I came across that phrase from a clay artist named Chris Staley, and he had gotten it from somebody else. In order to trust your own perceptions, you have to recognize that certain stimuli— visual images, sounds, textures, smells—mean something to you. And not everything you notice has to conform to somebody else's perception; something may be art to you, and not the next person. You know, what's the standard of what makes this "something" artful? Or what gives it the status? Who determines what art is? Not the writer, not the curator, not the critic. It's you who are in charge of determining what's art, and what will be art. So, getting them to be convinced of that what they noticed today is important, and then to collect what was noticed today and that's where we'll make some art. You know, keep that sketchbook, use that little camera, and you're going to start to see patterns of what

you in particular can continually notice, like the kinds of things that you notice if you're looking for your inside sources.

GOODE BRYANT All of us have the ability, innate ability to imagine and transform what we imagine into something tangible that others can experience or perceive. We all have that. That is, in my opinion, the most valuable resource we have. We're socialized in other ways, and often don't recognize that. We get socialized outside of realizing that we have that power.

CARPENTER Well, yeah, that's about conformity. You can't exist as a citizen of a certain kind of ideology if you're thinking for yourself. That will not be tolerated. We have all allowed this world to be created.

GOODE BRYANT If we feel we need to change that, we have the power to change it, right?

CARPENTER Students and people in general announce early on: I can't draw, I'm not an artist, I don't see things. And then I'll say to the nineteen-year-old in my class, but look at what you're wearing. You know, that is so off the charts wonderful! They don't even see that they are making art by just getting dressed.

VALERIO Syd, it would be great to talk about the other three sculptures around the circle. What about Sana Musasama's piece—it seems like the most architectonic of the three works (fig. 6.5).

CARPENTER Yes, it's architectural, and there appear to be windows and tower-like forms. But it's also growing, and the vertical structures are soft, intertwined, and wavy—organic and plantlike. Sana is amazing with color and she paints her forms with leaves and flowers. So the pot asks questions: What does it mean to live and strive, to build physical and psychological spaces with life-giving force?

GOODE BRYANT That makes a great dialogue with the piece by Yinka, which is so organic, sensuous (fig. 6.6).

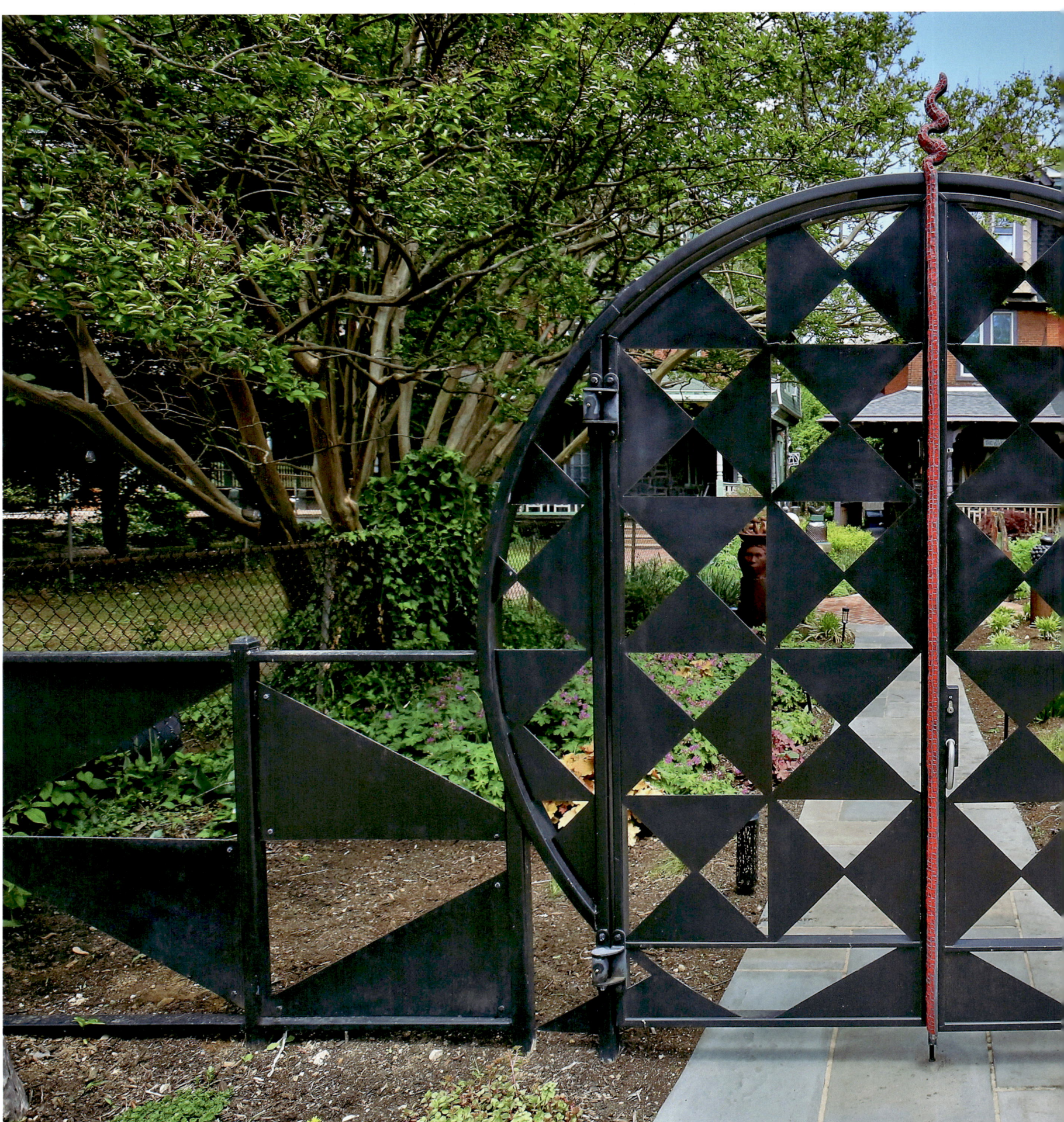

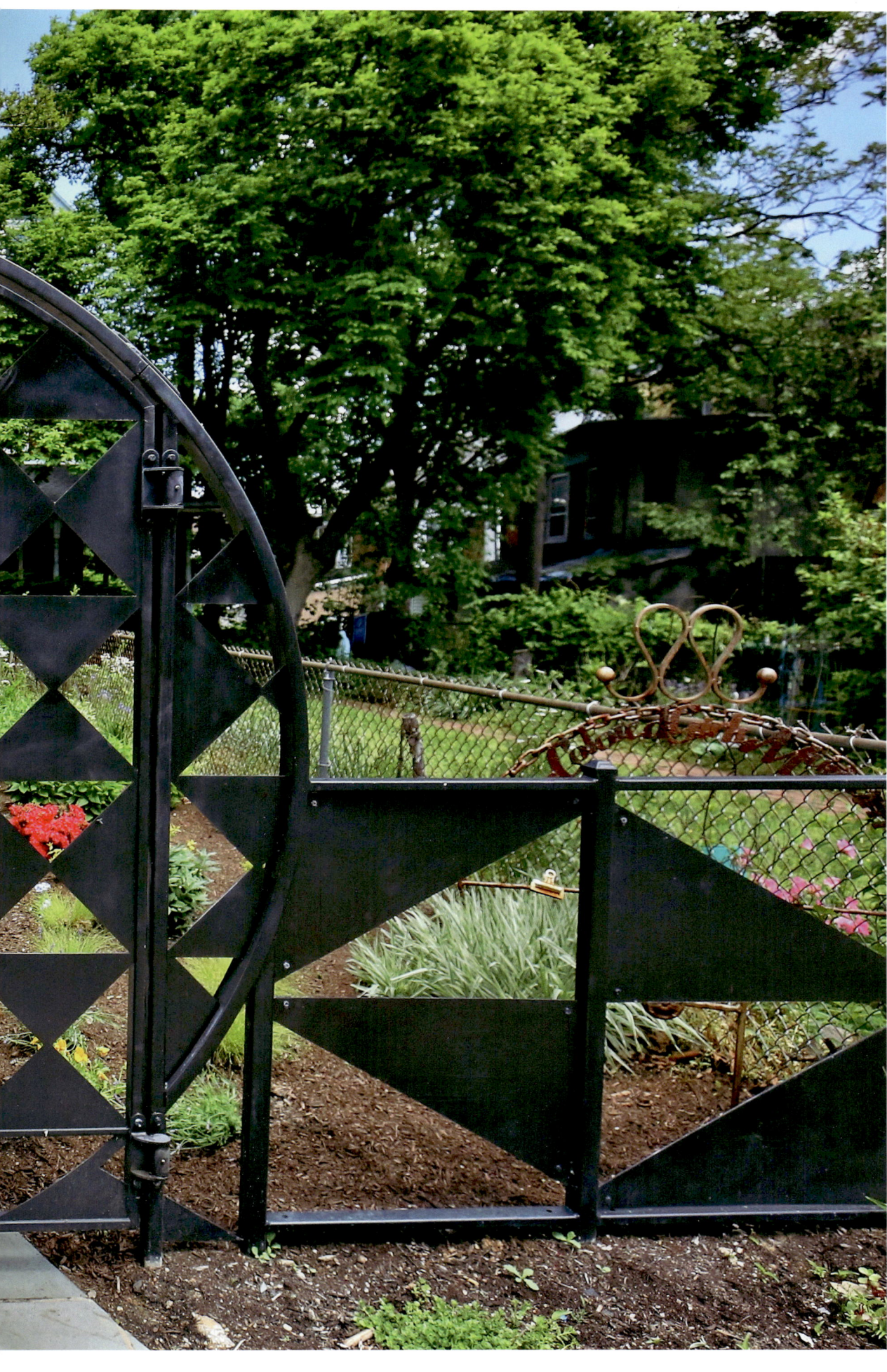

FIG. 6.11 Martha Jackson Jarvis, *Gateway Mosaic Astral*, 2024 (The Colored Girls Museum)

VALERIO The roundness of Yinka's dark, earthy pot is stunning. The coiled form seems to be carefully, lovingly placed in a pattern that covers the fertile belly of the pot. They are at the same time tangible and recognizable as hair braids or ropes, but then also mysterious, like some strange coiled seeds of something that's to come. I love it!

VALERIO Well finally, Syd, we talked about the symbolism of the mother pins, and so I see that your mother is here in the Colored Girls Museum garden (fig. 6.7).

CARPENTER Yes, she's here: two mother pins on the sculpture's head, actually a double self-portrait that I made years ago, looking back and looking forward, crowned with the mother pins and a bowl with beans, fruit, berries, and vines. The face is contemplative, and I'm thinking about myself as a producer, like my mother was a producer, and the issue of time. There's a certain mythical quality to looking backward and looking forward at the same time.

VALERIO The Janus figure of Greek and Roman mythology has two faces, and sees the past and the future.

CARPENTER That's it.

GOODE BRYANT Can you talk about the collaboration with material?

CARPENTER My sense is that different artists are drawn to the different textures, shapes, and properties of different material, and this is tied to being drawn to the different gestures of making, of using our bodies in different ways. As a ceramic artist I don't use my body the same way a printmaker does, or the same way a welder and metalsmith does. You combine your body's inclinations with what the material allows you to do with it. When I'm working with clay or sometimes when I work with paper (or another material) I have to figure it out—what I want it to do; what it wants or will allow me to do to it. That can be a limitation as well as an advantage, because I'm not always imagining what

the material really could do. It does other things for other artists, and other things for me at different times in my life. That's part of what's been so fascinating to me about the process of preparing for the retrospective and the shows at the Maguire Museum and at the Berman. I've been looking at all the work I've done, and I've wondered how I did it. And the answer is that at different times, my body was moving in a different way. My experiences were different. Also, I look at some works and I don't know how I made them. I would never be able to make them again. The material and me at that time were in collaboration, and I was able to do things, imagine things and get the material to do things. So always, when I approach a new clay project, I don't approach it with a sense of authority. Because I know that it's going to be a collaboration that I'm going to have to engage. Over the years I've built up certain skills, but I'm not good at replicating what I did because that was it in its own time. And so every time I approach it, if I'm doing a new body of work, it's a reteaching. I have to restart the engines again. Obviously I have a reservoir of things. I'm old enough that there damn well better be a reservoir of things. And so they're there in place. But new materials; I can't physically work with glass, but I collaborate with artists who work with glass or work with steel, or with wood. I'm not a woodworker, I'm not a glass blower, I'm not a welder, but I like those materials. I sometimes I want those materials in the work. So I have to find people who do, who do it every day. I've had great collaborations with Jack Larimore working in wood, with Warren Holzman in metals, with Theophilus Annor making the steel eggs.

VALERIO I heard about those eggs!

CARPENTER Well, I could have thrown them on the wheel. I know how to throw. I could get an egg on a wheel in a minute. But I was thinking about this different way of making, and I wanted a certain kind of pristine perfection that comes from this chicken making this egg. I could estimate that on the wheel, but I wanted to test the use of technology and digital process, so I made the connection with Theophilus, who is a master with using the scanning, enlarging, and casting. I would not get that pristine elegance on the wheel. And so it's just back and forth and being aware of these different materials, and how that they can be manipulated. I'm just fascinated by the abundance of things that can be manipulated and changed and engaged with and that there's no limits. When I started painting my ceramics many, many years ago instead of glazing, folks would say, oh but you're cheating. And I thought, excuse me? You know, I'm making and who said clay always has to be glazed or buffed up? I'm like what? And I'm not trying to belong to a club. I recognize folks who are working in the tradition. Fine. They're working. I'm not working in the tradition.

VALERIO On the subject of materials, what are these elements that read as the hair on your double self-portrait, that look like coiled rope?

CARPENTER They're rope. That's rope that's painted. Yes, it's real rope. It's dipped, dipped in a solution of a very impervious glue that can sit outside. This is its first winter, but that stuff's not going anywhere.

GOODE BRYANT I think we must talk about the gate (fig. 6.11).

CARPENTER Yes, we should start on the other side. We have to go out and appreciate what it does from the other side. This gate was designed by Martha Jackson Jarvis, who in her own right is iconic to me in terms of her artistry. She's an amazing painter, a designer of public art, and maker of magnificent installations. I was fortunate enough to be in school at the same time with her at Tyler. But this gate was something that needed to be here. When we were thinking about the garden, I knew there had to be an entrance that was symbolic of, and indicative of, what was happening in this building, at this museum. There had to be something to announce this place. The kind of potency that, as you can see, is now present in this doorway. To go through this doorway, you know that you're passing into something special. This isn't your average way of entering a space. She has evoked West African architecture where you'll see the painted buildings that are not rectangular, that are round, that are ovoid, that are very, very

luscious in their shapes and the way they meld into the ground, and into the surface and the earth around them. It's something that once again, in terms of slowing down and stopping you, you recognize the power of the design and what it does for this space. There is this kind of regal quality to it, and the shield suggests strength. And that you can also see through the shield speaks to the dual ability for this thing to protect, as well as to invite. Martha was brilliant in terms of her design and the way she related this gate to the house and the museum.

GOODE BRYANT What about the red snake? Thinking in terms of potent symbols . . .

CARPENTER The vitality of the red is blood to me. I always use red, whether you can see it or not; in my work it's always an underpainting and it speaks to the potential vitality of whatever object it's on. In terms of the visual impact it says shield, emblem, guardian. It's all of these different things. You know that something is happening as you move through this space. The house has a mojo now. And I just think that that's what that is.

GOODE BRYANT I can't help wanting to peer through it, and then I'm rewarded by the beautiful sculptures.

VALERIO And then you see the signage, the Colored Girls Museum. It really draws you in. Like a portal.

CARPENTER You're going to have layers of experience moving from here into there. Vashti, thank you for the opportunities you created, and Bill, Linda, this was a wonderful conversation.

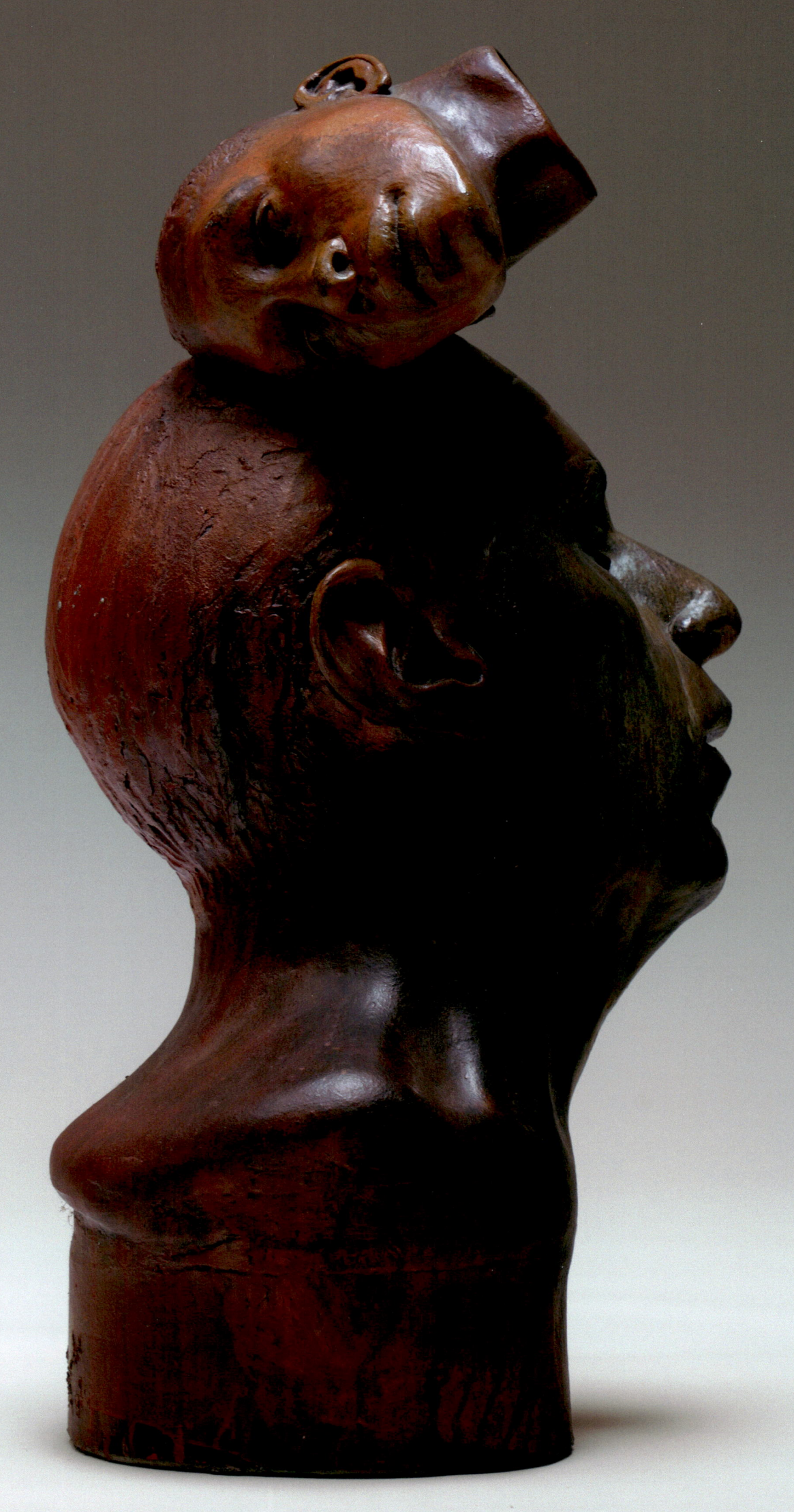

Selected Chronology

1953
Born on January 7, in Pittsburgh, Pennsylvania.

1970
Moves to Philadelphia to study painting at the Tyler School of Art, Temple University. Transfers to the ceramics department because of the mentorship of Rudy Staffel and the friendship of fellow students including Martha Jackson Jarvis, Judy Moonelis, Sana Musasama, and Winnie Owens-Hart.

1974
Earns a Bachelor of Fine Arts (BFA) in ceramics from the Tyler School of Art.

1976
Receives a Master of Fine Arts (MFA) in ceramics from the Tyler School of Art.

1981
Co-founds 915 Studios at 915 Spring Garden Street in Philadelphia with Steve Donegan; the 70,000-square-foot building houses over 100 artist studios.

1985
Awarded a Visual Arts Fellowship by the Pennsylvania Council on the Arts.

1986/1987
Recherché/Den Flexible (Danish artist group based in Copenhagen) exchange; works included in catalogue.

Charlottenborg Museum Copenhagen/Port of History Museum Philadelphia; works included in catalogue.

1988
Receives the Best of Show Award at the State University of New York at Buffalo National Exhibition.

Travels to Brazil with Recherché, a group of African American artists, to exhibit and celebrate the freeing of enslaved people in 1888.

1989
Granted a fellowship from the National Endowment for the Arts, Mid Atlantic.

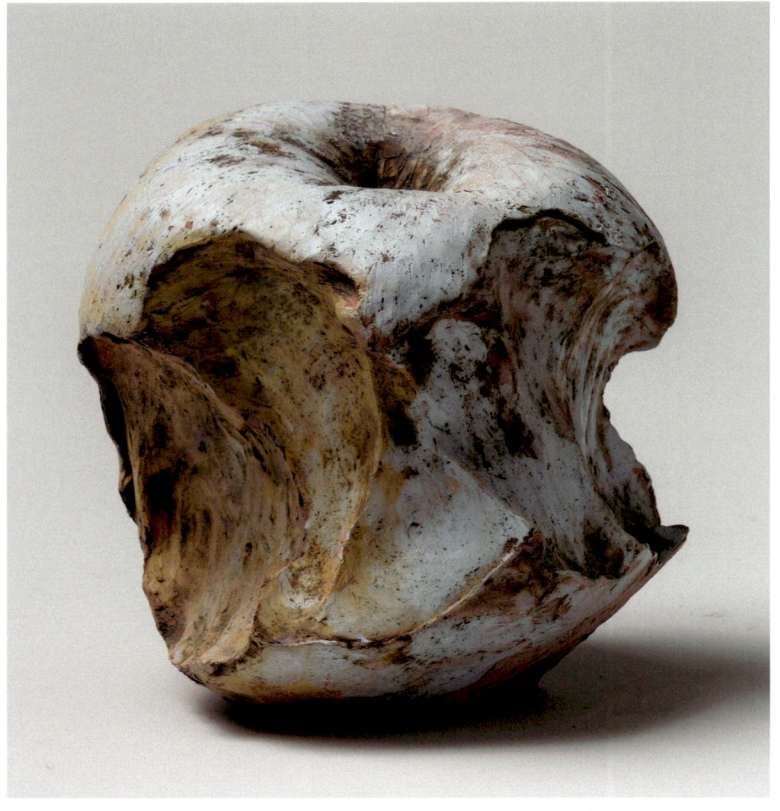

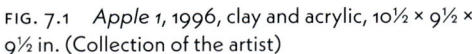
FIG. 7.1 *Apple 1*, 1996, clay and acrylic, 10½ × 9½ × 9½ in. (Collection of the artist)

Group exhibitions: Westby Gallery, Rowan University, Glassboro, NJ; *Artists' Selections: Six African American Artists Select Six Emerging Artists*, Nexus Gallery, Philadelphia; *Urban Interpretations in Fiber, Clay, Photography, and Metal*, Colorado College, Colorado Springs, CO; *Altered States: Contemporary American Ceramics*, Metropolitan State College of Denver, CO.

1998
Group exhibitions: *Twenty Philadelphia Artists: Celebrating Fleisher Challenge at Twenty*, Philadelphia Museum of Art; *20 × 12: A Generation of Challenge Artists*, Fleisher Art Memorial, Philadelphia; *In Her Voice: Self-Portraits by Woman*, Berman Museum of Art, Ursinus College, Collegeville, PA; *Constructions in Multiple Hues*, Painted Bride Art Center, Philadelphia.

1999
Receives a Leeway Foundation Fellowship.

Group exhibitions: Leeway Foundation Fellowship Exhibition, Art Alliance, Philadelphia; *A More Perfect Union*, Abington Art Center, Jenkintown, PA; *Thunder in the Cathedral*, Rush Gallery, New York, NY.

2000
Awarded her first Eugene Lang Swarthmore Faculty Fellowship (also awarded in 2004, 2008, and 2012).

Solo exhibition: Sande Webster Gallery, Philadelphia.

Group exhibitions: Biennial Exhibition, African American Museum, Philadelphia; *Figures: Alone and Together*, Craft Alliance, St. Louis.

2001
Solo exhibition: Philadelphia International Airport.

Group exhibition: *Reconstructing the Shards*, Howard University, Washington, DC.

1990
Receives a Master Fellowship in Visual Arts from the Pennsylvania Council on the Arts.

1991
Begins teaching as a professor of studio art at Swarthmore College.

Buys a house and studio in Mt. Airy with husband Steve Donegan.

1992
Awarded the Pew Fellowship in the Arts.

1995
Group exhibition: *Contained, Uncontained: Syd Carpenter, Martha Jackson Jarvis, Magdalene Odundo, James Watkins*, Dallas African American Museum.

1996
Group exhibitions: *Exploring a Movement: Feminist Visions in Clay*, Wignall Museum, Rancho Cucamonga, CA; *Art of the State*, State Museum of Pennsylvania, Harrisburg, PA; *Artists Select Artists*, Trenton City Museum, NJ.

1997
A Snake without a Head Is Just a Rope is acquired by the Philadelphia Museum of Art for its permanent collection.

Solo exhibition: Sande Webster Gallery, Philadelphia.

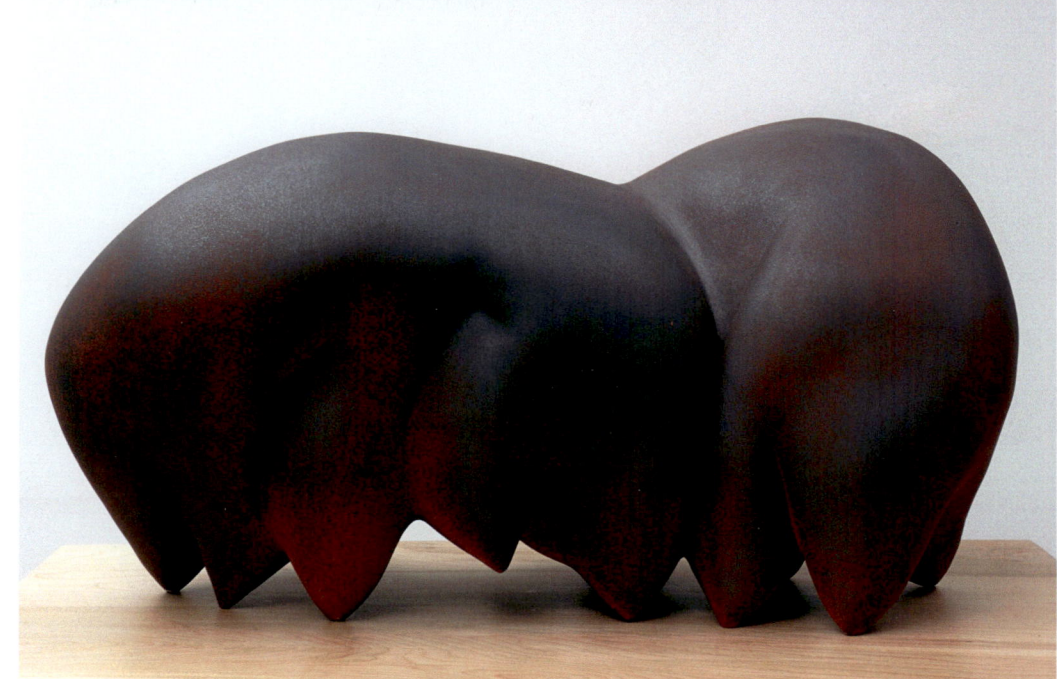

FIG. 7.2 *Old Soul*, 2006, clay, underglaze, and oxide, 20 × 36 × 20 in. (Collection of the artist)

2002

Two-person exhibition: *Sonya Clark and Syd Carpenter*, Stella Jones Gallery, New Orleans.

Group exhibitions: *21st Century Philadelphia Sculptors*, Samuel T. Freeman & Co., Philadelphia; Everson Ceramic National, Crocker Art Museum, Sacramento, CA.

2003

Two-person exhibition: *Syd Carpenter/Steven Donegan*, Sande Webster Gallery, Philadelphia.

2004

Curates the traveling exhibition *Shades of Clay: A Cultural Look at Contemporary Clay* at the Louisiana Art and Science Museum, Baton Rouge; Museum of Texas Tech University, Lubbock; Baum Gallery of Fine Art, University of Central Arkansas; Bergstrom-Mahler Museum, Neenah, WI (runs until 2007).

2005

Group exhibitions: *Chemistry of Color*, Pennsylvania Academy of the Fine Arts, Philadelphia; *Tour de Clay Afrique*, Baltimore Clay Works, Baltimore, MD.

Solo exhibition, Sande Webster Gallery, Philadelphia.

2006

Solo exhibition, Delaware Center for Contemporary Art, Wilmington, DE.

2007

Group exhibition: *From Taboo to Icon: Africanist Turnabout*, Icebox Gallery, Philadelphia.

2009

Carpenter begins to create farm portraits.

Solo exhibition, John Jay College, New York, NY.

Group exhibition: *Mass and Meaning: Clay Sculpture*, Armory Art Center, West Palm Beach, FL.

2010

Solo exhibition: *A Place of Our Own*, Sande Webster Gallery, Philadelphia, PA.

Curates the exhibition *Fertile Ground* at the Philadelphia Horticultural Center.

2011

Deep Roots and *Familiar Figure* are acquired by the Metropolitan Museum of Art for its permanent collection.

Receives a second Leeway Foundation Artists Fellowship.

915 Studios closes.

Group exhibitions: *Informed by Fire*, Philadelphia Museum of Art; *Garden as Muse: Sally Apfelbaum, Markus Baenziger, Syd Carpenter, Lois Dodd, Sarah McEneaney* (curated by Andrea Packard), Walton Arts Center, Fayetteville, AR.

2012

Travels to Georgia, South Carolina, and the Gullah Islands to research African American farm history.

Receives a third Leeway Foundation Fellowship.

Group exhibitions: *Earth and Alchemy*, Massachusetts College of Art and Design, Boston; *Creative Hand, Discerning Heart*, Michener Art Museum, Doylestown, PA.

2014

Solo exhibition: *More Places of Our Own*, African American Museum, Philadelphia.

2016

Group exhibitions: *Shaping Minds: Philadelphia's Clay Mentors*, Clay Studio and Leonard Pearlstein Gallery, Drexel University, Philadelphia; *Faces of Politics: In/Tolerance*, Fuller Craft Museum, Brockton, MA.

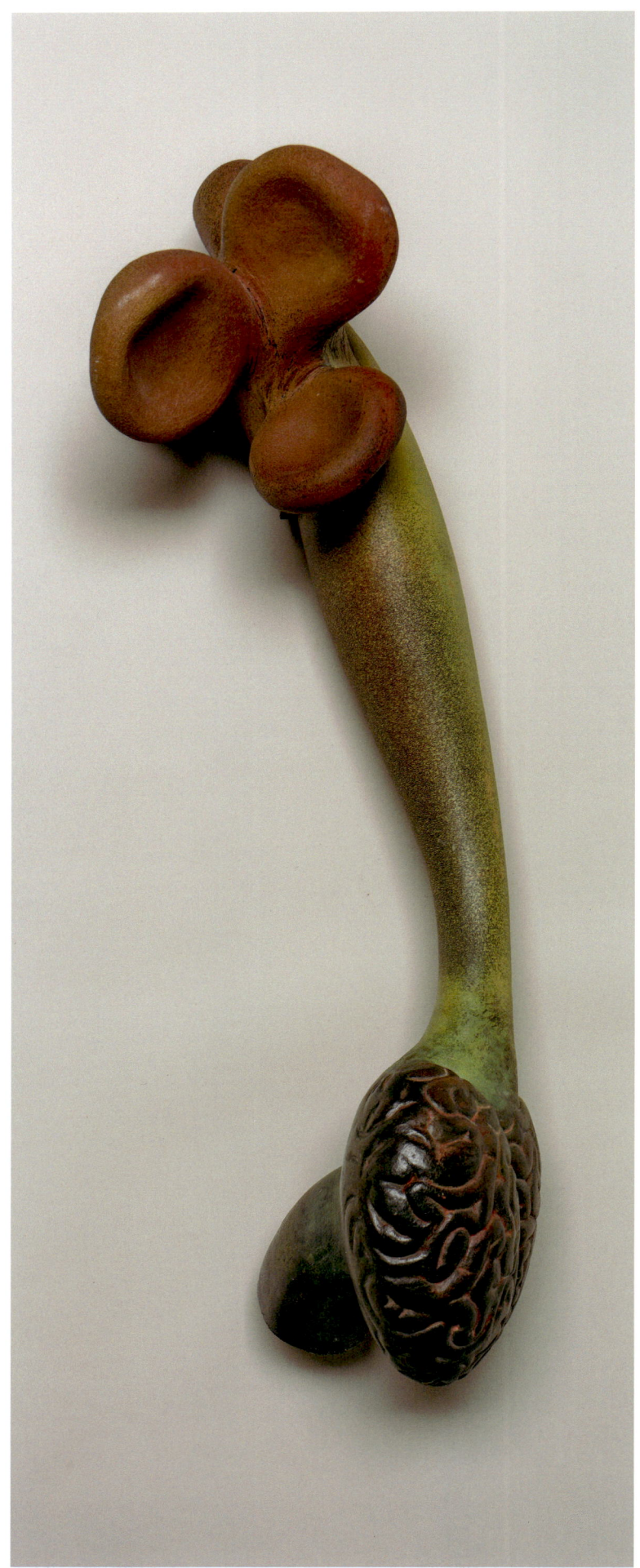

2017
Group exhibition: *Preservation: Objects Registering the Past and Future*, Clay Studio in collaboration with PhilaLandmarks at the Hill-Physick House, Philadelphia.

2018
Solo exhibition: *Mother Pins*, Center for Emerging Visual Artists, Philadelphia.

Group exhibitions: *Making a Difference: Social and Political Activism in Clay*, Clay Studio, Philadelphia; *The Woodmere Annual: 77th Juried Exhibition*, Woodmere, Philadelphia.

Society for Art in Craft, National Conference on Education in Ceramic Arts (NCECA), Pittsburgh, PA.

2019
Group exhibition: *An Essential Presence: The Petrucci Family Foundation Collection of African American Art*, Allentown Art Museum, Allentown, PA.

2020
Solo exhibition: *Portraits of Our Places*, Michener Art Museum, Doylestown, PA.

Group exhibitions: *Never Done: 100 Years of Women in Politics and Beyond*, Tang Museum, Saratoga Springs, NY; *Women Working with Clay: Ten Years of Telling the Story*, Valentine Museum, Richmond, VA, and the Eleanor D. Wilson Museum, Hollins University, Roanoke, VA.

2021
Appointed to the Endowed Peggy Chan Professorship of Black Studies at Swarthmore College.

Group exhibitions: *Shapes from Out of Nowhere: Ceramics from the Robert A. Ellison Jr. Collection*, Metropolitan Museum of Art, New York; *Voices and Visionaries*, Philadelphia Sculptors at the Cherry Street Pier, Philadelphia.

FIG. 7.4 *Heart of the Yam*, 2006, clay, underglaze, and oxide, 26 × 26 × 14 in. (Collection of the artist)

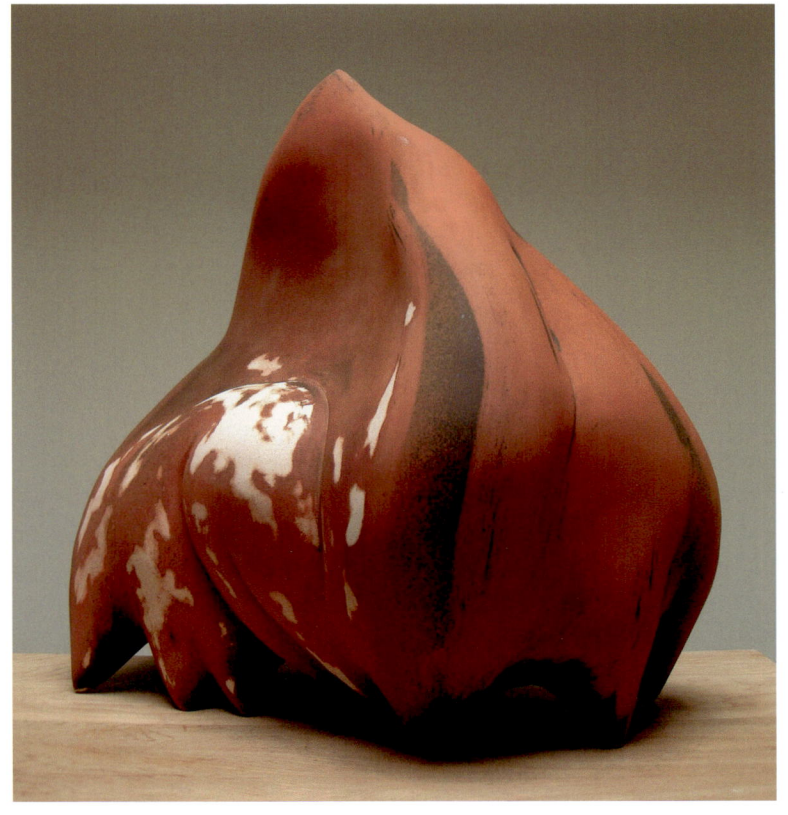

2022

Solo exhibition: *Earth Offerings: Honoring the Gardeners*, Rowan University Art Gallery, Glassboro, NJ.

Retires from Swarthmore College as professor emerita of studio art.

Featured in the "Home" episode of the PBS series *Craft in America* (broadcast on December 16, 2022).

2023

Receives the United States Artists Fellowship.

Awarded the Anonymous Was a Woman grant.

2024

Group exhibition: *Founders and Foundations: 50th Anniversary*, Clay Studio, Philadelphia.

2025

Group exhibitions: *2025 NCECA Annual: True and Real*, Utah Museum of Contemporary Art, Salt Lake City; *Yesterday's Dreams Are Real: Collecting Black Art and the Legacy of Lewis Tanner Moore*, Michener Art Museum, Doylestown, PA; *State Fairs and Farms*, Renwick Gallery of the Smithsonian Institute, Washington, DC.

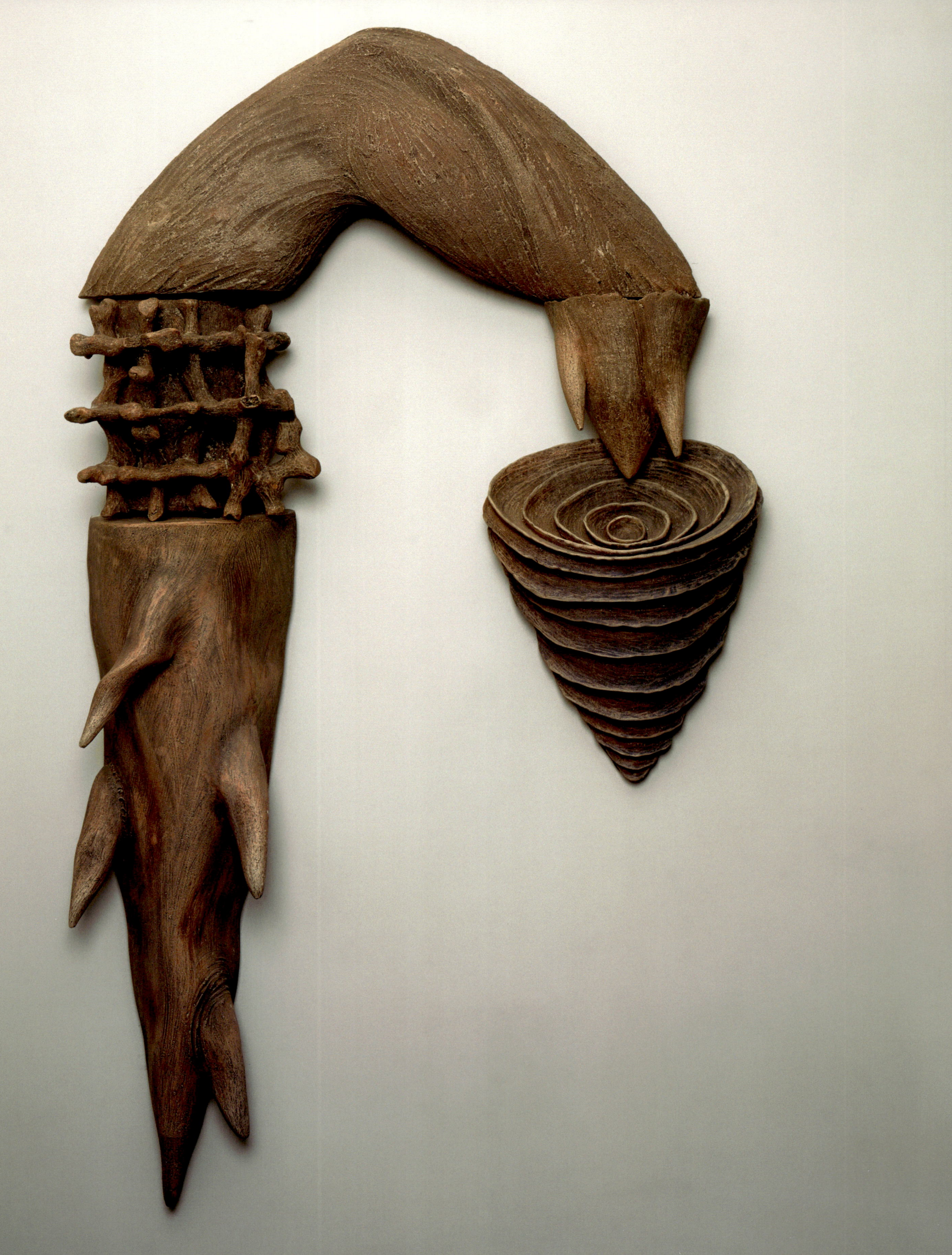

Works in the Exhibitions

AS OF AUGUST 22, 2025

This checklist includes works on view at the three Philadelphia venues: Woodmere, the Philip and Muriel Berman Museum of Art at Ursinus College, and the Frances M. Maguire Art Museum at St. Joseph's University. All works are by Syd Carpenter (American, born 1953), unless otherwise indicated.

Works are listed chronologically. Dimensions are given as height × width × depth, unless otherwise indicated.

Not all works in the exhibition are illustrated in this publication.

WOODMERE

House for Mr. Biswas, 1982
Clay with underglazes, 20 × 10 × 10 in.
Collection of James Brantley

Green Seed, 1983
Ceramic with acrylic paint, 16 × 15 × 15 in.
Collection of the artist

Late Season, 1984
Clay with oxide washes, 12 × 12 × 12 in.
Collection of James Brantley

Untitled (Lorraine's Pot), 1985
Terracotta and black copper oxide, 15 × 10 × 10 in.
Woodmere: Gift of Lorraine and Benjamin Alexander, 2023

Of a Like Mind, c. 1986–87
Ceramic, 26 × 18 × 4 in.
Collection of James Brantley

A Part of the Whole, 1989
Ceramic mounted on plywood, 41 × 64 × 6 in.
Woodmere: Gift of the Wind Family, 2024

Below Ground, 1990
Paint over clay, 69 × 36 × 8 in.
Collection of the artist

Check Your Sources, 1990
Ceramic on wood, 88 × 49½ × 8 in.
Pennsylvania Academy of the Fine Arts: The Harold A. and Ann R. Sorgenti Collection of Contemporary African American Art

Child 3, 1990
Clay and terra sigillata, 17 × 21 × 16 in.
Collection of the artist

Child 4, 1990
Clay and terra sigillata, 14½ × 21 × 21 in.
Collection of the artist

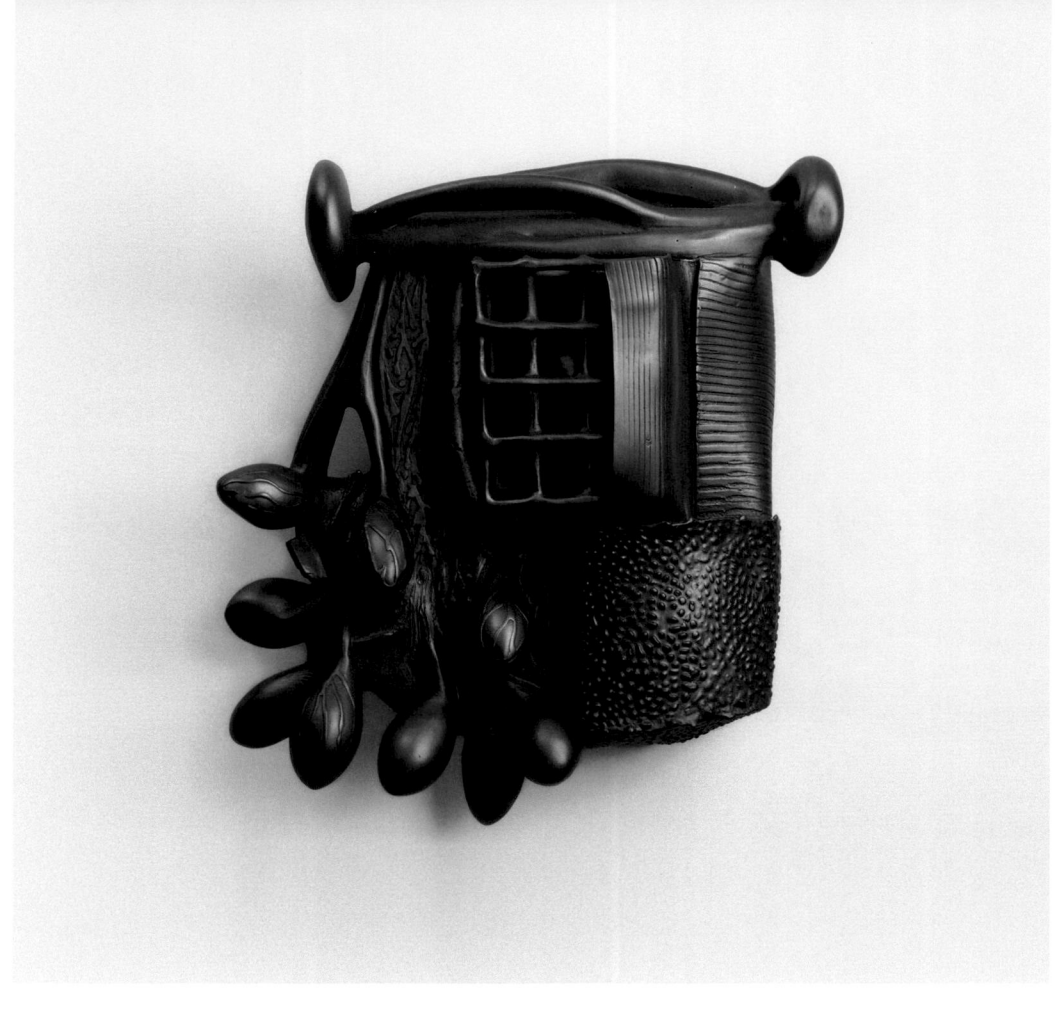

FIG. 8.1 *Willie and Jelena Gray*, 2009, clay and graphite, 28 × 24 × 7 in. (Private collection)

Child 5, 1990
Clay and terra sigillata, 15 × 22 × 22 in.
Collection of James Brantley

Then, Now, When, 1991
Clay and slip, 41 × 42 × 12 in.
Collection of the artist

A Snake without a Head Is Just a Rope, 1994
Glazed earthenware, 59 × 20 × 16 in.
Philadelphia Museum of Art: Purchased with funds contributed by The Women's Committee and the Craft Show Committee of the Philadelphia Museum of Art, 1995-19-1

Apple 1, 1996
Clay and acrylic, 10½ × 9½ × 9½ in.
Collection of the artist

Apple 2, 1996
Clay and acrylic, 10½ × 10 × 12 in.
Collection of the artist

Apple 3, 1996
Clay and acrylic, 6¾ × 7 × 7 in.
Collection of the artist

Love Letter, 1996
Ceramic with acrylic paint, 23 × 12 × 12 in.
Collection of the artist

Frank's Peace, 2002
Paint over clay, 38 × 12 × 12 in.
Collection of the artist

Breathe, 2004
Watercolor over clay, 20 × 42 × 15 in.
Woodmere: Gift of the Wind Family, 2024

Brain Food, 2005
Clay, graphite, and acrylic, 12 × 42½ × 12 in.
Collection of the artist

Frank as Sun King, 2005
Mixed media, 50 × 50 × 20 in.
Promised gift of the artist

Daughter of Old Soul, 2006
Ceramic, 10½ × 17 × 7½ in.
Collection of Lewis Tanner Moore

Frank Portrait, 2007
Clay and watercolor, 15 × 15 × 10 in.
Collection of the artist

Two Birds Dancing, 2007
Clay, slip, and oxide, 26 × 24 × 12 in.
Collection of Andrea Packard

Frank in Tow, 2008
Graphite on clay, 12 × 52 × 8 in.
Courtesy of the Petrucci Family Foundation Collection of African American Art

Mother Pin, 2008
Clay and graphite, 24 × 9 × 7 in.
Collection of Lewis Tanner Moore

Ramshackle Fence, 2008–12
Earthenware, graphite, and acrylic, 30 × 75 × 9 in.
Everson Museum of Art: Museum Purchase, Deaccession Fund

Everelena Cannon, 2009
Clay, acrylic, and graphite, 41 × 35¾ × 23¾ in.
Woodmere: Museum purchase, 2018

Inez Faust, 2009
Clay, watercolor, and graphite, 28 × 24 × 8 in.
Collection of the artist

Percy Robinson, 2009
Clay, watercolor, graphite, 24 × 22 × 6 in.
Rhode Island School of Design Museum: Gift of Thomas Daley and Donna Weaverling Daley, 2020

Thomas Evans, 2009
Clay and graphite, 18¼ × 19½ × 8½ in.
Collection of the artist

Willie and Jelena Gray, 2009
Clay and graphite, 28 × 24 × 7 in.
Private collection

Ellis and Anna Mae Thomas, 2009–10
Earthenware, acrylic, and graphite, 26 × 20 × 8 in.
From the series *Places of Our Own*
The Frances Young Tang Teaching Museum and Art Gallery at Skidmore College: Gift of the artist, 2017.30

Albert and Elbert Howard, 2014
Clay, steel, and graphite, 49 × 42 × 27 in.
Courtesy of the Petrucci Family Foundation Collection of African American Art

Joseph and Helen Fields, 2014
Clay, found objects, and steel, 43 × 27 × 27 in.
James A. Michener Art Museum: Gift of the artist, 2021.1.2ab

Sara Reynolds, 2014
Clay and steel, 50 × 27 × 26 in.
James A. Michener Art Museum: Gift of the artist, 2021.1.1a–e

Mother Pin Afire, 2017
Clay, graphite, and watercolor, 27 × 16 × 12 in.
Collection of the artist

Mother Pin with Shirt, 2017
Clay and graphite, 19 × 8 × 7½ in.
Collection of the artist

Mother Pin Arise, 2018
Clay, graphite, and watercolor, 28 × 19 × 19 in.
Courtesy of Martin Weinstein and Teresa Liszka

Mary Howard Farm Bowl, 2020
Stoneware, 15 × 20 × 22 in.
Collection of the artist

Albert and Elbert Howard Farm Bowl, 2021
Stoneware, 15 × 24 × 21½ in.
Collection of the artist

Green Farm Bowl, 2022
Clay and acrylic, 12½ × 27 × 19 in.
Collection of the artist

Untitled, date unknown
Ceramic with glaze, 15 × 20 × 20 in.
Collection of Danny Simmons

PHILIP AND MURIEL BERMAN MUSEUM OF ART AT URSINUS COLLEGE

Bite Down, 2006
Clay, underglaze, and oxide, 26 × 22 × 12 in.
Collection of the artist

Black Bird, 2006
Clay and graphite, 27 × 28 × 10 in.
Collection of the artist

Heart of the Yam, 2006
Clay, underglaze, and oxide, 26 × 26 × 14 in.
Collection of the artist

Merge, 2006
Clay, underglaze, and oxide, 26 × 24 × 15 in.
Courtesy of the Petrucci Family Foundation Collection of African American Art

Mind of Its Own, 2006
Clay, slip underglaze, and graphite, 26 × 14 × 12 in.
Collection of the artist

Of and About the Skin, 2006
Clay, underglaze, and oxide, 25 × 25 × 12 in.
Collection of Sarah Willie-LeBreton and Jonathan LeBreton

Old Soul, 2006
Clay, underglaze, and oxide, 20 × 36 × 20 in.
Collection of the artist

Helen and Joseph Fields, 2014
Clay, found objects, and steel, 43 × 26 × 24 in.
Collection of the artist

Troy Johnson, 2014
Clay and steel, 48 × 24 × 24 in.
Collection of the artist

Williams Muscadine, 2014
Clay and steel, 48 × 26 × 24 in.
Collection of the artist

Mother Pin Awash, 2016
Clay and acrylic wash, 21 × 28 × 23 in.
Collection of the artist

Mother Pin with Beans, 2021
Clay and acrylic wash, 22 × 15 × 12 in.
Collection of the artist

Mother Pin with Floating Beans, 2021
Clay, lentils, and acrylic wash, 16 × 28 × 24 in.
Collection of the artist

Release, 2021
Steel, clay, and papier-mâché, 28 × 64 × 64 in.
Collection of the artist

Home Places, 2025
Corrugated steel and wood, 12 × 10 × 10 ft.
Collection of the artist

Mother Pin Ascending, 2025
Wood, clay, and steel, 65 × 60 × 60 in.
Courtesy of the Petrucci Family Foundation Collection of African American Art

Mother Pin Embedded #1, #2, #3, 2025
Clay, offset lithograph, aluminum, and acrylic, 57 × 49 in. each
Collection of the artist

FRANCES M. MAGUIRE ART MUSEUM AT ST. JOSEPH'S UNIVERSITY

Cure in a Bottle, 1994
Painted clay, 15 × 36 × 30 in.
Collection of the artist

Potion, 2004
Earthenware and graphite, 60 × 10 × 8 in.
Collection of the artist

Adjust Pressure to Normal, 2005
Clay, graphite, and acrylic, 78 × 10 × 8 in.
Collection of the artist

Apothecary, 2005
Clay and graphite, 52 × 20 × 10 in.
Collection of the artist

Blood Ties, 2005
Ceramic, 18 × 42 × 12 in.
Collection of the artist

Three Mother Pins on a Vine, 2021
Clay and mixed media, 18 × 37 × 26 in.
Collection of the artist

Martha Jackson Jarvis
American, born 1952
Crossing Land, 2020
Oil, acrylic, watercolor, black walnut ink,
and canvas, 84 × 120 × 2 in.
Collection of the artist

Martha Jackson Jarvis
American, born 1952
Red Road of Dissemblance, 2020
Oil, acrylic, watercolor, black walnut ink,
and canvas, 94¾ × 83¼ × 3 in.
Collection of the artist

Martha Jackson Jarvis
American, born 1952
Fire Flies, 2021
300 lb paper, canvas, oil, acrylic, watercolor, and black walnut ink, 125 × 79½ ×
3 in.
Collection of the artist

Judy Moonelis
American, born 1953
*Blood Cell (Cell Block 2, #27/29), Eastern
State Penitentiary, Philadelphia*, 2010
Photographic print, 36 × 48 in.
Collection of the artist

Judy Moonelis
American, born 1953
*Brain Cell (Cell Block 10, #21), Eastern
State Penitentiary, Philadelphia*, 2010
Photographic print, 36 × 48 in.
Collection of the artist

Judy Moonelis
American, born 1953
*Celestial Bodies (1), Basilica of Saint Mary,
Minneapolis*, 2019
Photographic print, 36 × 48 in.
Collection of the artist

Judy Moonelis
American, born 1953
*Celestial Bodies (2), Basilica of Saint Mary,
Minneapolis*, 2019
Photographic print, 36 × 48 in.
Collection of the artist

Judy Moonelis
American, born 1953
Double Lancet with Neuron, 2022
Chain, wire, glass, and plastic, 48 × 21 ×
4 in.
Collection of the artist

Judy Moonelis
American, born 1953
Neural Home, 2023
Clay and mixed media (clay, wire, chain,
paper, ink, gouache, root, repurposed
materials, and slate), 102 × 36 × 67 in.
Collection of the artist

Judy Moonelis
American, born 1953
Neural Greenhouse, 2025
Clay and mixed media (clay, wire, chain,
branches, acrylic paint, gouache, glass,
safe deposit box, repurposed materials,
and slate), 72 × 48 × 84 in.
Collection of the artist

Judy Moonelis
American, born 1953
Neural Well, Barnes Foundation, 2026
Clay and mixed media, 25 × 32 × 32 in.
Collection of the artist

Sana Musasama
American, born 1957
House Series, 1983
Ceramic, 12 × 14 × 9 in.
Collection of the artist

Sana Musasama
American, born 1957
House Series 7, 1983
Ceramic, 67 × 14 × 9½ in.
Collection of the artist

Sana Musasama
American, born 1957
House Series, Returning to Ourselves, 2020
Ceramic, 14 × 11 × 5 in.
Collection of the artist

Sana Musasama
American, born 1957
House Series, Returning to Ourselves, 2023
Ceramic, 24 × 15 × 12 in.
Collection of the artist

Sana Musasama
American, born 1957
House Series, Returning to Ourselves, 2023
Ceramic, 13 × 9 × 8 in.
Collection of the artist

Sana Musasama
American, born 1957
House Series, Returning to Ourselves, 2023
Ceramic, 31 × 10 × 8 in.
Collection of the artist

Sana Musasama
American, born 1957
House Series, Returning to Ourselves, 2024
Ceramic, 24 × 16 × 12 in.
Collection of the artist

Winnie Owens-Hart
American, born 1949
Helmet Mask, 1978
Stoneware, slip, and fiber, 13 × 12½ ×
11¾ in.
From the series *Scream… You're Black in
America*
Collection of the artist

Winnie Owens-Hart
American, born 1949
Wall Mask #2, 1978
Stoneware and slip, 13 × 15 × 6 in.
From the series *Scream… You're Black in
America*
Collection of the artist

Winnie Owens-Hart
American, born 1949
UDO Drum #13, 1979
Raffia and stoneware, 9 × 9 × 9 in.
Collection of the artist

Winnie Owens-Hart
American, born 1949
Adorned #2, 2005
Porcelain, 5 × 3 × 3½ in.
From the series *Little Women*
Collection of the artist

Lenders to the Exhibitions

James Brantley

Everson Museum of Art

James A. Michener Art Museum

Judy Heggestad and the Lewis Tanner Moore Collection

Andrea Packard

Pennsylvania Academy of the Fine Arts

Petrucci Family Foundation Collection of African American Art

Philadelphia Museum of Art

Private Collection

Rhode Island School of Design Museum

Danny Simmons

Frances Young Tang Teaching Museum and Art Gallery at
Skidmore College

Martin Weinstein and Teresa Liszka

Sarah Willie-LeBreton and Jonathan LeBreton

Artist Acknowledgments

I'VE BEEN FORTUNATE to work as an artist for over fifty years and have the greatest appreciation for those who made this retrospective a reality.

Choosing to become an artist was a life-altering decision made decades ago. At that time, as a young person with limited confidence and little awareness of other Black women artists, there was uncertainty about the future and how I would make use of my talents. My family, particularly my mother, Ernestine Carpenter, always encouraged me. Her commitment to her three children prevented her from pursuing the intellectual and artistic life she desired, but her sacrifice enabled me to become an artist in her name. To her I will always be grateful.

My ceramics professor Rudolph Staffel allowed me to develop without restriction or judgment. My very good friends and fellow artists, Martin Weinstein and Teresa Liszka, consistently supported my art and provided companionship and humor, greatly enriching my life. My students at Swarthmore College gave me an avenue to share the value of making, seeing, and communicating through art.

I am deeply grateful to collectors James Brantley, Sarah Willie-LeBreton, Andrea Packard, Franz Rabauer, Danny Simmons, Lorraine and Ben Alexander, Tom and Donna Daley, Dina and Jerry Wind, and Garth Johnson, curator of ceramics at the Everson Museum of Syracuse University. Judy Heggestad and Lewis Tanner Moore collected my work and that of other Black artists with a vigor previously unknown. Gallerist Sande Webster organized my first one-person exhibition and gave me the opportunity to build a career. Adrienne Spinozzi, associate curator of American decorative arts at the Metropolitan Museum of Art, is a champion, and Jim Petrucci, Claudia Volpe, and artist-curator Berrisford Boothe of the Petrucci Family Foundation of African American Art are giving my work new visibility, making it accessible to new audiences. Jack Larimore and Co., Erica Ehrenbard and Zachary Steinheiser of Carriage Creative, and Jim Innis of the Challenge Program are also to be thanked for their expertise and facility. I extend my gratitude to the lenders to the exhibition: James Brantley, Everson Museum of Art, James A. Michener Art Museum, Judy Heggestad and the Lewis Tanner Moore Collection, Andrea Packard, Pennsylvania Academy of the Fine Arts, Petrucci Family Foundation Collection of African American Art, Philadelphia Museum of Art, a private collection, Rhode Island School of Design Museum, Danny Simmons, Frances Young Tang Teaching Museum and Art Gallery at Skidmore College, Martin Weinstein and Teresa Liszka, and Sarah Willie-LeBreton and Jonathan LeBreton.

I am honored by the participation of the esteemed trio of Lowery Stokes Sims, Leslie King-Hammond, and Linda Goode Bryant, whose words appear in these pages. Ryan Polich, design director at Marquand Books, and Jack Ramsdale, photographer, made this book beautiful. Many thanks to William R. Valerio, the Patricia Van Burgh Allison Director and CEO of Woodmere; Lauren McCardel, executive director of the Philip and Muriel Berman Museum of Art at Ursinus College; and Emily Hage, director, and Jeanne Bracy, associate director, both of the Frances M. Maguire Art Museum at Saint Joseph's University—together they orchestrated an extraordinary multi-institutional retrospective.

I am grateful to the staff at the three museums. At Woodmere, thank you to Rick Ortwein, deputy director of exhibitions; Amy Gillette, associate curator; Laura Heemer, registrar; Julianna Liska, assistant registrar; Hildy Tow, Robert L. McNeil, Jr. Curator of Education; Lya Rodgers, assistant curator of school and family programs; Amanda Monroe, assistant curator of education; Lily Williams, director of development; Anne Standish, Klorfine Foundation Director of Institutional Advancement; Sara Stewart, development manager; Erin Lawrence, development associate; Amy Ferracci, director of marketing and communications; Marie Latham, marketing manager; and Bryce Long, director of facilities and grounds. At the Berman Museum, thank you to Deborah Barkun, creative director; Catherine Sirizzotti, collections manager; and Betsy Witt, operations manager. At the Maguire Art Museum, thank you to Emily Hage, director; Jeanne Bracy, associate director; Erin Downey, assistant curator; and Jane Allen, education and community engagement coordinator.

Vashti DuBois, founder and executive director of the Colored Girls Museum, has, for me, provided a cultural and creative home.

I've been sustained in my work by many artists with whom I share friendship, inspiration, and creative support, and these include Martha Jackson Jarvis, Judy Moonelis, Sana Musasama, Winnie Owens-Hart, Angelica Pozo, Yinka Orafidiya, and MaPó Kinnord-Payton.

I am forever grateful to my sister, Dr. Adrienne Carpenter.

Finally, I give unending thanks to my husband, Steven Donegan, for his strength and love.

Biographies

LINDA GOODE BRYANT

Goode Bryant is a New York–based artist whose long career has seen her move successfully between roles as educator, gallerist, activist, filmmaker, and farmer. In the mid-1970s, she founded Just Above Midtown (JAM), one of the city's first galleries to show work by African American and other artists of color. Open from 1974 until 1986, JAM's legacy was cultivated as a self-described laboratory and a place where Black art flourished; in 2022 JAM was the subject of a retrospective exhibition at the Museum of Modern Art, New York.

Goode Bryant's latest ongoing work is Project Eats, which aims to increase food sovereignty by growing and distributing fresh produce in New York communities that have limited access to nutritious food while also providing residents with farm and culinary opportunities for employment and management.

LESLIE KING-HAMMOND

An artist, curator, and art historian, Dr. King-Hammond is the founding director of the Center for Race and Culture at the Maryland Institute College of Art, where she is also graduate dean emerita, and board chair of the Reginald F. Lewis Museum of Maryland African American History and Culture. Dr. King-Hammond has curated several exhibitions, including the Global Africa Project, co-organized with Lowery Stokes Sims.

Dr. King-Hammond was the recipient of a Lifetime Achievement Award from the Studio Museum in Harlem in 2002; an artist grant from the National Endowment for the Arts in 2001; an Andy Warhol Foundation Curatorial Fellowship in 2008; and the Alain Locke International Prize in 2010. While at the Maryland Institute College of Art, she earned the Trustee Award for Excellence in Teaching in 1986.

LAUREN MCCARDEL

McCardel is the executive director of The Philip and Muriel Berman Museum of Art at Ursinus College, an AAM accredited academic museum dedicated to cultivating dialogue and understanding through exhibitions and programs. Her work is driven by an interest in evolving the ways we engage with art and our communities, especially within the dynamic landscape of contemporary art. McCardel's curatorial approach at the Berman has led to the implementation of inquiry-driven programming, with exhibition concepts emerging through collaborative development. She and her team work closely with exhibiting artists, guest curators, students and faculty, and community partners to activate initiatives that are intellectually stimulating and socially relevant, functioning as catalysts for cultural exchange and creativity.

McCardel has organized and produced numerous exhibitions, among them *Mark Thomas Gibson: Overture* (2025), *New Neighbors* (2025), and *Enrique Bostelmann: Apertures and Borderscapes* (2024). She held previous positions at the Philadelphia Museum of Art and Tyler School of Art and Architecture at Temple University.

JUDY MOONELIS

A New York–based artist, Moonelis has exhibited in numerous solo and group exhibitions nationally and internationally, including the Ninth International Frankfurt Triennial; Katonah Museum of Art, New York; Temple Gallery, Rome; The Basilica of St. Mary, Minneapolis; Eastern State Penitentiary, Philadelphia; the Church of St. Paul the Apostle, New York; and the Kehila Kedosha Janina Synagogue and Museum, New York. Her artist grants include two National Endowment for the Arts Fellowships, two New York Foundation for the Arts Fellowships, and the Virginia A. Groot Grant.

Her work is represented in major public collections, including the Smithsonian Institution, Washington, DC; Museum of Arts and Design, New York; Museum of Fine Arts, Boston; Hermitage Museum, Moscow; Museo de Arte Moderno, Santo Domingo, Dominican Republic; Philadelphia Museum of Art; Pennsylvania Academy of the Fine Arts, Philadelphia; High Museum, Atlanta; Everson Museum, Syracuse; and the Frederick R. Weisman Art Foundation, Los Angeles.

SANA MUSASAMA

Musasama began traveling as a way to recover identity and cultural place. Clay was a geographical catalyst that brought her first to West Africa. She studied Mende pottery in Sierra Leone and ventured later to Japan, China, South America, and Cambodia. She has continued her quest, expanding her interests to tribal adornment practices in various Indigenous cultures. She is challenged by the concerns surrounding the safety of women, specifically the rituals involving rites of passage, female chastity, and the "purification" of the female body.

Musasama's travels have transformed her and her approach to clay. Realizing that clay is universal, she believes that there is no dichotomy between her life and her work. Her trekking has taught her valuable lessons in observation; her mission speaks of a global citizen who walks through the artwork, heart first. Musasama's work is informed by history, women's studies, culture, and her travel journal.

LOWERY STOKES SIMS

A specialist in modern and contemporary art, Sims is known for her particular expertise in the work of African, Latino, Native, and Asian American artists and for her decades-long commitment to diversity and inclusion in the art world.

Sims is curator emerita of the Museum of Arts and Design, New York, where she served as senior curator between 2007 and 2014 and chief curator from 2014 to 2015. She was executive director, president, and adjunct curator for the permanent collection at the Studio Museum in Harlem from 2000 to 2007. She curated more than thirty exhibitions as a member of the education and curatorial staff of the Metropolitan Museum of Art from 1972 to 1999.

Sims has lectured and guest curated exhibitions nationally and internationally. She is currently on the board of the Center for Curatorial Studies at Bard College and the Robert Pousette-Dart Foundation.

WINNIE OWENS-HART

Owens-Hart is a cultural researcher, author, ceramic artist, and documentary filmmaker. Her life's work and passion revolve around the creative process, the historical significance of clay workers globally, and the preservation of all aboriginal ceramics.

She is founder of the ILE AMO Research Center, dedicated to world aboriginal ceramics, and the Women's Pottery House, dedicated to improving the lives of traditional female potters and their children through their clay work. Owens-Hart is a professor emerita in the Department of Art at Howard University. Her honors include a National Endowment for the Arts Individual Craftsmen Fellowship; Renwick Fellow, Smithsonian American Art Museum; Faculty Research Fellow, Smithsonian American Art Museum; and several faculty research grants at Howard University.

She has exhibited nationally and internationally for more than three decades. Her work is in the collections of the Smithsonian American Art Museum, Renwick Gallery, universities, and in other public and private collections.

Index of Works Illustrated

This book is published in conjunction with the exhibitions *Re-Union: Syd Carpenter, Martha Jackson Jarvis, Judy Moonelis, Sana Musasama, and Winnie Owens-Hart* at the Frances M. Maguire Museum at St. Joseph's University (January 14–March 29, 2026); *Syd Carpenter: Home Bound in Wood, Steel, and Clay* at the Philip and Muriel Berman Museum of Art, Ursinus College (January 22–April 5, 2026); and *Syd Carpenter in Planting in Place, Time, and Memory* at Woodmere (January 23–May 25, 2026).

Funding was provided by The Pew Center for Arts & Heritage, with additional support from National Endowment for the Arts (NEA), The Edna W. Andrade Fund, a Donor Advised Fund of the Philadelphia Foundation and the Philadelphia Committee of the Garden Club of America.

Library of Congress Control Number: 2025947730
ISBN: 979-8-9931280-0-9

Published by Woodmere Art Museum, Philadelphia
www.woodmereartmuseum.org

Distributed by the University of Pennsylvania Press
www.pennpress.org

Produced by Marquand Books, Seattle
www.marquandbooks.com

Edited by Gretchen Dykstra, with assistance from Irene Elias
Designed by Ryan Polich
Typeset in Neue Kabel and Untitled Serif by Maggie Lee
Proofread by Emily Holt
Color management by I/O Color, Seattle
Printed and bound in China by Artron Art Group
Photography by Jack Ramsdale and Darryl Moran
Videography by Patrick Dolan

Title page: *Albert and Elbert Howard Farm Bowl*, 2021, stoneware, 15 × 24 × 21½ in. (Collection of the artist)

Contents: *Mother Pin Ascending* (detail), 2025, wood, clay, and steel, 65 × 60 × 60 in. (Courtesy of the Petrucci Family Foundation Collection of African American Art)

Page 6: *Untitled*, date unknown, ceramic with glaze, 15 × 20 × 20 in. (Collection of Danny Simmons)

Page 10: *Mary Howard Farm Bowl*, 2020, stoneware, 15 × 20 × 22 in. (Collection of the artist)

Page 50: *Indiana Hutson Farm Bowl*, 2021, stoneware, 11 × 24 × 23 in. (Collection of the artist)

Page 72: *Sara Reynolds*, 2014, clay and steel, 50 × 27 × 26 in. (James A. Michener Art Museum: Gift of the artist, 2021.1.1a–e)

Page 104: *Mind of Its Own*, 2006, clay, slip underglaze, and graphite, 26 × 14 × 12 in. (Collection of the artist)

Page 116: The Colored Girls Museum, Philadelphia, with garden designed by Carpenter

Page 136: *Love Letter*, 1996, ceramic with acrylic paint, 23 × 12 × 12 in. (Collection of the artist)

Page 142: *Below Ground*, 1990, paint over clay, 69 × 36 × 8 in. (Collection of the artist)